"The most complete home-buying book you will find… doesn't leave out any of the essentials. On my scale of one to 10, this superb new book rates an off-the-chart 12."
—Robert Bruss, syndicated real estate columnist

"Coming from a gal that knows tools, this book is a must-have tool for any home buyer. It offers so much essential information, purchasing a home without it would be like trying to drive a nail without a hammer!"
—Norma Vally, host of *Toolbelt Diva* (Discovery Home) and author of *Chix Can Fix: 100 Home Improvement Projects* and *True Tales From the Diva of Do-It-Yourself*

"Any first-time homebuyer owes it to him or herself to get this book. It's packed with information you won't find anywhere else, yet is remarkably accessible, even when covering complex financial issues."
—Elisabeth DeMarse, CEO, Creditcards.com,
former CEO, Bankrate.com

"Enthusiasm, hints and tips all rolled into a great read for first-timers."
—Pat Lashinsky, President of ZipRealty

"…Provides in-depth insight and helpful advice that is easy to understand and use."
—Rob Paterkiewicz, CAE, IOM,
Executive Director, American Society of Home Inspectors

"Like having over a dozen real estate experts over for dinner."
—Steve Kropper, President, Bank on Real Estate,
founder of Domania.com

"Nolo's excellent guide for novice home buyers provides fresh, updated information about the whole process that even those in the know will find useful."
—Library Journal

NOLO® Products & Services

⇨ Books & Software

Get in-depth information. Nolo publishes hundreds of great books and software programs for consumers and business owners. Order a copy—or download an ebook version instantly—at Nolo.com.

⇨ Legal Encyclopedia

Free at Nolo.com. Here are more than 1,400 free articles and answers to common questions about everyday legal issues including wills, bankruptcy, small business formation, divorce, patents, employment and much more.

⇨ Plain-English Legal Dictionary

Free at Nolo.com. Stumped by jargon? Look it up in America's most up-to-date source for definitions of legal terms.

⇨ Online Legal Documents

Create documents at your computer. Go to Nolo.com to make a will or living trust, form an LLC or corporation or obtain a trademark or provisional patent. For simpler matters, download one of our hundreds of high-quality legal forms, including bills of sale, promissory notes, nondisclosure agreements and many more.

⇨ Lawyer Directory

Find an attorney at Nolo.com. Nolo's consumer-friendly lawyer directory provides in-depth profiles of lawyers all over America. From fees and experience to legal philosophy, education and special expertise, you'll find all the information you need to pick the right lawyer. Every lawyer listed has pledged to work diligently and respectfully with clients.

⇨ Free Legal Updates

Keep up to date. Check for free updates at Nolo.com. Under "Products," find this book and click "Legal Updates." You can also sign up for our free e-newsletters at Nolo.com/newsletters.

3rd edition

Nolo's Essential Guide to
Buying Your
First Home

Ilona Bray,
Alayna Schroeder
& Marcia Stewart

THIRD EDITION	JANUARY 2011
Editor	ILONA BRAY
Cover Design	SUSAN WIGHT
Book Design	SUSAN PUTNEY
CD-ROM Preparation	ELLEN BITTER
Proofreading	ROBERT WELLS
Index	JEAN MANN
Printing	DELTA PRINTING SOLUTIONS, INC.

Bray, Ilona M., 1962-
  Nolo's essential guide to buying your first home / by Ilona Bray, Alayna Schroeder & Marcia Stewart. -- 3rd ed.
    p. cm.
  Includes index.
  Summary: "Presents a detailed view of how home purchases take place across the U.S. in easy-to-understand terms. The new edition emphasizes that careful research is necessary before deciding what price and terms to include in an offer and warns of the changing requirements to secure financing."--Provided by publisher.
  ISBN-13: 978-1-4133-1322-2 (pbk.)
  ISBN-10: 1-4133-1322-1 (pbk.)
  ISBN-13: 978-1-4133-1348-2 (e-book)
  ISBN-10: 1-4133-1348-5 (e-book)
  1. House buying. I. Schroeder, Alayna, 1975- II. Stewart, Marcia. III. Title. IV. Title: Essential guide to buying your first home.
  HD1390.5.B734 2010
  643'.12--dc22

                                2010031334

Please note

We believe accurate, plain-English legal information should help you solve many of your own legal problems. But this text is not a substitute for personalized advice from a knowledgeable lawyer. If you want the help of a trained professional—and we'll always point out situations in which we think that's a good idea—consult an attorney licensed to practice in your state.

Acknowledgments

We didn't really write this book.

Well, we did, just not by ourselves. This book was a 100% team effort and couldn't have been written without the advice, stories, and ideas of real estate experts and homebuyers from around the United States. First and foremost, we thank the members of our advisory board, who spent countless hours reviewing chapters, explaining local practices, and sharing the best and worst memories from their professional experiences. Special thanks to **Broderick Perkins,** a real estate journalist based in San Jose, California, and founder and Executive Editor of DeadlineNews.Com (www.deadlinenews.com), who reviewed and contributed to every chapter.

Our other invaluable sages included:

- **Nancy Atwood,** Designated Broker with ZipRealty in Framingham, Massachusetts (www.ziprealty.com)

- **Marjo Diehl,** Mortgage Adviser at RPM Mortgage in Alamo, California (www.rpm-mtg.com)

- **Steve Elias,** attorney, author, and community radio programmer in Lakeport, California. He writes blogs on bankruptcy and foreclosure law, and books on a variety of subjects, all of which can be accessed at www.nolo.com.

- **Stephen Fishman,** Bay Area attorney, tax expert, and author (many of his books are available from www.nolo.com)

- **Sandy Gadow,** expert on real estate closing and escrow, and best-selling author of *The Complete Guide to Your Real Estate Closing* (www.escrowhelp.com)

- **Paul Grucza,** author, radio host, and Executive Vice President and Corporate Trainer for Classic Property Management AAMC® in Arlington, Texas (www.classicpm.com)

- **Mary I. Husk,** Vice President of Faculty Development for The National Alliance for Insurance Education & Research in Austin, Texas (www.scic.com)

- **Richard Leshnower,** New York-based real estate attorney

- **Mark Nash,** Associate Broker with Coldwell Banker, who serves the Chicago, Evanston, Skokie, and Wilmette areas of Illinois (www.marknashrealtor.com), and author of *1001 Tips for Buying & Selling a Home*

- **Paul A. Rude,** professional inspector and owner of Summer Street Inspections, in Berkeley, California (www.summerinspect.com)

- **Bert Sperling,** city and neighborhood expert and author in Portland, Oregon, and founder of www.bestplaces.net

- **Fred Steingold,** attorney and author in Ann Arbor, Michigan (many of his books on small business and other legal matters can be found on www.nolo.com)

- **Russell Straub,** founder, President, and Chief Executive Officer of LoanBright, a mortgage intermediary service based in Evergreen, Colorado (see www.loanbright.com and www.compareinterestrates.com).

A number of other experts provided additional advice—you'll see many of them quoted in this book. They include Neil Binder, New York real estate investment expert (www.bellmarc.com); Elisabeth DeMarse, CEO, Creditcards.com, former CEO of Bankrate.com, and New York-based real estate industry expert (www.demarseco.com); Kartar Diamond (www. fengshuisolutions.net); Debbie Essex, child and family therapist based in Berkeley, California; Joanna Hirsch, real estate agent with Pacific Union in Oakland, California (jhirsch@pacunion.com); Joel Kinney, attorney with Goldstein & Herndon, LLP, in Chestnut Hill, Massachusetts (www. brooklinelaw.com); Annemarie Devine Kurpinsky, associate with George Devine, Realtor® (www.georgedevinerealtor.com); Pat Lashinsky, President, ZipRealty (www.ziprealty.com); Jeff Lipes, President of Family Choice Mortgage in South Yarmouth, Massachusetts (www.familychoicemortgage. com); Maxine Mackle, Connecticut Realtor® (www.country-living.com); Paul MacLean, retired home inspector in Austin, Texas; Carol Neil, Realtor® with Pacific Union in Berkeley, California (www.pacificunion.com); Fiore Pignataro, Realtor® with Windermere Realty in Seattle, Washington (www. windermere.com); Lorri Lee Ragan, of the American Land Title Association (www.alta.org); Mary Randolph, attorney and author at Nolo (www.nolo. com); Frank Rathbun, Vice President of Communications, Community

Associations Institute (www.caionline.org); Ira Serkes, Berkeley Realtor® with Pacific Union (www.berkeleyhomes.com); Debbie Stevens, Oregon real estate agent (www.ramsayrealty.com); Rich Stim, attorney and Nolo author (www. nolo.com); and Craig Venezia, real estate author (www.craigvenezia.com).

No amount of advice can substitute for a personal story, so we'd also like to thank the many homebuyers who shared the good, the bad, and the ugly of their own experiences or told us what they'd like from this book, including Amy Blumenberg, Laurie Briggs, Dave and Danielle Burge, Karen Cabot, Linda Chou, Jennifer Cleary, Jaleh Doane, Phil Esra, Lisa Guerin, Gabrielle Hecht, Pat Jenkins, Ellie Kania, Justin and Tamara Kennerly, Chris and Libby Kurz, Talia Leyva, Willow Liroff, Meggan O'Connell, Evan and Tammy Ohs, Leny and Frank Riebli, Leah Scheibe, Diane Sherman, Bruce Sievers, Luan Stauss, Tom and Heather Tewksbury, Josh and Gillian Viers, Julie and Malachi Weng-Gutierrez, and Kyung Yu.

Within Nolo, we got huge amounts of help from our talented colleagues. Special thanks to Lexi Elmore, who gave us a 20-something, Internet-savvy perspective—and a lot of stellar research and writing help. Rich Stim did an excellent job with the audio interviews on the CD-ROM. Other colleagues who lent a hand, researching everything from 50-state legal matters to fun facts, included Cathy Caputo, Stan Jacobsen, Terry McGinley, Leah Tuisavalalo, and Joe Warner. Sandy Coury and Sigrid Metson helped line up advisory board members.

Big thanks go to our colleagues in the editorial department, who supported us through the (long) process of writing this comprehensive (and yet fun!) text. Kudos to Susan Putney in Nolo's Production Department who took a challenging compilation of information and turned it into a beautifully designed book. And to Ellen Bitter in Nolo's Application Development Department for helping put together the capital Homebuyer's Toolkit on the CD-ROM.

Thanks also to Nolo founder Jake Warner, who championed this book idea for many years.

Our basements may be cluttered, our gardens may need weeding, and our floors may need a good scrubbing—but we love our homes. Thanks to the people who helped us get there—professionals (some who taught us what to do, others who taught us what not to do!) and our families, who share the joy of homeownership with us.

About the Authors

Ilona Bray is an attorney, author, and legal editor at Nolo. Her other real estate books include *The Essential Guide for First-Time Homeowners* and *Selling your House in a Tough Market*, both coauthored with Alayna Schroeder. Her working background includes solo practice, nonprofit, and corporate stints. She recently sold her first home at a profit—despite being in the middle of a real estate downturn—and bought a larger home. Her fantasy house would be a Greene & Greene mansion of the same style (like the Gamble House in Pasadena), with a large sun porch and lots of surrounding trees.

Alayna Schroeder is an attorney whose legal experience has included everything from work at a corporate law firm to editing and writing to a stint in the Peace Corps. According to *Sacramento Magazine*, the home she shares with her husband, twin babies, and Bolivian-born dog, Luna, is in one of the Sacramento area's ten Great Neighborhoods—a fact Alayna tries to remember as she redoes the aging plaster and desperately searches for adequate closet space into which to stuff modern-day baby gear. Alayna's idea of a fantasy house is always changing, but she'd settle for an A-frame in the woods with a lake view, big deck, and gourmet kitchen.

Marcia Stewart is the author or editor of many Nolo real estate books, including the best-selling *Every Landlord's Legal Guide*. Years ago, she found the perfect "starter" house in one of her favorite neighborhoods. As her family started to grow, so did the house, with a new second story and deck. Someday, Marcia may even get around to remodelling her 1950s kitchen—if she doesn't give it up for her fantasy house first. That would be a Queen Anne Victorian on a tropical beach, with a sunny kitchen, home theater, and a detached cottage office.

Table of Contents

 Your Homebuying Companion

4 Stepping Out: What's on the Market and at What Price

5 Select Your Players: Your Real Estate Team

6 Bring Home the Bacon: Getting a Mortgage

7 Mom and Dad? The Seller? Uncle Sam? Loan Alternatives

8 I Love It! It's Perfect! Looking for the Right House

9 Plan B: Fixer-Uppers, FSBOs, Foreclosures, and More

10 Show Them the Money: From Offer to Purchase Agreement

11 Toward the Finish Line: Tasks Before Closing

12 Send in the Big Guns: Professional Property Inspectors

How to Use the CD-ROM

List of Forms and Resources in the Homebuyer's Toolkit on the CD-ROM

Tools for Househunting

Dream List Directions

Dream List

Questions for Talking With Locals

Common Real Estate Abbreviations

House Visit Checklist

Questions for Seller Worksheet

First-Look Home Inspection Checklist

Condo/Co-op Worksheet

Cobuyer Discussion Worksheet

Homeowners' Insurance Terminology

Financial Tools

Debt-to-Income Ratio Worksheet

Financial Information for Lenders

Gift Letter

Private Loan Terms Worksheet

HUD-1 Settlement Statement

Tools for Choosing Professionals

Real Estate Agent Interview Questionnaire

Real Estate Agent Reference Questionnaire

Mortgage Broker Interview Questionnaire

Mortgage Broker Reference Questionnaire

Attorney Interview Questionnaire

Attorney Reference Questionnaire

Home Inspector Interview Questionnaire

Home Inspector Reference Questionnaire

Tools for Evaluating a House's Physical Condition

Indiana Seller's Residential Real Estate Disclosure

California Real Estate Transfer Disclosure Statement

California Natural Hazard Disclosure Statement

Sample Home Inspection Report

Final Walk-Through Checklist (Existing Home)

Final Walk-Through Checklist (New Home)

List of Interviews on Homebuyer's Toolkit CD-ROM

Author Interviews with Ilona Bray, Alayna Schroeder, and Marcia Stewart

Househunting, an interview with adviser Mark Nash

House Inspections, an interview with adviser Paul A. Rude

Getting a Mortgage, an interview with adviser Russell Straub

Loans From Family and Friends, an interview with adviser Asheesh Advani

Closing the Purchase, an interview with adviser Sandy Gadow

Your Homebuying Companion

B uying a house may be one of the first certifiably grown-up things you ever do. And no matter how ready you feel, taking a major step like this—particularly one where there are so many zeros on the price tag—can make you want to just close your eyes and *get it over with*.

But if you're going to invest your time and money, you want to make sure you don't find just any house—you find the *right* house, at the *right* price, with the *right* loan. A house you're happy to stay in for a long time, no matter what the market does. To do that, you need a lot of information.

This book is full of nuts-and-bolts information about the homebuying process. But it's also got anecdotes and advice that we hope will remind you to enjoy this exciting, if sometimes frustrating or nerve-wracking process. Keep in mind what you're aiming for: your own home, where you're free to pound nails in the wall, get a cat, or paint your bedroom any color you want, without asking the landlord!

By the time you've read the key information here (don't worry, you won't have to read every chapter or every section), you'll truly be ready. We'll show you how to:

- choose the right house in the right neighborhood, whether it's an old bungalow on a tree-lined street, a condo in the city center, or a custom-built home in a new development
- narrow in on a realistic price range based on your budget, and strategize ways to afford more
- select from a variety of financing options, from a 30-year fixed rate mortgage (like the one Mom and Dad got) to a private loan from a relative or friend
- pick a great real estate agent, mortgage broker, home inspector, and other professionals
- negotiate and sign an agreement to buy a house (find out what's important in all that fine print)
- wrap up your financing, get inspections, and take care of other last tasks, and finally
- close the deal, arrange your move, and settle into your new home.

You're going to benefit from the expertise of a number of different people, not just one author. We put together a team of 14 advisers from around the country who have reviewed this book and added the kinds of insights you usually get only in personal conversations. For instance, you'll meet a mortgage broker who explains why you should avoid oral loan preapprovals; a real estate agent who cautions against dressing too well at open houses (it can hurt your negotiating position); a closing expert with straightforward advice on why you should care about things like "easements" and title insurance; and a lawyer who suggests how to save on attorney's fees.

The CD-ROM that comes with this book includes a Homebuyer's Toolkit—over two dozen forms, checklists, and letters to help keep you organized and on track during every stage of the process. Whether it's a "Dream List" that prompts you to set out your priorities, checklists to carry when you tour a house or condo, or a set of interview questions for potential real estate agents, you'll find it there. And as a bonus, it includes MP3s with interviews of several of our advisers, plus this book's authors, who share their insider insights.

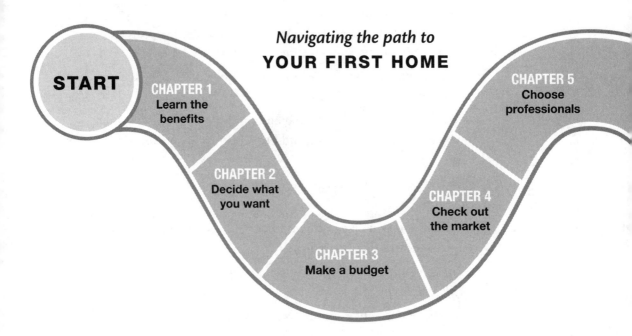

Navigating the path to
YOUR FIRST HOME

START

CHAPTER 1
Learn the benefits

CHAPTER 2
Decide what you want

CHAPTER 3
Make a budget

CHAPTER 4
Check out the market

CHAPTER 5
Choose professionals

The three authors of this book, Ilona, Alayna, and Marcia, bring not only years of legal and real estate expertise, but also different first-time homebuying perspectives of our own. One of us bought with a 15-year mortgage that's paid off and is now paying her daughter's college tuition. Another bought with the help of family members and now has probably the lowest mortgage payment on the block in one of the city's up-and-coming neighborhoods. And the third bought a modest starter home with a hybrid adjustable rate mortgage and has been fixing it up with the hope of selling someday.

Our varied experiences help us understand that everyone has different objectives when buying and special challenges when buying for the first time. You may just be looking for a place—any place—to get started, you may want the challenge of a fixer-upper, or you might need the convenience of a low-maintenance condo. We know that you might be doing this alone, with your spouse or partner, or even with a friend. No matter who you are or what your goals and objectives may be, we hope you recognize yourself in some of the stories and experiences reflected in this book.

So hang on tight—to this book, that is. It will be your companion, providing advice, information, and inspiration all along the path to your new front door.

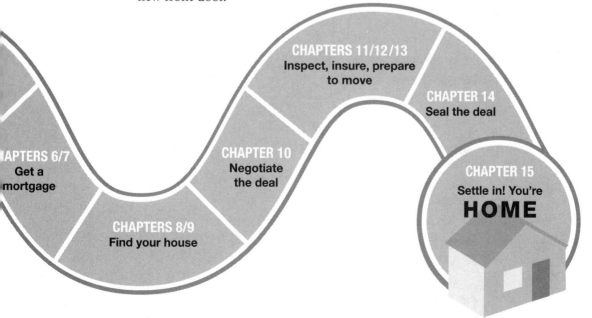

CHAPTERS 11/12/13
Inspect, insure, prepare to move

CHAPTER 14
Seal the deal

CHAPTERS 6/7
Get a mortgage

CHAPTER 10
Negotiate the deal

CHAPTER 15
Settle in! You're
HOME

CHAPTERS 8/9
Find your house

What's So Great About Buying a House?

Meet Your Adviser

Broderick Perkins, an award-winning real estate journalist based in San Jose, California, and founder and Executive Editor of DeadlineNewsGroup, which provides real-estate related editorial content for online and print publications.

What he does   Broderick tirelessly follows real estate and consumer news and trends nationwide, having been a journalist specializing in these areas for more than 30 years. His company provides in-depth articles, analysis, and breaking news. He has provided real estate news stories for *The Wall Street Journal*, Move.com, *Better Homes & Gardens*, and RealtyTimes.com, among other publications. In his former life as a journalist with the *San Jose Mercury News*, Broderick participated in Pulitzer Prize-winning coverage of the 1989 Loma Prieta earthquake. Today, he focuses on residential real estate topics from the consumer's perspective, everything from appraisals to zoning. He says, "I try to tell consumers not just what the current news is, but what it means to them as a buyer, seller, owner, or renter."

- -

First house   "Despite being a real estate journalist, I hadn't even thought about buying a place yet, when the owner of my apartment said she'd need to either raise the rent or sell. It was a one-bedroom, 750-square-foot condo in a historic part of San Jose. Rents were going up—this was just before the big tech boom. I felt like, this is it, it's time. We arranged for me to buy it, and without an agent. Since I was already familiar with how real estate worked, and was on good terms with the owner, all went smoothly. We didn't even have to get a home inspection, since I knew the place inside and out. It was funny that while I was writing about defects with condos, mine was in great shape! I bought it for $134,000, and sold it for $354,000 after five years."

Fantasy house   "A loft on the beach. Any beach on the West Coast, maybe in a warm spot like San Diego or Malibu. I like the openness of lofts, the high ceilings and big windows—I have one now. My ideal would be brick or stone masonry, but now we're really talking fantasy, because no one would put masonry on top of soft sand, especially in earthquake country. That would need some serious engineering."

. . . .

Likes best about his work   "Aside from the fact that I don't have to go into an office every day, I appreciate the learning aspect of it. I used to get kidded a lot at the *San Jose Mercury News* when I didn't own a home and was working on a real estate story—people from the realty industry would say, 'How can you write about home ownership when you don't even own a home?' I'd say, 'Do I have to rob a bank to write about crime?' Now that I've been writing about real estate for years, I realize there's no end of stuff to learn—details of mortgages, appraisals, the physical structure of homes, unique homebuying experiences, and more. I figure this learning aspect will help prevent my brain from turning to mush as I get older!"

. . . .

Top tip for first-time homebuyers   "Check out your finances with a professional even before you think you're ready to buy. Most people who don't own a home don't think they can. They think they won't qualify. The biggest thing that stops them is that they haven't sat down with a mortgage person or financial planner. Like me: I'd been renting for five years and was writing about real estate, and still didn't think it was possible, until I was forced to take a closer look. (I got in with $10,000 down—money I borrowed from a friend!) Even if you're not yet thinking about buying, sit down with a pro to find out what steps you can take now to get ready."

Picking up a book on homebuying for some light reading? We're guessing not. If you're reading this, you're probably seriously interested in buying a house. But before we launch into how, let's explore why— just in case you've got any lingering doubts about whether it's a good idea. This chapter will preview some of the primary financial and personal benefits to buying a home (and you'll find details on many of the subjects covered, such as tax benefits, in later chapters). Then we'll talk about some common myths and fears, and how to get over them.

> ⭐ **Best thing I ever did**
>
> **Buy my first home.** Although Leah was happy with her rental place, she says, "I wanted a place that I could call my own, with a backyard for my cats, and space for an office so I could work at home full time. After three weeks of looking, I found it! And after a year, some of the best parts of homeownership are things I wasn't even expecting—like having already gotten to know more neighbors than I did during a whole six years in my apartment. Plus, although I've never thought of myself as domestic, I've had a surge of interest in decorating—I put up Roman blinds, have been picking out paint colors, and just bought my first Christmas tree!"

Investment Value: Get What You Pay For ... And Then Some

You've probably heard people talk about real estate as a great investment. But what exactly do you get out of the deal? Well, a few things: You'll build equity instead of spending cash on rent, you gain immediate benefits (a place to live!), and you'll eventually have full ownership of an asset that—at least over the long term—has a good chance of appreciating in value.

Equity, Baby

Over time, as you patiently pay your mortgage, two things may start happening—your principal loan balance will go down, and the house's market value may go up. Both of these mean that you're accruing *equity*. Equity is the difference between the market value of a house (what it's currently worth) and the claims against it (what you have left to pay on any mortgages or loans you've taken out against it). You'd be hard-pressed to find another investment where you can borrow a large amount of money, pay a modest interest rate, and reap every bit of the gain yourself.

EXAMPLE: Hugo buys a home for $300,000 with a $30,000 down payment and a $270,000 mortgage. If the market value of the house is $300,000, Hugo's current equity in the home is $30,000 (market value minus mortgage debt). A few years later, Hugo has reduced the principal on the mortgage by $5,000, to $265,000. Meanwhile, the house's value has risen to $310,000. Hugo now has $45,000 in equity: ($310,000 minus $265,000). That's $15,000 more than he originally invested.

Of course recent history has shown that the value of a property doesn't always increase: It can also decrease, sometimes dramatically. Fortunately, history shows that houses rarely drop in value permanently. For example, median existing U.S. home prices increased an average of 6.5% every year between 1972 and 2005, according to the National Association of Realtors®, though homeowners experienced some precipitous value drops during that time period, too.

It Beats Paying Rent

A good chunk of the money you'll use to finance your home is money you're already spending anyway, on rent. When you buy a house, that cash is actually going into your investment.

You Can Live in Your Investment

Some people like to call a mortgage a forced savings plan, because it makes you sock a little cash away every month in the form of a mortgage payment— money you will, with any luck, get back when you sell the place. On the other hand, we like to call it a smart investment plan, because it gives you both a roof over your head *and* a way to convert your cash into a potentially appreciating asset.

That House Is *Yours*

One benefit to buying a house is kind of obvious ... you're becoming a home*owner*, and when the loan is paid off, you won't have to pay for a place to live. You could keep renting the same place you're in now for 50 years, and at the end of that time you'll still have to pay monthly rent checks to your landlord.

Tax Breaks: Benefits From Uncle Sam

You'll get to claim various federal tax deductions and credits for home-related expenses. These can add up to some serious savings.

Tax Deductions Versus Tax Credits

Be careful not to confuse a tax deduction with its more valuable cousin, a tax credit. A tax deduction is an amount you subtract from your gross income (all the money you earned during the year) to figure out how much of your income is subject to tax. For example, if your gross income is $80,000, and you have a $2,000 tax deduction, your taxable income is reduced to $78,000.

A tax credit, by contrast, is a dollar-for-dollar reduction in your tax liability. If your taxable income is $80,000, and you qualify for a $2,000 tax credit, your taxable income is still $80,000, but you get to reduce the amount of tax you ultimately owe by $2,000.

Tax Credits

As a new homeowner, you may be entitled to certain tax credits.

- **Tax credit for first-time homebuyers.** At the time this book went to print, all the tax credits for first-time homebuyers had expired—but check the news and www.irs.gov for the latest.
- **Tax credits for energy-efficiency.** In 2010, if you make your home more energy-efficient by putting in insulation, replacement windows or doors, water heaters, or certain high-efficiency heating and cooling equipment,

you may be eligible for a tax credit of 30% of the cost up to $1,500. For more information, visit www.energystar.gov (search for "tax credit"). Another tax credit, good through 2016, lets you claim 30% of the cost of installing geothermal heat pumps, small wind turbines, or solar energy systems.

Mortgage Interest

One of the biggest deductions will be the interest you pay on your home mortgage (available for mortgages up to $1 million for individuals and married couples filing jointly and $500,000 for marrieds filing separately). This one's particularly advantageous during the first few years of a fixed rate mortgage, when most of your payment will be put toward interest.

Other Tax-Deductible Expenses

You can also deduct certain other expenses, such as:

- **Property taxes.** While the amount varies between states and localities, most people pay around 2%–4% of the home's value each year in state property tax. This amount is deductible from your federal taxes if you itemize, or, through 2010, can be added to your standard deduction if you don't itemize (see IRS Tax Tip 7).

- **Points.** Points are additional and usually optional fees paid when you buy your mortgage (you get a reduced interest rate in return). They're tax-deductible in the year you pay them.

- **Private mortgage insurance (PMI).** If you get a mortgage for more than 20% of your home's purchase price, the lender will probably require you to buy PMI. (Though you pay the premiums, PMI protects the lender from loss if you don't make your payments.) Through 2010, PMI is tax-deductible, though the amount of the deduction decreases as the taxpayer's income increases.

- **Interest on a home improvement loan.** If you take out a loan to make improvements that increase your home's value, prolong its life, or adapt its use—for example, by adding a deck or a new bathroom—you can deduct the interest on that loan, with no limit. But you can't deduct interest on loans used to make normal repairs, such as repainting the kitchen or fixing a broken window.

- **Interest on home equity debt.** Sometimes you can deduct interest on a home equity loan even if the money isn't used to buy, build, or improve your home, for example, if you use it toward a child's college tuition or family medical bills. The deduction is limited to a maximum loan amount or the total fair market value of the home less other mortgages. The maximum loan amount is $100,000 for an individual or married couple filing jointly and $50,000 if married but filing separately.

- **Home office expenses.** If you use part of your home exclusively for a home-based business, you may be able to deduct a portion of the related expenses—including the costs of some home repairs.

- **Moving costs.** If you move because of a new job that's more than 50 miles from your current residence, you may be able to deduct your moving expenses.

- **Prepayment penalties.** Although we advise against getting a mortgage with a prepayment penalty (as discussed in Chapter 6), if you do, and then you make a prepayment, the penalty you pay will be tax-deductible.

Itemizing Your Deductions

To take advantage of house-related tax deductions, you'll need to *itemize* your tax deductions, rather than take the standard deduction (for 2010 tax returns, $5,700 for individuals and $11,400 for marrieds filing jointly). The true tax savings comes in the difference between your tax liability when you take the standard deduction and your tax liability when you itemize. Itemizing involves a step up from the good old 1040EZ, but it's not all that complicated. To make it worthwhile, your itemized deductions should exceed the standard deduction. With the high price of real estate these days, it's not usually too hard to outpace the standard deduction with deductible homeowner costs, not to mention other deductible expenses like donations to your favorite charity.

EXAMPLE: Let's say you get a $200,000 fixed rate loan at 6% interest. You're looking at paying around $12,000 the first year in interest alone. That doesn't count property taxes, points on the mortgage, or any other tax-deductible expenses.

If you're single, the standard deduction is $5,700. But if you itemize your deductions, you could deduct the $12,000 in interest payments instead. By itemizing even this one deduction, almost $7,000 less of your income will be taxed.

TIP

Keep good records. You'll be able to reap the benefits of itemizing your deductions only if you know about them and are prepared to prove them to the IRS—all of them, not just the house-related ones. Keep a file of receipts for the more common deductions, such as unreimbursed business expenses (office equipment and travel); educational expenses (tuition and books); charitable contributions; and unreimbursed medical expenses. Consider getting help from a tax professional— even your meeting might be tax-deductible!

CHECK IT OUT

Go straight to the source. See IRS Publication 530, *Tax Information for First-Time Homeowners*, available at www.irs.gov. This publication will give you more detailed information about the tax benefits of buying a home.

Capital Gains Tax Relief When You Sell

While it may be too soon for you to imagine selling your first home, another important benefit is available if and when you do. Thanks to the Taxpayer Relief Act of 1997, you don't pay capital gains tax (usually 15%) on the first $250,000 you make on the place. Double that to $500,000 if you're married and filing jointly, or to $250,000 per person if you co-own the place. To qualify, you usually must have lived in the home two out of the previous five years before selling. Many first-time buyers use this tax break to move from modest starter homes to roomier homes that cost more.

Personality and Pizzazz: Your Home Is Your Castle

If you've always been a renter, you know the drill: Things stay the way they were when you moved in. White walls stay white, ugly carpeting stays ugly, and funky bathroom light fixture stays funky.

When it's your home, you get to make your mark. There's just no way to quantify the psychological advantage of personalizing your space. Even people who've never taken an interest in home decorating, repair, or gardening find themselves hooked on the creativity and self-expression possible with home projects.

No More Mr. Roper: Say Goodbye to Renting

Expressing your personality isn't the only advantage to leaving rental living behind. Say goodbye to things like waiting around for things to get fixed, wondering whether the landlord will raise your rent or kick you out anytime soon, and being surprised by landlords who stop by at their own convenience.

Even reasonable landlords who make prompt and thorough repairs and never raise the rent can pull surprises or sell the property. Owning your own house reduces the stress and uncertainty of renting. You're in charge of when you move on, who comes in the front door and when, and what gets done to the place. While that means you've got some extra responsibilities, you've definitely got some extra security and benefits, too.

The Future's So... Expensive!

If you pay $1,000 in monthly rent now, approximately how much will you be paying in 40 years, assuming average inflation (4% per year) and no rent control?

a. $2,500   b. $3,400   c. $4,800

d. None of the above, because I'll own a home.

Answer: c or d.

★ **Best thing I ever did** — **Make monthly payments to myself, not the landlord.**
At age 25, Talia had only toyed with the idea of buying a house—she'd thought that, despite her full-time job, it was financially impossible.

But then her landlord raised the rent. Talia says, "I looked into loan options—and to my surprise, I qualified. Within two months, I bought a converted first-floor apartment with a little patio, in a safe neighborhood. I love not having to share a washer and dryer with other people anymore. But even better is the feeling of independence of having my own place: Because I'm building equity, I like to think I'm making those mortgage checks to myself—and they're not that much higher than my rent checks were, plus I can claim some significant tax deductions."

You Can Do It … If You Want To

Are you still on the fence about homebuying? Some people just don't feel ready to take the plunge. Below are a list of common "I can't do it because . . . " excuses. Don't get us wrong: Not every excuse is a *bad* excuse. You just need to know whether yours are based on solid facts rather than plain old fear.

"But … I Like Renting"

Maybe you're thinking, *I really love my apartment* or, *I'm getting such a good deal.* But even if your current rent seems cheap, cheap is never as good as free. Yes, we're aware that buying a house isn't free. But at some point, you won't be paying a mortgage anymore. That will *never* be true if you rent.

 CHECK IT OUT

Run your own numbers. These calculators compare the costs of renting and buying:

- www.myfico.com (search for "Am I better off renting?")
- www.nolo.com/legal-calculators (click "Should I rent or buy?")
- www.ginniemae.gov (under "Homeownership," click "Buy vs. Rent Calculator").

While you'll need to guess how much you'll spend on a home to use these calculators, the result will at least give you a rough comparison. Revisit the calculators after you've looked at Chapters 3 and 6 (covering the financial details of buying a house).

All that being said, renting might be best in the following situations:

- **You plan on moving from the area within the next few years.** Buying is a long-term strategy, with some significant up-front costs. Plus, it's easier to move out of a rental than a home you own—selling is almost as complicated as buying.

- **You need flexibility.** Buying is best for people whose lives are fairly stable. If your first priority is being able to quit your job any time a friend proposes a round-the-world sailing trip, maybe homeownership will feel more like a trap than a positive step. (Then again, we've met travelers who've sublet their house and supported their travels with the rent payments!)

- **You expect your income to decrease soon.** If you're planning to return to school or quit your 9 to 5 to pursue an acting career, you might not want to lock yourself into a mortgage. Still, you may be a potential homebuyer if you can afford something more modest within your anticipated future income or can pay the mortgage by co-owning the property or taking in renters.

- **It will cost you far more to buy than to rent.** Run those numbers, using calculators like the ones listed above. In some markets, you can still rent for much less than you can buy—even after you factor in tax deductions and inflation. If that's the case, you might be better off renting and investing elsewhere.

"But ... I Can't Afford It"

Maybe your main reservation about buying a home is that you simply can't afford one. Scraping together a 20% down payment can be no small task when you've already got your plate full with your current bills. Or perhaps you're afraid you won't qualify for the gigantic loan you'll need or won't be able to pay it once you get it.

Best thing we ever did **Focus on the spaghetti.** Caryn and her husband Alec were stretching to their financial limits to buy a house, and Caryn says, "We were nervous, but our agent told us, 'You'll just need to eat spaghetti for about a year, and then things will even out.' For some reason, that image stuck in my head, and I thought, okay, I can handle eating spaghetti for a while. In fact, that's about the way it worked. The first year, we depleted our savings, not only with the house closing but with repainting and buying furniture. Now we've settled in, and owning a home doesn't feel like such a big load on our shoulders anymore."

If you're trying to get a down payment together and finding your efforts frustrated, don't lose heart. There are alternatives: For example, you may be able to augment your down payment with a loan from a family member, or even enter into a cobuying arrangement with a friend.

As for the mortgage payment, people who think they can't afford it often focus only on the big number—the five, six, or even seven-digit figure that says what a house is going to cost. But a mortgage allows you to spread that number out over a big portion of your life.

Finally, let's not forget that the first home you buy isn't necessarily going to be the one you'll live in forever. By remaining flexible, and starting with a not-quite-perfect house, you can break into the housing market. That's why they call it a "starter" house—it's only the beginning. The equity that you accrue may very well help you get into that next place.

> ### Small Can Be Beautiful
>
> If you think living in a small space means you'll be cramped, uncomfortable, and aesthetically disappointed, check out www.apartmenttherapy.com. Under "house tours," your secret voyeur can look at tiny spaces other people have transformed into fabulous homes. Be inspired!

"But ... I'm Single"

Some people are reluctant to buy a house because they're single. But did you know that more than one-fifth of homebuyers today are single women? Obviously those women have figured out that there's no secret rule that says only couples get to buy houses.

Best thing I ever did   **Invest in my present as well as my future.** Real estate agent Joanna knows about not wanting to buy a house as a single woman—she's seen it in many of her clients. But, says Joanna, "The problem with waiting to do something the traditional way is, what do you lose during that waiting period? I was in my early 30s and ready to have a place of my own. Plus, it makes sense to spend the money and get a tax write-off rather than pour it into rent. This isn't to say that buying alone wasn't stressful—I stretched financially to make it work. But since buying, my house has gone up in value."

Maybe you're worried that you'll have to move as soon as you meet Mr. or Ms. Right. While that admittedly is possible, it's also possible that in the meantime, the increased value of your place will help, not hinder, your happily-ever-after. If the value of your home increases and you pay down the mortgage, the two of you will have equity you can use to buy a place together. Besides—a house that's perfect for one may accommodate two just fine.

Best thing we ever did   **Combine our homes.** Hannah says, "I was a young professional and *very* single when I bought a condo. Two years later, I met Chad, who also owned a small home. Before I knew it, we were married and living in the house, renting out the condo. Then we had kids, and the house was just too small. We sold my place and Chad's, using the equity to buy a house big enough to accommodate our kids. It's nice to have a place that we chose together, with our family in mind."

"But … It's Too Much Responsibility!"

For some, the idea of owning a home just seems like too much to handle. Admittedly, renting is much simpler than owning. You write a rent check, and you're covered for the month. And in many rental arrangements, you can leave with just a month's notice—perfect for those with wanderlust.

Telling yourself that renting doesn't involve responsibility isn't really true, though. After all, what happens if you don't pay the rent? You get evicted—and then where do you go? Back to Mom and Dad's? Most people would rather do whatever it takes to make that monthly payment happen.

So if you've already lived away from home, you're familiar with what's needed to make monthly payments and handle monthly finances. Of course, when you buy you'll have other responsibilities, like taking care of your yard or doing repairs, but you're in charge of prioritizing what happens when. If you decide you don't want to repair the creaky stairwell until you've redone your kitchen cabinets, that's up to you.

"But … I'm Still Scared!"

Buying a home may seem overwhelming, even if you've always wanted to do it. The process is unfamiliar, there's a lot of money at stake, and you may fear getting swept up into buying a place you don't even like or that will drop in value. But fear shouldn't stop you from realizing your homebuying dreams. To help calm the butterflies, take constructive steps such as these:

- **Know your strengths and weaknesses going in.** Then find ways to address them, for example with self-education or by hiring professionals.
- **Learn what you can expect from professionals.** Understand what real estate agents, mortgage brokers, home inspectors, and other professionals do, and put them to work for you, saving time and money.
- **Observe your local real estate market.** We'll show you how to research the trends in your area, in order to reassure yourself that you're not buying an asset that will immediately drop in value, and has long-term appreciation potential.
- **Understand the process.** Read up on all steps of the homebuying process now, so that you won't be confused—or need to do any late-night remedial study—when the process kicks into high gear.
- **Get organized.** Use all the worksheets and checklists in the Homebuyer's Toolkit on this book's CD-ROM to stay on top of all your key tasks, such as choosing a real estate agent or inspector or pulling together financial papers for the lender.

This book will help you accomplish all those goals. It will tell you where you are at every step, so that you can breathe, get your bearings, and proceed with confidence. Get the facts, and you'll be ready.

What's Next?

Once you've decided you're ready to buy, it's time to figure out what's important to you. In the next chapter, we'll discuss how to examine and settle on your priorities regarding types of houses and neighborhoods.

What Do You Want?
Figuring Out Your Homebuying Needs

Meet Your Adviser

Paul Grucza, a community association expert and educator, author, and TV show host based in Coppell, Texas.

What he does With 29-plus years of real estate-related experience, Paul is an active faculty member for (and former President of) the Community Associations Institute (CAI, at www.caionline.org), which provides nationwide guidance and resources to the volunteer homeowners who govern community associations. Paul received CAI's 1999–2000 "Educator of the Year" award and hosted a community association issues television program for the Dallas-Fort Worth market, viewed by well over one million people per week. He's also the Executive Vice President and Corporate Trainer for Classic Property Management AAMC® in Arlington, Texas (www.classicpm.com), which provides professional management and consultant services for a variety of condominiums and planned communities.

First house "It was an absolutely rundown but gorgeous Mission-style bungalow built around 1922, in one of the first incorporated subdivisions outside Buffalo, New York. The house was the builder's model for that subdivision, so it had all the features, including inlaid floors, woodwork, and leaded glass. I spent the next 11 or so years lovingly restoring it—regrouting the bathroom tile, refinishing the woodwork, rebronzing the heat duct covers, replacing the modernized light fixtures through a restoration company, and much more. It turned out to be the most beautiful home I've ever owned."

Fantasy house "That would be a 5,300-square-foot combination Frank Lloyd Wright and modernistic house on a cliff or hill overlooking Newport Beach, California. I would fill it with 1950s or early 1960s period furniture. And it would be a technologically smart house—with voice-command lights, A/C, and garage door, all cutting-edge. Why 5,300 square feet? I had a house in Florida that size once, and it was comfortable—anything bigger feels overwhelmingly large."

Likes best about his work "My daily interaction with a wide variety of people. They include homeowners, developers, service professionals, managers, and board members. This brings me more joy than anything—and after nearly 30 years, I'd better enjoy my work!"

Top tip for first-time homebuyers "Regardless of the type of property you're looking for—whether a house, a condo, a cabin, a doublewide, or whatever—leave your emotions at home. Look at the property and its practical application in your life, and at what it will cost to turn it into your home."

You know you're ready to buy but are probably wondering, "Where do I start?" There's a lot to think about, like what kind of home or neighborhood you want, and what features you can't *possibly* live without. This chapter will help you:

- identify neighborhood characteristics that fit your personality and that maximize house-resale value

- understand how your lifestyle and plans should play into your choice of house

- learn the benefits and drawbacks of different types of properties (single-family houses, condominiums, or co-ops, plus new or old places), and finally

- create a Dream List, describing and organizing your priorities, to use when house shopping.

Later chapters will teach you how to do the looking, how to figure out whether you can afford what you want, and what to do once you've found a place. For now, focus on organizing your thoughts and priorities.

Test Your Knowledge of Famous Neighborhoods

Match these famous neighborhoods to their descriptions:

1. Bel Air, Los Angeles

2. Mr. Rogers's Neighborhood

3. SoHo, New York

4. Beacon Hill, Boston

5. The French Quarter, New Orleans

a. Formerly known as the Cast Iron District, this neighborhood shares its name (spelled slightly differently) with another big city neighborhood.

b. Open alcohol containers along with other debauchery, are permitted in this partying hot spot.

c. It's long been a hub for famous folk, including John Hancock, Charles Sumner ... and David Lee Roth.

d. Once home to a former President—and one "fresh" prince.

e. Probably the safest neighborhood in America.

Answers: 1-d, 2-e, 3-a, 4-c, 5-b.

Know Your Ideal Neighborhood: Why Location Matters

If you're a lifetime renter, you've probably always thought about location in the short term, knowing you could move at the end of your lease. Buying is different: You're committing yourself to a location for at least a few years. And you'll probably feel a sense of investment in your community that you didn't before. So get serious about identifying your location preferences, then make sure these preferences won't mean buying a house with low resale prospects.

Neighborhood Features for Daily Living

Not everyone wants the same features in a neighborhood, and you're the one who's got to live there. Before letting anyone else tell you what the best neighborhoods are, consider your preferences and priorities regarding:

- **Character and community.** For some, the uniformity of well-planned developments is pleasing; others enjoy the variety of older, one-of-a-kind homes. Visualize your ideal neighborhood, whether it features trees and parks or restaurants and bars.
- **Safety.** While most everyone prefers less crime, safety often comes with a trade-off. For example, a rural neighborhood might be safe, but a city's resources and nightlife will be very far away.
- **Resources and accessibility.** Think where the important places and resources in your life are, like your workplace, child's school or day care, grocery stores, health care providers, public transportation or major roadways, cultural amenities, and more. How much time are you willing to spend traveling to those places?

- **Schools.** If you're planning on sending children to public schools, the quality of nearby schools will be important.

- **Zoning and other restrictions on owners.** If you want the freedom to remodel your home, you'll have to be in an area that allows that. Or, if you appreciate community uniformity, you'll like living somewhere that limits the changes owners can make to their houses or property.

This isn't a complete list, and you should think about features that are unique to your needs. For example, adviser Bert Sperling notes, "If you're lucky enough to be a stay-at-home parent, you may find yourself lonely during the day if you have to travel a considerable distance to find some community for you and your youngsters."

Neighborhood Features That Boost Resale Value

When it comes to the long-term value of your home, location really *does* matter. If you have a desirable piece of property that's also in a desirable location, more people will want to buy it. That keeps its value relatively high compared to nearby homes in less sought-after locations (which people may buy partly because they can't afford anything else).

Not surprisingly, many of the features that attract first-time homebuyers boost resale value, like high-quality schools, low crime rates, convenient amenities, and neighborhood character and community. Another major factor affecting resale value is conformity. Buying a house that's much bigger than the houses around it is usually a bad idea. That house will appreciate at a slower rate, because buyers drawn to a neighborhood of smaller homes won't be able to afford the larger home, and buyers drawn to larger homes won't be drawn to that neighborhood. And if a house is just

They Call That a House?

You won't believe what people live in! Here are a few creative houses:

- The Golden Pyramid House in Wadsworth, Illinois: The largest 24-karat gold-plated object ever created.

- The Shoe House in Hellam, Pennsylvania: Just what it sounds like—in the shape of a work boot, made of light-colored stucco and featuring shoe-themed stained-glass windows in every room.

- A live-in water tower in Sunset Beach, California: from the 1940s, converted to a three-story house.

too unique—because the owner has customized it too much—it's going to stick out like a sore thumb.

Finally, try to get an idea of whether a neighborhood is up and coming. You can tell by looking at whether there seems to be a lot of remodeling, new landscaping, or trendy-looking shops. Bert Sperling adds, "If you read the signs correctly, you could get in on the ground floor of the next hot new neighborhood."

Know Yourself: How Your Lifestyle, Plans, and Values Affect Your House Priorities

Later in this chapter, we'll show you how to prepare a Dream List to help you find the right house. Before making your list, reflect on what you want the house for. (To live in, duh, we got that.) Although it may be hard to imagine where your life will be in a few years, do your best to consider:

- **Who is going to live in the home?** You may be on your own now, but in the future, might you bring in a roommate, significant other, child, elderly parent, or pet? If so, factor this into your priorities for things like number of bedrooms, quality of the school district, or availability of outdoor space.

- **What do you plan to do in the home?** If you plan to work at home, spend a lot of time in the kitchen, or entertain frequently, plan adequate space for that. Conversely, consider whether you really need to spend extra for a huge gourmet kitchen if you eat takeout every night.

- **What does your lifestyle require?** If you travel for business, you might want the convenience of a condo with easy airport access. Or if you're into nightlife, you might want to be able to stroll home and crash at 2 a.m.

- **How do you like to spend your time at home?** Do you love the idea of remodeling an old home or creating a beautiful garden? Are you scared to death of anything that hints at the word "handy"? If you'd rather be throwing a cocktail party than mowing the lawn, the big house in the suburbs may not really be right for you.

Best thing I ever did

Look for a house with scope for my artistic side. A graphic designer and yoga teacher, Diane had wanted to buy a house for years—but knew it would be a financial challenge. She says, "I scraped together enough to buy a small cottage, with a disastrous backyard—and I turned it into my art project. I painted those white walls celery green, brick red, and tan. I spent all winter pulling weeds, then put in flagstone and flowers. And eventually I sold it for a large profit—enough to buy a duplex, so now I'm a property investor!"

"Where *Could* I Be in Five Years?"

Instead of planning where you think you'll be in five years, why not play "Where *could* I be in five years?" Try it with a friend or partner over a glass of wine, or while walking in the park. You'll have to be a little realistic—do you *really* think you'll win the lottery?—but optimistic, too. You may see yourself finding a better job in another city, or having your first baby. Imagining the possibilities can help you not only define your housebuying objectives, but see how those goals fit into your life's priorities.

Know Your Ideal House: Old Bungalows, New Condos, and More

You probably have a vision in your mind of the house you want, whether it's a cozy cottage with fruit trees; an elegant brick townhouse with no yard; or a modern, glass-enclosed loft with views of the city. For an overview of your options, read on. (And when you're reading the bios of our advisers in this book, take a peek at their fantasy houses!)

Isn't my house classic? The columns date all the way back to 1972.

Cher, Clueless

Of course, where you live will play a huge role in what you can buy. For example, in Chicago or New York City, you may be looking at apartments in high-rise buildings, while in less urban areas, most of the homes may be single-story ranch houses or newly built homes within developments.

Would You Like Land With That? Single-Family Houses

You wouldn't think we'd have to define "house," would you? But since a number of different house types are available, let's be clear about what each one is. Technically speaking, a "house" is a detached, single-family dwelling. When you own a house, you own both the structure and the property that it sits on, all by yourself. Your house won't be attached to the next one, and you won't be cursing an upstairs neighbor for stumbling across the floor at 3 a.m.

Even if you know you want a house, however, an important question remains—new or previously lived in? Each has its own benefits and headaches.

> **CHECK IT OUT**
>
> **Interested in house styles?** To decide whether you prefer a "Colonial," a "Victorian," or an "Italian Renaissance," look online at sites such as:
>
> - www.architecture.about.com (search for "house styles")
> - www.oldhouses.com (click "Old House Style Guide")
> - www.wikipedia.org (search for "List of house styles").

Old (or Not-So-New) Houses: Benefits and Drawbacks

If you're in an uber-urban area or your price range dictates it, older houses may be all that are available to you. Or you may just prefer a touch of historical charm. Either way, you'll get all these benefits:

- **Affordability.** Older homes tend to cost less to purchase than new, customized homes. (Though this isn't a universal rule—in large cities, where the majority of new building is far outside the city, it can be the reverse.)

- **Established neighborhood.** Instead of looking at mounds of dirt while perusing architectural drawings, you'll be able to get a feel for the neighborhood by taking a stroll.

- **Established landscaping.** You're not likely to find a tree-lined street, or a wisteria arbor over your front gate, in a new development.

- **Construction.** Older homes are often built with high-quality materials such as thick beams, solid-wood doors, and heavy fixtures.
- **Character.** Crown molding and built-in cabinetry are just a few of the fun features found in older homes—but rarely in newer homes.

There are also drawbacks to previously loved homes, including:

- **Lower resale value.** Older homes, on average, sell for less than their newer counterparts.
- **Replacement costs.** The years take a toll on appliances, water heaters, and roofs—and replacing them isn't cheap.
- **Efficiency.** Older houses tend to be less energy efficient than newer ones.
- **Style.** Although you can probably switch out the former owner's unique style choices (like magenta bathroom tile), it may require a fair amount of sweat equity (meaning *your* sweat builds equity).
- **Layout.** Older houses were built for another era ... an era before plasma screen TVs and home offices. Rooms may be smaller and laid out differently than you'd like, with too few electrical outlets.

Of course, not every used home is *old*. If you buy one that was built only a few years ago, some of the drawbacks described above will be eliminated. Likewise, you'll lose some of the benefits.

Newly Built Houses: Benefits and Drawbacks

Nearly 1.6 million new homes are built in the United States each year, often in planned communities or developments. (Of course, you can always buy a piece of land and build a custom home—but that's a different book, with its own unique set of issues.) No surprise—buying a new home has unique benefits, including:

- **It's mine! It's new!** A new house is a blank slate, clean and virtually untouched.
- **It's custom-built.** Although most builders offer a limited choice of floor plans, you usually get to define details like paint colors, flooring, and fixtures (though good taste comes at a price).

- **All the modern conveniences.** New houses are built for today's lifestyles, so you'll be able to find features like a three-car garage, great room, or high-speed data lines. Also, you shouldn't have to worry about replacing a water heater or roof anytime soon.

- **Livin' green.** New houses are generally more energy efficient than older homes, so per square foot, you'll probably spend less money on things like heating and cooling costs. And with some searching, you might find a "green builder" who uses environmentally friendly building techniques and materials (see the U.S. Green Building Council's website at www. usgbc.org).

- **Community planning.** Many new homes are built in Planned Unit Developments (PUDs). Like condominiums, PUDs often have rules and amenities like swimming pools and community centers. If you like the conformity and resources you often get from a community association, but want the privacy of a detached home, a new home in a PUD might be a perfect compromise.

But buying new also has these drawbacks:

- **It costs HOW much?** New houses are generally worth more, but they tend to cost more, too. Developers often offer unique financing alternatives (discussed in Chapter 7), which may make a new house purchase more affordable.

- **Who's this guy?!** You might have to deal with the developer's salesperson or representative, without the benefit of your own real estate agent to protect you. If you hope to use an agent, be sure to bring him or her along on your first visit—otherwise, you may lose your chance.

- **Not time-tested.** While it's exciting to get a brand-new home, you'll be the first to discover whether all the lights work, the dishwasher runs, the water heater heats, and more.

- **It will be done *when*?!** Developers don't always finish houses when they expect to, and often don't compensate purchasers for the delay. Instead, the fine print may release them of liability. Worse yet, during the recent real estate downturn, the less financially stable builders had an unfortunate tendency to go bankruptct before the houses were finished at all, or before adding amenities such as a golf course or swimming pool.

- **More rules?** As we'll discuss when we get to condos, some PUDs require all owners to live by a set of written rules. Short of selling, there's often little you can do to get out of these rules if you don't like them.

Sharing the Joy, Sharing the Pain: Common Interest Properties

Maybe a traditional house isn't for you—perhaps it's out of your price range, you're looking to avoid all the maintenance, or you want to live in an area that just doesn't have many regular houses. In that case, you may want to consider an alternative, like a condominium ("condo") or co-op.

These types of properties are often referred to as common interest developments (CIDs), because they involve shared ownership or responsibility for common areas like hallways, recreation rooms, or playgrounds. How a place looks physically doesn't really make a difference—any of these three might look like an apartment, flat, loft, or townhouse; old or new; in the city or the country. (Houses in PUDs count too, but since we've already covered those, we won't include them in this section.)

Are you picturing yourself out on the roof with a hammer, doing your share for the common good? Don't worry, you won't likely be asked to perform repairs or fix elevators. But you *will* have to become a member of a community association, which makes sure those things are done. Your monthly membership fee will help keep common areas in good shape and provide a cash reserve for unanticipated or larger projects like replacing a roof. If you want to actively participate in the association, you can attend meetings and voice your opinion—or even get yourself elected to the board of directors. If you don't, you just write the check and hope the more active owners are like-minded.

There are three types of community associations: planned community associations (for PUDs and townhouses), condominium associations, and co-op associations. We'll point out any significant differences among them as we go.

> **TIP**
> **What the association leaders do.** Though every CID homeowner must join the community association, the board of directors handles the day-to-day work and decision making, such as coordinating repairs and collective services like trash pickup; managing amenities such as swimming pools, playgrounds, and tennis courts; preparing annual budgets; and conducting meetings.

Condominiums: Benefits and Drawbacks

When you buy a condo, you buy the interior space of your home. Your walls, ceiling, and floors define your boundaries instead of fences and sidewalks. Everything in the common space—be it stairwells, swimming pools, sidewalks, or gardens—the whole community owns together and is financially responsible for. Some of the benefits of condo life include:

- **Affordability.** A condo often costs less to buy than a house (although in major metropolitan or resort areas, the opposite is sometimes true). Maintaining a condo can also be less expensive, since costs that otherwise might be duplicated—like landscaping, roofing, and some insurance— are shared.

- **Convenience.** If you aren't into maintenance, you'll appreciate that the condo association—particularly in a larger complex—is likely to hire a management company to take care of the common areas. You may also get valuable on-site amenities like a gym or pool.

- **Community.** Because you're all part of the same community association, you'll get the opportunity to know your neighbors, whether you wish to or not.

Every rose has its thorns. Some of the drawbacks to condo living include:

- **Rules, rules, rules.** You'll be subject to a document called the master deed or Declaration of Covenants, Conditions, and Restrictions (CC&Rs). This sets forth not only rules for the community association management to follow, but rules governing all owners. You'll be told what you can do in the common space, and even what you can do with or in your own unit.

- **Buy for less, sell for less.** Condos generally appreciate at a slower rate than houses. And some have gotten into serious financial trouble in recent years, leaving homeowners unable to sell at all.

Diet-Time for Fido?

What kinds of things do CC&Rs limit? Common examples are:
- whether you can have a pet, and if so, its maximum height or weight
- whether you'll get a parking space, or whether your guests can park in the lot
- whether you can change the color of your curtains or paint the outside of your unit
- the location or appearance of things like your mailbox, clothesline, TV antennas, and wreaths
- how long visitors can stay with you
- whether you can rent your unit to someone else, and
- whether you can smoke in your unit.

- **Privacy.** Since you'll be sharing common areas and usually walls or ceilings, too, you'll be giving up some privacy. Also, if having a large outdoor space to garden, entertain, or keep a pet is important, you might be frustrated by the outdoor spaces, which are usually either miniscule or communal.

- **You share all costs, whether you want to or not.** It may be frustrating to see your monthly membership dues spent on things you never use, like the swimming pool. And if you're the kind of person who can live without a repair until you have spare cash, tough luck—you'll be forced to pay your share on the association's schedule, sometimes in excess of your regular fees. If you get behind on paying your dues, your condo association may have the power to foreclose on you (even if you're up to date on your mortgage)!

- **It can cost more than you expect.** In addition to your monthly membership dues, you may have to pay additional fees called "special assessments." These are one-time fees collected for major purchases the association can't afford to make with its current reserves (for example, to replace the roof). Do your research: In recent years, with many new buildings not fully occupied, the few owners in some CIDs have found their special assessments very high.

TIP

Size matters in condo developments. Your experience will be a lot different in a Boca Raton megaplex than in a Brooklyn brownstone. In a building with fewer units, you may find the rules less constricting—but you may also be more responsible for day-to-day operations and costs.

Townhouses and Duplexes: Benefits and Drawbacks

One compromise between a single-family dwelling and a traditional condo is a townhouse. Townhouses are usually built in rows and share at least one common wall (also called "row houses"). Like single-family houses, each townhouse owner has title to the building and the land it sits on. Like condos, townhouses may share some common areas, governed by a community association (but unlike condos, the community association usually owns the common area).

Just be sure, when you start househunting, to find out for sure what type of property you're looking at. If a careless ad or agent calls a property a townhouse, but it's really a condo, you'd own a little less personally (because the land isn't yours, nor is the outside of your unit) and should pay less accordingly.

> *Celebrities Who've Owned Co-ops*
>
> Among the big names who've made a co-op home (or maybe one of their homes) are Jimmy Fallon, Chloe Sevigny, Sean Combs (a.k.a. Diddy), Matthew Perry, and Kelis.

Co-ops: Benefits and Drawbacks

Co-ops sound so glamorous, don't they? But what are they, other than swanky apartments in New York City for the rich and famous?

Like condos, co-ops are defined by their ownership structure. When you own a house or condo, you own a piece of physical property. When you own a co-op, however, you own shares in a corporation. The corporation, in turn, owns the building you live in, and you get a proprietary lease to live in a specific unit within the building. The lease allows you to live there as long as you own your shares and spells out any restrictions on your use of the unit.

As with any corporation, your shares also give you voting rights. Shareholders elect the board of directors, who make most of the decisions and manage daily operations or hire staff to do so. The shareholders pay a monthly "maintenance fee" to cover these and other costs. Usually, the more desirable the unit a shareholder has, the higher the maintenance fee.

Because of your limited ownership and other financial issues (discussed in Chapter 6), co-ops are sometimes difficult for the average first-time homebuyer to afford. The limitations also mean that co-ops tend to be quite slow to appreciate in value.

Factory Made: Modular and Manufactured Homes

Buying a prefabricated home no longer means living in an insubstantial-looking box. In fact, it's a creative possibility and a growing trend. Modern, multistory dwellings, now known as "modular homes," are built in blocks in factories and transported to properties, where they're fully assembled to comply with local building codes. If you decide to buy a property and build a home on it, a modular home might be a relatively low-cost option.

Million-Dollar Mobile Homes?

Yes, you'll find them in Malibu: Even the rich and famous (like Minnie Driver) sometimes retreat to manufactured home communities.

However, you'll have to consider additional expenses like transporting the home; getting the proper permits and access to utilities and sewer lines; hiring professionals for installations; and adding features like landscaping, driveways, or fences. A local contractor may be able to give you a brief overview of the costs, players, and timeline.

CHECK IT OUT

Check out modular homes styles, from the traditional to the ultra-modern, at:

- www.modularcenter.com
- www.mkd-arc.com
- www.cusatocottages.com (the famous "Katrina cottage")
- www.maplehomes.com.

Another low-cost option is the manufactured house, once commonly referred to as a mobile home. These too have come a long way. Manufactured homes comply with federal building standards but aren't constricted by local or state building codes.

Manufactured homes are typically transported to communities of other, similar homes, and the owners lease the land the homes sit on. If the lease is terminated or the land is sold, the owners can be required to leave and take their homes with them. Since a lot of the value of a home is in the land, these homes tend to *lose* value over time, and moving one may cost more than it's worth. Manufactured homes are often more difficult to finance, too. The bottom line is that they're low-cost options to more permanent properties but don't usually offer the same equity-building advantages.

Putting It All Together: Your Dream List

Now it's time to fill out what we call your "Dream List." This is a handy worksheet where you'll write down your "must haves," such as number of bedrooms, size or type of house, neighborhood, maximum price, and anything else you consider a minimum requirement in a home, such as a garden. There's also space for you to note your "would likes," features you'd prefer but could live without or possibly add later (such as a deck). Of course, expressing your preferences

> Ooh! I forgot about the washer and dryer! I've been dreaming about that my whole New York life!
>
> Carrie, *Sex and the City*

doesn't mean you'll *get* all of them. But later, when you're out househunting, carrying a copy of your Dream List will help make sure you keep your priorities straight.

The Dream List also includes a section for things you absolutely won't accept, under any condition, such as a kitchen with bad lighting. You might need this reminder one day, when you find a house that's perfect in every other respect.

TIP
Check in with your partner. If you're buying the house with another person, make sure you assess your priorities and complete the Dream List *together*. It won't help to make a list of priorities, only to find out they're in direct conflict with your fellow buyer's.

Best thing I ever did

Put my practical needs as a single woman first. Hope thought she was looking for a cute Craftsman with wainscoting, high ceilings, and a yard. "In fact," she says, "I almost bought a house that fit my supposed ideal. But at the last minute, I realized it wasn't going to work. My work hours don't leave time for home maintenance, and my safety was an issue in that neighborhood. So I switched gears and bought a late '80s townhouse with a drive-in garage with direct access to the house, in a nicer neighborhood. It's architecturally boring, but I'm comfortable there, the homeowners' association deals with most of the maintenance, and I haven't had a moment's regret."

CD-ROM
The "Dream List" can be found in the Homebuyer's Toolkit on the CD-ROM. A partial sample is shown below.

Dream List			
Address:		**Date visited:**	
General Features	**Must Have**	**Would Like**	**This House**
Type (house, condo, etc.) or Style (Colonial, loft, etc.)			
Upper price limit	$	$	
Age above/below			
Min. square footage			
Min. lot size			
Number of bedrooms			
Number of bathrooms			
___ car garage			
Parking			
Fireplace			
Other:			
Other:			
Other:			
Floor Plan:			
Formal living/dining			
Great room			
Number of floors			
Basement/attic			
Other:			

Dream List Directions

This Dream List includes the more common features found in many homes, but you can add others to this list (perhaps a must-have hillside location with a view) or delete some features. Add as many details as you want in the left-hand column ("General Features"). At the end of the Dream List, there's a section for those things you absolutely will not accept, under any condition. There's also a section at the end for notes, such as comments about a particular house or neighborhood—something you want to be sure to remember, such as a quiet location at the end of a cul de sac. These last two sections are not shown on the Sample Dream List, but they are on the complete form, which is available on the CD-ROM.

Fill in the "Must Have" column with your minimum requirements and the "Would Like" column with features you'd prefer but could live without. For example, for the "Number of Bedrooms" feature, you might write "3" in the "Must Have" column and "4" in the "Would Like" column. For some features, you can simply place a check mark to show that yes, you must have or would like that feature (such as a dishwasher). In some cases, you'll add additional information: For example, you might put a checkmark indicating that a house meets your upper price limit, and then note the actual price of the house. If a "Must Have" can be added when you move in, such as a deck or second bathroom, you can also note this.

If you fill out the left columns of the Dream List now and print more copies, you can use this sheet over and over again. Each time you visit a house, simply write in the address and note how it compares in the right-hand column ("This House"). Save copies for homes that seem like good possibilities.

What's Next?

Now that you know what features you're looking for, it's time to figure out whether you can afford them all. In Chapter 3, we'll explain how a lender is going to evaluate your finances and what you should do to evaluate them yourself.

Does This Mean I Have to Balance My Checkbook? Figuring Out What You Can Afford

Meet Your Adviser

Russell Straub, a former mortgage broker and founder, President, and Chief Executive Officer of LoanBright, a mortgage intermediary service based in Evergreen, Colorado, whose services involve two websites, www.loanbright.com and www.compareinterestrates.com.

What he does Helps LoanBright serve its goal of giving homeowners a convenient way to find the right mortgage broker as well as a loan with favorable terms. Homebuyers visit the company's website, Compare interestrates.com, enter some basic information, receive a list of lenders or brokers and available loan terms, and consent to being contacted. At the other end of the transaction, LoanBright helps mortgage brokers (particularly sole proprietors or independent ones) meet these potential clients.

First house "It was a condo in Boston, a 350-square-foot studio—big enough for me, by myself. I bought it during a run-up in real estate prices—at the peak, as it turned out! I was working as a manufacturing engineer and didn't know a thing about real estate. I chose my mortgage broker because she lived two floors up from me in my apartment building, but she managed to shepherd me through. Although the 1980s real estate crash hit not long afterward, I held onto the place. In fact, even though I now live in Colorado, I still own the condo and rent it out, and it has since tripled or quadrupled in value."

Fantasy house "Right on the ski slopes at Vail. I already spend some time there, but not enough. If you've been there, you know the style I'd like—wood, European looking, with a wood-shake tile roof, ski in/ski out."

Likes best about his work	"My short commute from home is great. Also, I like how each of us at LoanBright brings something different to the table, with varying interests and viewpoints, which we can combine into something new. I'm also conscious of the fact that we have the ability to change the lives of the solo or small-business mortgage and loan brokers whom we consider our primary customers. Many of them are honestly struggling—some are single moms—and it's a competitive business, with more people doing the jobs than there are transactions. We're trying to do the right thing for them. It's also satisfying to be able to help homebuyers get competitive loan quotes, potentially saving them thousands of dollars on their new mortgage."

• •

Top tip for first-time homebuyers	"Do your homework. Read about the process, ask your questions, and talk to more than one broker and lender. It can take a while to get the hang of it. But I read a survey recently saying that consumers booking a hotel room online spend an average of one hour or more selecting a hotel. If homebuyers would spend a proportionate amount of time researching their prospective purchase and mortgage, they'd come out way ahead. But I've met many who spent less than an hour getting educated about buying a home!"

CD-ROM

For more tips from Russell Straub, check out his audio interview on the CD-ROM at the back of this book.

U p to this point, we've been able to focus on the fun stuff—finding out all the great reasons to buy a house and imagining what the new place will look like. Now it's time to take a step into the world of finances—nothing that will require an accounting degree, fortunately. You may be wondering why we're even bringing up boring financial stuff before you've started seriously househunting. That's what a mortgage broker is for, isn't it?

But wouldn't it be horrible to put an offer on a house and begin shopping for a loan, only to discover that you couldn't qualify for the amount you needed or the terms you expected? Even worse, what if you were able to get a loan, but discovered after moving into your new home that you'd borrowed more than you could handle—at least, without moonlighting?

Don't Play the Multiplication Game

You may have heard of a formula where you multiply your household's gross annual income by two and a half to find out how much you can afford to spend. This may be fun and easy, but it won't help you draw realistic conclusions. It fails to factor in important things like how much debt you currently have, the terms of your mortgage, or how much you already have saved for a down payment. If you really want to guess how much you can spend before reading this chapter, you're better off using a reliable online affordability calculator like the one at www.nolo.com/legal-calculators.

Getting familiar with your finances before there's a prospective property in sight—even if you just sit down for an hour or two—will show you how much you can realistically afford to spend and prepare you to choose the best possible loan. This chapter will help you by:

- explaining the costs of purchasing a house
- demystifying the process mortgage lenders use to decide how much you can borrow
- providing simple ways to calculate what you can *really* afford based on your lifestyle and finances

- showing you how to boost your financial profile, and
- explaining what it means to get preapproved for a loan and why you should do so.

If you've already found a place and are trying to figure out how to pay for it, don't skip this chapter. A quick look at your finances will still help you decide whether your prospective home's cost is within your budget and whether you're likely to get the loan terms you're counting on.

Beyond the Purchase Price: The Costs of Buying and Owning a Home

Buying a house means some new expenses beyond the purchase price. A first-time homebuyer should plan to drop some cash for:

- the down payment
- the loan principal, loan interest, taxes, and insurance
- up-front costs, mostly to close the deal, and
- recurring ownership costs.

The exact amounts of these expenses depend on you, the house you buy and where you buy it, and the type of mortgage you get. But even if you can't predict exact amounts, understanding these expenses and what drives them will save you some sticker shock.

Do We *Have* to Talk About Money?

We know, all this talk about numbers makes watching an MP3 download seem fascinating. But if you're one of those people who never balances a checkbook, this exercise is even more important—unless you think it's worth thousands not to deal with the hassle. If you pay just half a percent more than you could have if you'd done some research—say, 5% instead of 4.5%, on a 30-year, fixed-rate mortgage for $200,000—you could end up paying almost $22,000 more in interest over the life of the loan.

Down Payment

You may be plunking down a hefty chunk of change, in the form of a down payment, to buy your home. Due to recent tightening up of lending practices, it's rare to find a lender who will make you a loan if your down payment is anything less than 20% of the house's purchase price, although the most pristine borrowers may be able to go as low as 5%–10%.

Nevertheless, there are many benefits to making a large down payment:

> *Tick, Tick, Tick*
>
> Finding the house you want to buy might not take as long as you think. According to a 2008 survey by the National Association of Realtors®, the typical homebuyer spent ten weeks searching before settling on a house.

- **No PMI.** If you pay 20% of your purchase price, you don't have to pay private mortgage insurance, or PMI, which lenders routinely require of homebuyers who borrow more than 80% of the home's value, to protect the lender if you default.

- **Smaller monthly mortgage payments.** If you borrow less money, you'll have less to pay back, leaving you more cash for other things.

- **Less interest overall.** If you borrow less, you'll owe less in total interest. For example, if you got a 30-year, fixed rate loan for $200,000 and paid 6.5% interest, you'd pay approximately $255,090 in interest over the life of the loan. But you'd pay only about $204,070 over the life of a $160,000 loan with the same terms. The bank would get over $51,000 more in interest just because you didn't put $40,000 down at the beginning.

- **It's like money in the bank.** No matter what the market does, putting cash into your home is a low-risk way to use it.

- **Lower interest rate.** Borrowers who take out mortgages for more than a certain amount ($417,000 in most places in 2010, but it is higher in high-cost areas such as Hawaii and New York City—up to $729,750 in 2010—and can change annually) get what are called "jumbo" loans, with higher interest rates. If making a down payment will lower your loan to below that amount, your interest rate will probably drop, too. Likewise, if you're a borrower with poor credit, you might be able to obtain better loan terms if you fork over more cash at the beginning—the lender figures you've got more incentive to keep paying if you stand to lose your down payment when the lender forecloses.

Where Will I Get Down Payment Money?

If you're interested in making a down payment but haven't saved the cash, here are some alternative sources:

- **A gift or loan from family or friends.** If you have a loved one with available cash, you may be able to get a low-interest loan, or even a gift. Around one third of first-time homebuyers get help from friends and family—either as a gift or a loan—for the down payment. However, you'll need to keep an eye on your lender's rules regarding the source of your down payment. Adviser Russell Straub notes, "If one gets an FHA mortgage, there are no restrictions on the amount or percentage of the gift so long as it comes from a blood relative. If one gets a conventional mortgage and the gift is for less than 20% of the purchase price, however, the borrower(s) must make at least 5% of the down payment from their own funds, and the gift(s) must be from a blood relative."

- **Withdrawal from your IRA.** You can withdraw up to $10,000, penalty-free, from an individual retirement account (IRA) to purchase your first home. Your spouse or cobuyer can do the same. For more information, see IRS Publication 590, *Individual Retirement Arrangements (IRAs)*, available at www.irs.gov.

- **Borrow from your 401(k).** Check with your employer or plan administrator about whether you can borrow from your 401(k) plan. Also ask how much you can borrow (usually, $50,000 at most). For more information, see IRS Publication 575, *Pension and Annuity Income*, available at www.irs.gov.

- **Current assets.** If you have other investments, like stocks or bonds, consider cashing them out—but be sure to factor in the taxes you'll owe.

- **Don't have a big wedding!** Okay, we're half joking here. But you wouldn't believe the number of couples we've met who said that, in retrospect, they wish they'd kept the wedding small and put that money toward a house.

B est thing we ever did — **Make a 30% down payment.** According to Nigel, "When Olivia and I decided to buy a house together, we were earning nonprofit salaries (low). But our parents were excited to see us settle down and gave us generous gifts. Between that and emptying our savings account, we had about 30% to put down—which convinced the seller to choose our bid from among the many others, because we'd obviously have no trouble financing the rest. Now we have absurdly low monthly payments—less than we'd be paying in rent—and the house has appreciated in value. Also, we're in a position to help our parents out financially, if they need it."

Principal, Interest, Taxes, and Insurance

Ever heard of PITI (pronounced "pity")? It stands for principal, interest, taxes, and insurance, all of which must be factored into your homebuying plans. Here's the breakdown on these expense items:

- **Principal.** The amount you borrow from the lender and must pay back, month by month.

- **Interest.** A percentage of the overall borrowed amount that the lender charges you to use its money. The exact rate varies widely.

- **Property taxes.** Taxes vary by state and sometimes by local area, but expect to pay between 2% and 4% of the house purchase price each year, if the place you live fits the national average.

- **Homeowners' insurance.** Coverage for theft, fire, and other damage to the property (required by your lender) and usually for your liability to people injured on your property or by you. Average rates run upwards of $600 per year.

It makes sense that these four items have their own acronym, PITI, because for some homebuyers (usually those whose down payment is less than 20%), all four must be paid straight to the mortgage lender each month. The lender turns around and pays the appropriate party. The lender's rationale is that if you don't pay these bills (or your mortgage) and the lender gets the property, it doesn't want to get stuck with your tax or insurance bill, too.

> **TIP**
> **PITI is paid differently when you buy a condo or co-op.** Instead of paying the lender, you may have to pay your community association or co-op board for your portion of the mortgage and real estate taxes (on a co-op), or for insurance on the jointly owned parts of the property (on either a condo or a co-op).

Added together, your total PITI may come to a lot more than your current monthly rent. That makes owning a home look like an expensive proposition. But it's not an apples-to-apples comparison. First, remember that your mortgage payments typically reduce your loan principal, so your payment is building equity, not just going into a black hole. Second, your interest payments and property taxes are tax-deductible.

EXAMPLE: Mieko and Lyle buy a house for $250,000, putting down $25,000 and financing the remainder with a mortgage. Not only are their monthly mortgage payments $1,350 a month, but the mortgage lender also collects $450 each month to pay their homeowners' insurance and annual property taxes, for a total monthly payment of $1,800. The money for the tax and insurance bills is held in an escrow account, which the lender draws on to pay the bills when due. At the end of the first year, Mieko and Lyle will be able to deduct about $15,800 from their taxable income: $2,400 for property taxes and about $13,400 for interest paid on the mortgage.

Up-Front Costs

Until now, we've been talking about costs associated with the house itself. But you'll also have to spend some pretty serious cash at the beginning to make the sale happen. (Sort of like paying first and last month's rent.) Particularly if you're trying to save up for a decent-sized down payment, you'll need to plan for the following additional up-front costs:

- **Closing costs.** An array of miscellaneous and sometimes aggravating charges—for everything from couriers to loan points (discussed below) to insurance premiums—are lumped into a category called "closing costs." These vary across the country, but are usually 2% to 5% of the house purchase price.

- **Points.** Borrowers often agree to pay a "loan origination fee" or "points" to obtain a specific loan. Each point is 1% of the loan principal (so one point on a $100,000 loan is $1,000). Paying points can lower your interest rate, so you pay less in the long term. But you'll probably need to pay the cash up front (although points can be amortized into your loan—meaning added on, with interest accruing).

- **Moving costs.** How high these will go depends on how far you're moving, how much stuff you have, and whether you use a professional moving company.

- **Service setup costs.** You may have to pay fees to set up cable, phones, DSL, and similar services in your new home.

- **Emergency fund.** It's a good idea (and sometimes a lender requirement) to have a couple months' worth of PITI payments saved, in case something goes unexpectedly awry.

- **Remodeling costs.** If you buy a fixer-upper or a planned remodel, you might need thousands of dollars in cash early on, just to make the place livable. Estimate high for these expenses—they're almost always more than anyone expected.

Recurring Costs

Yes, there's more. Whether new or old, your house will need regular maintenance—gutters cleaned and trees trimmed regularly, a paint job every few years, new appliances when the old ones die, and so on. If you buy in a common interest development, your own maintenance costs may go down, but you'll have to pay monthly dues and sometimes special assessments for unanticipated projects like resurfacing a damaged parking lot. While not part of your PITI, all of these expenses will affect your monthly cash flow.

TIP

Adjust your deductions. Once you know the details of your mortgage, work with a financial professional to change your withholdings to account for your lower tax liability, freeing up more money for other expenses.

Spend Much?
How Lenders Use Your Debt-to-Income Ratio

Once you understand what you'll be paying for, and that you'll probably need a mortgage to make it happen, the obvious question is, how much can you borrow? To know that, you need to understand how lenders think. Just as you're trying to get the best loan, lenders are looking for the best borrowers.

Without knowing you personally, lenders need some criteria to figure out how risky it is to lend you money. If you make your payments, they'll turn a profit, either in interest or by selling your loan on the secondary market (more on that in Chapter 6). If you don't, they'll have to chase you down for the cash or sell the property to try to get it.

One of the criteria that lenders use is the comparison between your income and your debt load, called your "debt-to-income" ratio. They also look at your track record for paying previous debts, or your credit history, discussed below.

The concept of "debt-to-income ratio" isn't as complicated as it sounds. The lender simply looks at your household's gross monthly income, then makes sure that your combined minimum debt payments—for your PITI (including any community association fees), credit card, car, student loan, and others—don't eat up more than a certain percentage of that amount. The idea is to make sure you have enough cash left over for your mortgage payment.

Maximum Acceptable Ratios: The 28/36 Rule

How high can your debt-to-income ratio go? Traditionally, lenders have said that your PITI payment shouldn't exceed 28% of your gross monthly income, and your overall debt shouldn't exceed 36%. (Your gross monthly income means the amount you earn before taxes and other monthly withdrawals, plus income from all other sources, like royalties, alimony, or investments.)

EXAMPLE: Fernando and Luz have a gross annual income of $90,000 ($7,500 per month) and a moderate amount of existing debt. If they plan to spend 28% of their gross monthly income on PITI, they'll pay $2,100 each month. Assuming they spend about $300 of that on taxes and insurance, they can borrow about $315,000 using a 30-year, fixed rate loan at 5% interest.

Khanh and May also have an gross annual income of $90,000, but they're debt-free, so they can spend 36% of their gross monthly income on PITI. Spending the same on taxes and insurance, they can borrow about $363,000 using a 30-year, fixed rate loan at 5% interest. With the same income but a higher debt-to-income ratio, Khanh and May can spend a lot more money on a house than Fernando and Luz.

CHECK IT OUT

Ready to run some numbers? Online affordability calculators show how a traditional lender will use your debt-to-income ratio to set your maximum monthly mortgage payment. Find such calculators at www.nolo.com/legal-calculators, www.hsh.com, www.bankrate.com, and www.interest.com. Make sure any calculator you use factors in the amount of your down payment, your income and your debts, and your estimated taxes and insurance.

Calculating Your Own Debt-to-Income Ratio

All you need to figure out your own debt-to-income ratio is your combined gross monthly income figure plus that of anyone buying with you. This will tell you approximately what a lender will say you can afford to spend each month on a mortgage payment. See the sample Debt-to-Income Ratio Worksheet below.

CD-ROM

You'll find a blank version of the "Debt-to-Income Ratio Worksheet" in the Homebuyer's Toolkit on the CD-ROM included in this book.

Sample Debt-to-Income Ratio Worksheet		
Gross monthly income:	$2,000	
Gross monthly income × 0.28	$560	Maximum monthly PITI payment
Gross monthly income × 0.36	$720	Maximum monthly debt overall

Blasts From the Past: How Your Credit History Factors In

Aside from your available income, your lender's main preoccupation will be with your credit history. Most lenders want to know whom they'll be competing with to get your monthly dollars, how much you're borrowing from those various sources, and how good you've been about paying money back in the past. You've probably undergone credit history checks before, like when you applied for a car loan or rented a new apartment.

Managing Your Money Is So Easy!

You just use your credit cards! You pay your American Express with your Discover, your Discover with your Visa, your Visa with your MasterCard. Before they catch up with you, you're buried in a glorious crypt in Bel-Air!

Camilla, character on TV series *The Naked Truth*

Credit reporting bureaus exist to keep track of your borrowing habits. The three major companies are Equifax (www.equifax.com), Experian (www.experian.com), and TransUnion (www.transunion.com). They use a formula compiled by the Fair Isaac Corporation to calculate your "FICO" score (which we'll call your "credit score"; but beware when you see this term other places, because anyone can compile a number and call it a "credit" score).

How Lenders Use Credit Scores

Lenders use your credit score to decide whether to lend you money and, if so, how much and on what terms. If you'll be financing your home jointly with others, the lender will look at each person's credit score. Unfortunately, that means that if one of you has a low score, it will probably affect the terms of the loan offered to all of you. If any of you has serious skeletons in the financial closet, either clear out the closet, reconsider the joint purchase, or get creative with your financing strategies.

Getting Your Own Credit Report and Score

The best way to know exactly what prospective lenders will be looking at is to look at it yourself first. Federal law requires each of the three major consumer reporting companies (named above) to provide you with a free copy of your credit report once every 12 months.

 CHECK IT OUT

The only authorized source for free credit reports: Go to www. annualcreditreport.com. Other websites may advertise a "free report" but try to sell you something in the process. This site also links you directly to the websites for the big three reporting bureaus.

essons learned the hard way **Being financially responsible left me with no credit history!** When Willow decided to buy her first house, she didn't expect her lack of debt to create a problem. Willow explains, "I'd worked my way through school and taken out a student loan that I'd paid off almost immediately. And I'd always used a debit card instead of a credit card. As a result, I had to jump through all sorts of extra hoops, providing a letter from my old landlord showing that I paid the rent on time; showing records of my payments of phone bills, cable bills; and even having my parents add my name to their credit card account. (That last strategy worked faster than I expected—within one month, my credit score was the same as theirs.) Here I thought I'd been so good at controlling my finances, yet I discovered I'd been completely naïve when it came to creating a record of debt payments."

It's a good idea to ask all three agencies for your credit report. They sometimes have different information, and your lender may be looking at all three reports. You can do this simultaneously, but it means that you won't be able to get another free report from any of them for another full year.

Federal law doesn't require the agencies to give you your credit *score*, which is different from your report. You'll probably have to pay extra to get the score (unless you live in a state like California that requires that consumers be given their scores for free when getting a mortgage). You can get your credit score either from the individual consumer reporting company websites or by going to www.myfico.com.

What Your Credit Score Means

When you get your credit score, it will be a number somewhere between 300 and 850—the higher the better. If your score is in the 700s, it's considered pretty strong. Most people are in the 600s or 700s. A higher number tells the lender you pay your debts on time, have limited sources of revolving credit, and have an established record of using credit prudently, making you a good credit risk. A lower number means you look more risky—perhaps because you have enough revolving credit that if you maxed it all out you couldn't pay all your bills plus a mortgage; you've missed payments in the past; or you've never used any credit source, so the lender doesn't know what to make of you.

A low score will make it difficult to find a willing lender. And any lender you do find will expect you to pay more for that privilege of lending you money, probably in the form of higher interest. (If your credit is less than perfect, you can clean it up, as we'll discuss below.)

CHECK IT OUT

What makes up a FICO score? It includes your payment history (35% of the score), how much you currently owe (30%), how long you've been a borrower (15%), whether you have any new credit accounts (10%), and the types of credit you use (10%). To learn more, go to www.myfico.com, a Fair Isaac website for consumers.

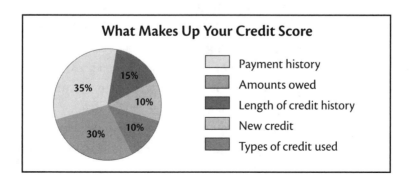

What Makes Up Your Credit Score

- 35% — Payment history
- 30% — Amounts owed
- 15% — Length of credit history
- 10% — New credit
- 10% — Types of credit used

Understanding Your Credit Report

Get ready: Your credit report may go on for *literally* pages and pages. Focus on making sure the most critical information is mistake-free, particularly these bits of data:

- **Name, Social Security Number, and addresses.** Especially if your name is a common one, you may have multiple aliases. And an address you don't recognize may mean someone with the same name is incorrectly listed on your report.

- **Creditors.** Make sure you actually borrowed money from the creditors that appear, and that the amounts borrowed are accurate. Keep in mind that some types of loans, like student loans, can be sold or transferred. In that case, all creditors that have held the loan will appear, but the pre-transferred or sold accounts should no longer be designated "open."

- **Open credit lines.** Make sure any lines of credit you've closed are no longer shown as open. Different reporting companies use different terminology, so if you're not sure, call to clarify.

- **Collections and judgments.** Make sure any collections actions or judgments are reflected accurately.

- **Late payments.** These notations will usually indicate a late payment of 30, 60, or 90 days. Make sure they're accurate.

Correcting Credit Errors

Credit reporting mistakes happen frequently. Inaccuracies in the report affect your score, and if your score drops, so does the likelihood of you getting the best possible loan. You'll want to spot and correct any errors before a lender sees your report, not after you've applied for a loan and been rejected.

All manner of mistakes are possible—from bits of credit history that aren't yours to a false claim that you paid a bill late. To correct such errors, contact the reporting agency in writing. If all three agencies misreported the information, you'll have to contact all three. Each agency may have a different procedure and forms to use for disputing the report. When you discuss issues over the phone, make sure to document conversations, including the date and name of the person you spoke with. Finally, if you have any documentation that supports your claim, send a copy with an explanatory cover letter.

The credit reporting agency has 30 days to investigate your complaint and give you its findings. If it can't verify that its version of events is correct, the agency is supposed to remove the information from your file. If it won't, you have the right to place a statement in your file giving your version of what happened.

Sometimes you can also work directly with your current and former creditors to correct inaccuracies or solve problems. If you're willing to pay the disputed amount, or the creditor is willing to settle for a lesser amount—which it sometimes is—the creditor may also agree to clear the item from your credit history. Likewise if you have proof of an error, it may be faster to go directly through the creditor than to correct it through the reporting bureau.

CHECK IT OUT

Need help patching up your credit? See *Credit Repair*, by Robin Leonard and John Lamb (Nolo). It offers plain-English explanations and over 30 forms and letters to help you negotiate with creditors, get positive information added to your credit record, and build a financial cushion.

Repairing Your Credit

Rome wasn't built in a day, and credit history can't be repaired in one, either. If you or a coborrower have a poor credit history, Fair Isaac suggests you start cleaning it up six to 12 months before applying for a loan. If your credit history is really messy, it may take even longer.

But here's some good news: Even if you have a long, ugly credit history, your score will be weighted in favor of your latest performance. Turn over a new leaf by following these strategies:

- **Pay on time from now on.** Don't miss due dates for credit cards and other bills. Setting up automatic payment plans can help, and your lender may reduce your interest rate in return.

- **Pay the worst first.** Start by paying off high-interest debt, like on credit cards. Also, keep your balances low on revolving lines of credit. Don't just move the debt around—that won't fool the credit scorers, nor will it free up cash for a mortgage payment.

TIP

Check out FHA-backed loans. Some low down payment federal loan programs are less strict about credit background. See Chapter 7 for details.

What's Your Monthly Budget? Understanding Your Finances

Now that you've seen what lenders look at to decide how much you can spend, it's time to think about what *you* believe you can spend. The point is to avoid taking on so much debt that you lose sleep or have to give up sushi for ramen noodles.

In fact, if you look closer at that debt-to-income ratio, you'll realize that it has a built-in problem. It's based on your *gross* income—the amount you theoretically make before your paycheck gets eaten by taxes and other withdrawals. Your mortgage payment could end up being at least half of what you actually take home. Depending on your lifestyle, spending that much on a house might sound either just fine or ridiculously impossible.

The easiest way to understand your current spending and savings pattern is to do a budget worksheet. You can do this using either special budgeting software, a spreadsheet like Excel, or the old-fashioned way, with a pencil and paper. List all your expenses, including food, entertainment, clothing, transportation and car-related expenses, health and dental care, child and pet care, student loans, and utilities. Hold onto your receipts, and if you use an ATM card or make electronic payments, look at your bank statement to see where it's all going each month. Include automatic monthly withdrawals on your budget worksheet—for your DSL line, online DVD rentals, or gym membership. Of course, you can leave your current rent and any rental-related expenses out of your calculations.

CHECK IT OUT

These websites have free budget worksheets you can print and fill out, or budgeting software to purchase:

- www.vertex42.com

- www.planabudget.com

- www.quicken.com.

Next, compare your monthly expense total to your monthly net income—what comes home, not what you make before taxes and the rest. The difference between that take-home pay and your expenses is the amount of disposable income that you can use for new house-related expenses.

Most people try to modify their spending habits if their disposable income isn't enough to cover the PITI. Having all your expenses in front of you helps you decide where to make such cuts. It also prepares you to draw the line if a lender or mortgage broker encourages you to pay more than your true budget allows. Remember, the lender mainly cares that you can pay back the money you borrow—not that you do it while living the life you want. If Pilates classes or Friday happy hours are important to you, then stick by your own budget and plan.

From Paperclip to House

Kyle McDonald set himself a challenge: to trade his way from a red paperclip to a house. He succeeded by bartering on Craigslist, working his way up through a pen, a doorknob, and a camp stove. It took McDonald only 14 trades (one with actor Corbin Bernsen) and about one year to reach his goal of homeownership. (He's now ready to trade the house, too.) Read his story at www.oneredpaperclip.com.

Getting Creative: Tips for Overcoming Financial Roadblocks

After running the numbers, you may feel that you can't afford a decent house, or maybe any house. But no matter your financial woes, there are steps you can take to ease them, including:

- **Reduce your debt.** This will free up cash for monthly house payments and reduce your debt-to-income ratio.

- **Make a new budget.** Revise your monthly budget, keeping your homebuying goals in mind. If you have targets, you're more likely to control your spending habits to meet them.

- **Reduce spending.** You may be able to get a roommate until you're ready to buy a place, apply an expected work bonus toward your fund, go back to basic cable, or shop more at thrift shops. Check out local freecycle groups (www.freecycle.org) for free items.

- **Borrow from a nontraditional source.** Consider different and creative options for borrowing money, from your family to the seller of the house you buy. For details, see Chapter 7.

- **Get a buying partner.** Perhaps you know someone who has cash and would be interested in jointly owning a property. Keep in mind that owning together doesn't have to mean living together, or even owning equal shares.

- **Cash out other investments.** Consider cashing out money invested in stocks, bonds, mutual funds, or other property to come up with a down payment, thus also reducing your monthly payment.

- **Consider other home types, sizes, conditions, or locations.** Remember that condominiums are often cheaper than houses and old houses generally cheaper than new.

- **Wait.** If you expect prices and interest rates to remain stable, your income to increase, and to save more money, you might delay your house purchase. With increased income, you may be able to borrow more; with an increased down payment, you may not need more.

The Power of Paper: Getting Preapproved for a Loan

Knowing what house-related costs will be laid at your feet, roughly how much a lender will let you borrow, and how much you'll really want to spend based on your income, lifestyle, and other factors, you can think about getting *preapproved* for a loan. Preapproval means you get a letter from a bank or lender committing to lend you a certain amount. It's often expressed as a monthly amount, because interest rates may vary, but the amount you can afford to pay each month does not.

> **CAUTION**
>
> **Preapproval is not a guarantee.** The bank will place several conditions on your final approval, and you'll need to comply with a host of requests for information. In fact, lenders have become more prone to declining final approval than ever before, so be prepared.

Preapproval does two important things: It gives you some certainty that you can afford the houses you're considering, and it makes you more attractive to sellers. You'll know exactly how much you can borrow, and sellers will know that if you've put an offer on their place, you can actually (subject to the bank's final approval) come through with the cash.

> **TIP**
>
> **You don't need to use the lender that preapproves you.** It would make matters easier if you did, but there's no need to feel bound. You (or your mortgage broker) might find a better deal by the time you've chosen a house.

Why Preapproval Is Better Than Prequalification

You may have heard of loan *prequalification*, but don't get it confused with preapproval. When you get prequalified, you give a lender some basic information about your income and debts, and the lender estimates what you'll likely be able to borrow. But the lender doesn't commit to lending you that money, so prequalification mainly helps you ballpark the price range you should be looking at and readjust your expectations if need be. Prequalification certainly won't wow any sellers. On the plus side, prequalification is free and easy to do (in person, over the phone, or on the Internet).

Preapproval is a different story. It will actually cost you a little money (in the $30–$40 range), because the lender will check your credit history. (This cost may be negotiable.) But preapproval will also give you more—a written commitment to lend you money. Don't accept a verbal preapproval.

Of course, the lender will attach a few conditions to that commitment. If, for example, you lose your job, the bargain is off. And make sure your preapproval letter doesn't contain too many conditions. For example, if the letter conditions the loan on a credit check, it means the lender hasn't really done its homework, and you're not really preapproved.

What You Need to Show for Preapproval

To get preapproved, you'll need to provide the lender with some financial data. This is actually a blessing in disguise—it's all stuff you'll need to dig up to get a loan anyway, and it's about the last thing you'll want to be thinking about later, when you've found a place to buy and are juggling other tasks.

Here's what you'll need to pull together and photocopy. If you're buying with someone else, both of you will need to give the lender every item on the list.

- pay stubs for the last 30 days
- two years' tax returns and W-2s or business tax returns if you're self-employed
- proof of other income
- proof of other assets (such as stocks or pension funds)
- three months of bank records for every account you have
- source of your down payment (for example, bank records from you and anyone gifting you money)
- names, addresses, and phone numbers of employers for the last two years
- names, addresses, and phone numbers of landlords for the last two years, and
- information about your current debts, including account numbers, monthly payment amounts, and so on.

CD-ROM

Use the "Financial Information for Lenders" checklist in the Homebuyer's Toolkit on the CD-ROM. It will help you keep track of everything you'll need for loan preapproval (and later, final loan approval).

You'll also need to fill out an application—if you're working with a mortgage broker, you'll probably get help with it, and can draw much of the information straight from the documents listed above. The lender will ask you for additional information once you've selected a property—that is, if you use that lender. If you switch lenders, you'll have to give the new one the whole works. The additional material includes:

- a property appraisal (you'll have to pay for that, usually about $300–$400 —the lender will set it up once you've selected a property), and

- proof that you've obtained homeowners' insurance.

Where to Go for Preapproval

Your options for getting preapproved include working with a mortgage broker, going directly to a local bank or institutional lender, or using an Internet aggregator—a website that compiles loan information from a lot of different lenders into one place. For more on how to research mortgages, see Chapter 6.

If you haven't yet found a mortgage broker, there's no harm in going straight to a lender for preapproval. First, make sure the lender is willing to do two things: give you the up-front letter stating that you're preapproved up to a certain amount, and then give you another letter later, when you actually bid on a home. This second letter will reflect a preapproval amount equal to the amount you're offering to pay for the property. The second letter is important because when you give a preapproval to a seller, the seller doesn't need to know that you can afford to pay more. That kind of revelation can hurt your bargaining position.

Preapproval is usually a quick process. If documents are transmitted electronically, you could be preapproved within hours. At its longest, it should take only a few days.

What's Next?

Confident that you're not going to break your personal bank or end up without a home loan, you can now start checking out the housing market. We'll show you how in Chapter 4.

Stepping Out:
What's on the Market and at What Price

Brett Patterson

Meet Your Adviser

Bert Sperling, a city and neighborhood expert based in Portland, Oregon. He's the founder of www.bestplaces.net and author of *Cities Ranked & Rated* (Wiley) and *The Best Places to Raise Your Family* (Wiley).

What he does   For over 20 years, Bert has been helping people find their own best place to live, work, play, and retire. As the foremost creator of best-places studies, he's in constant contact with the national media and regularly publishes his latest findings. His creative yet useful research topics cover everything from the best cities for dating to the worst ones for migraine headaches.

First house   "It was a 1920s Craftsman bungalow in Portland, Oregon. My wife found the house and said, 'We're buying it'—and she was absolutely right, it turned out to be a great place to raise our two sons. Affording it was a stretch, especially because interest rates were high. But we were tired of renting and were able to assume the seller's mortgage. We loved the neighborhood—only five minutes from downtown and close to shops, restaurants, and bus lines. Still, it had that neighborhood feeling—I'm a big fan of urban neighborhoods."

Fantasy house   "We've already found it! It's a cedar-shingled, Northwest coastal style place we bought in Depot Bay, Oregon. The house is right on the rocks overlooking the ocean—a wonderful getaway, though ocean living is a bigger challenge than many people realize. We're under assault by the weather, with winds up to 100 miles per hour. One of our requirements was high-speed Internet service so we can stay at the beach house for extended time periods and I can keep up on my work."

Likes best about his work	"I tell people I've got the best job in the world. It's wonderful to see all the differences in where people live and establish homes, and to be able to share their stories with others. I really believe there's no worst place to live. Every place is someone's home and has things that mean a lot to them, even though other aspects of living there might be challenging."

- -

Top tip for first-time homebuyers	"Start by figuring out what type of homebuyer you are. For example, are you a 'money is no object, because I'll live here forever'; an 'I don't care about resale, I just want to find a good fit for my family'; or an 'I've got to find a fixer-upper if this is going to work' type? Most of us have to watch how much we spend, so think about the long term, don't get in over your head, and don't buy the best place on the block."

Visualizing your perfect nest, and calculating what your budget will allow, was important. But now it's time to step out and see what the market really has to offer—before you turn into a serious house shopper, and possibly even before you find a real estate agent. Don't worry, this background work will take only a week or two. And it will be worth it, helping you to know when to leap at a house and what price to offer. You'll want to:

- get a feel for the communities where you might want to live (if you don't already know)
- look at the houses already on the market, including houses in developments, still under construction
- research the prices other sellers have recently paid for houses like the one you want, and
- gauge whether the local market is kinder to buyers or to sellers.

TIP

Eager to skip all this and just start shopping? It's possible to check out the market and keep your eye out for your dream house simultaneously—but it's harder. Without a sense of the market, you may waste your time, for example rushing to turn in a too-low bid in a hot market. Or you might waste your money, for example by bidding too high in a cool market. Give yourself time to explore.

What's the Buzz?
Checking Out Neighborhoods From Your Chair

Use the tips below to help you either find the right neighborhood for you, confirm your feelings about one you've already chosen, or open your mind to new possibilities. We'll start with the tasks you can accomplish online or by phone, then discuss visiting in person in a later section.

Where Do You Begin?

Most people have a good idea of where they want to live, sometimes right down to the street. But if you're moving from far away, you may not know your new town's uptown from its downtown, much less the names of the neighborhoods. And even if you're already a local, there are probably places on your map you haven't explored.

Starting with a blank slate lets you play tourist in your new hometown- (or neighborhood)-to-be and begin making friends and contacts. Here are some effective strategies:

- **Talk to friends, colleagues, and relatives about where they live.** Ask what they like best and least about the area—you're sure to uncover some surprises.

- **Out-of-towners: Start with whatever or whoever drew you to that town.** If it's a new job, ask your employer for staff contacts who'd be willing to share their experiences. The best people to talk to are those who've moved from far away themselves.

- **Call a real estate agent.** Even if you haven't hired an agent yet, you can call one and ask for information—the agent will probably jump at the chance to display knowledge to a potential client. Most agents know a lot about different neighborhoods, or at least about one neighborhood, since many of them specialize.

What's the Neighborhood Like?

One of your biggest questions will be the character of your prospective neighborhood. Is it a place where you walk to get tapas or drive to pick up cheeseburgers? Will the local hotspot be a sports bar or a blues bar?

 TIP

What about your neighbor's beliefs? Adviser Bert Sperling notes, "Perhaps the two biggest definers of local feel are things we've been told to avoid in polite conversation—religion and politics. Variety may be the spice of life, but you're going to find it very difficult to feel comfortable in your new town or neighborhood if you're the only person with a particular point of view. Do some research to find out which way a place is leaning."

Community character is one of the hardest issues to research (especially if you're completely new to the area), but these resources will get you started:

- **www.streetadvisor.com.** Enter a street address and see how the locals describe their area, whether it's seeing racoons at night or getting heckled by crackheads.

- **www.neighborhoodscout.com.** All you need is a zip code, and this gives you demographic data plus descriptions of neighborhood character and residents' age, ethnicity, and lifestyle.

- **Sperling's Best Places.** This website, at www.bestplaces.net, is known for its "best of" lists. Its studies will tell you the best and worst towns for everything from affordable housing to getting a good night's sleep. The site also gives statistical information, searchable by zip code. You can find out the percentage of your neighbors who vote Democrat or Republican or are affiliated with a particular religion, the cost of living, climate, local home characteristics, and more.

- **www.epodunk.com.** For smaller towns and communities—ones that could be described as "podunk"—try this site, which will link you to everything from population demographics to where you'll find local businesses, museums, and cemeteries.

- **your own, custom search. www.google.com.** Try plugging the name of your prospective neighborhood (if it has a name) into Google or your favorite search engine. Sites may come up for community associations, parents' associations, and more.

How Safe Is It?

If you're planning to live in your new home for a long time, make sure you feel secure there. Bert Sperling notes, "Smaller cities tend to have lower crime rates than large ones; that's part of the tradeoff you make for being part of a vibrant urban scene. Still, crime in large cities is often centered in certain areas, which you can avoid." Crime statistics for cities (but unfortunately not for neighborhoods) are available at www.homefair.com. Under "City Reports," enter the zip code.

The most accurate place to get neighborhood crime stats is from the local police department. Often you'll have to visit in person, though some larger cities put the information online. For examples, you can check out these cities by going to the website and searching for "crime statistics": San Francisco (www.sfgov.org), New York (www.nyc.gov), and Atlanta (www.atlantapd.org).

Best thing I ever did

Not assume an okay-looking neighborhood had low crime. Before buying her first house, Talia says, "I came close to buying a place in another neighborhood. It had looked fine when I was driving around. But my agent suggested I contact the local police station. I did and discovered that because this neighborhood was surrounded by areas where crime was much higher, it actually got its own share of break-ins and assaults. The crime rate was too high for me to feel comfortable living alone. I shifted focus to another area, where I now live and feel safe."

One crime issue that's easier to research online concerns registered sex offenders. Nearly every state has passed a law, usually called "Megan's Law" (after a young victim of abduction and sexual assault), requiring state governments to distribute information about sex offenders living in different communities. Many states have websites giving offenders' addresses. Search for "Megan's Law" and the name of your state. But take the information you find with a grain of salt—not all of these websites are regularly updated, and some contain inaccuracies or misleading information.

Safest Cities in the U.S.

These cities had the fewest violent crimes per capita, according to recent FBI statistics:

1. Irvine, California
2. Amherst, New York
3. Cary, North Carolina
4. Gilbert, Arizona
5. Sunnyvale, California
6. Thousand Oaks, California
7. Glendale, California
8. Provo, Utah
9. Bellevue, Washington
10. Simi Valley, California

Will the Services You Need Be Nearby?

The existence or proximity of schools, parks, shopping, and more could make or break your neighborhood decision. Fortunately, finding these is a relatively straightforward research task, with such websites as:

- **www.moving.com.** Provides free school reports and other demographic data, under the "Settling In" heading.
- **www.usnews.com/best-hospitals.** This is an annual report called "America's Best Hospitals," supported by *U.S. News & World Report*. Also see www.hospitalcompare.hhs.gov, by the U.S. Department of Health and Human Services.
- **www.mapquest.com.** To estimate your commute time, go to the "Directions" section of MapQuest, enter your work address and an address from the neighborhood where you might live, and receive a time and distance estimate.

Is It Zoned for How You Want to Use It?

After liberating yourself from your landlord's rules, you might be less than excited to discover that the home business you'd always dreamed of starting is prohibited, or that you can't turn the garage into an in-law cottage. Local zoning rules or other city regulations (even criminal laws) are usually to blame. It's also worth knowing what general uses the neighbors are allowed.

First, find out from the municipal planning and building department what zoning category each neighborhood you're interested in falls into. A classification called single-family residential is the norm. But some neighborhoods with ordinary houses might actually be zoned for multifamily residential, transitional, or a mixed use such as residential plus commercial. One of these other classifications might be good for you. For example if a home business is in your plans, mixed commercial and residential might be perfect. But these alternate classifications can also be a problem, particularly when it comes to your neighbors' future plans. Multifamily zoning, for example, might mean the house next door could be replaced with an apartment building.

Also realize that zoning ordinances usually deal with more than how the property can be used. They typically dictate the minimum square footage of a home and sometimes its maximum size, how tall it can be, and where it can be placed on the property. A home may have to be set back a certain distance from the street and be a certain distance away from neighboring homes. This can affect your plans to add an extra room or deck.

Research the zoning and other municipal rules further—ideally with the help of your real estate agent or attorney—if any of the following are true:

- **You intend to operate a home business.** In an area zoned residential, take a careful look at the local rules—they don't always give a clear thumbs up or down. Some, for example, prohibit home businesses in general but allow exceptions. Also talk to other local home-business owners about the restrictions, and whether their neighbors have raised any fuss.

> ## It's the Law!?
>
> There's probably a story behind these:
>
> - University City, Missouri: You're not allowed to have a garage sale in your front yard.
> - Texas: A hitching post must be placed in front of all houses on third-class roads.
> - Boulder, Colorado: You can't put indoor furniture outdoors in your yard.

RESOURCE

Planning on starting a home business? Find all the information you need, including more tips on zoning, in *Legal Guide for Starting & Running a Small Business*, by Fred Steingold (Nolo). Also check out *Home Business Tax Deductions: Keep What You Earn*, by Stephen Fishman (Nolo), which discusses issues like when you can deduct general home maintenance.

- **You plan to remodel the house or garage or add other structures (even a fence, pool, or child's tree house).** Rules for changing an existing house can be notoriously sticky and require permits. Local view ordinances may restrict your ability to add a second story. You might talk to a local architect in advance—they're used to dealing with, or getting around, the rules.

- **You plan to park a boat, RV, or large vehicle in your driveway.** Some city planners have decided this doesn't look so good.

- **The house has historic landmark status, or looks like it should.** Once a house is designated a historic landmark, any remodeling—even basic things like a new paint job—may be subject to rules on style and color. Still, owning a historic home can be personally satisfying and offer high resale value if you restore it.

- **You plan to cut down a large tree.** Yes, your landscaping may be a topic of separate regulation, excluding shrubs and flowers.

- **You have any other special plans for the property.** Local rules are limited only by the imagination of the local government, and bizarre ones sometimes pop up in response to one homeowner's inappropriate actions, like putting up too many holiday lights.

- **Vacant lots are widespread in the neighborhood, or you see a lot of new construction.** You'll want to know what might legally be built there.

- **You plan on keeping any farm animals such as roosters or a goat.** They may well be prohibited.

Is It a Planned Community, With Restrictions on Homeowners?

If you move into a community interest development (CID), you may find your choice of house paint colors limited to white, white, or white—and that's just for starters. Such communities often regulate how individual homeowners are expected to treat and use their property (such as fence style in a detached house or curtain color in a condo or co-op). A home located in a traditional subdivision consisting of lots may also be controlled by subdivision restrictions.

For now, just realize that these sorts of restrictions exist, and plan to research them further if you look at a CID.

How Good Are the Local Schools?

If you have children, or plan to, then the quality of the local school district is probably high on your list. But even if you don't plan on children, you should be concerned with school quality, because the *next* family who buys your home might want children. And they'll pay more if the local schools are great.

To get statistical information about how schools perform in your state, check your department of education website, usually accessible from your state's main Web page. Other good online resources include:

- **www.greatschools.org.** A national, independent nonprofit organization that helps parents choose schools, support their children's education, and more.

- **www.schoolmatters.com.** This site, run by the Council of Chief State School Officers, is mostly for people interested in public policy, but it offers information about student performance, school finance, and community and school demographics.

- **www.homefair.com.** (Click "School Reports.") This site lets you access information about "educational climate" and student/teacher ratios. If you provide your personal information, they'll tell you SAT scores, percentage of students going to college, and more.

Best thing I ever did

Visit local public schools. Violet says of her family's move from Connecticut to Pennsylvania, "Our criteria for choosing a neighborhood were: school district, school district, and school district. We'd heard there were two excellent districts close to my husband's new job. So I took my son and daughter to visit the principals and teachers and watch classrooms in action. The school in one of the neighborhoods had great classroom morale, lots of activities, and ethnic diversity. Wouldn't you know it, the houses in that neighborhood were mostly million-dollar-plus McMansions. But we found a fixer-upper we could afford. It was worth the hard work to make it livable—the kids love their school."

See for Yourself: Driving Through Neighborhoods

You can tell a lot about an area by cruising through it, most likely by car. When you get a real estate agent, he or she will also drive you around, but it's good to go on your own first, free to explore the seedier spots. You may find yourself thinking, "I could live here," or "Get me out, fast."

First, pull out your map, locate the areas where you might like to live, and circle them with a highlighter. Pay special attention to places on the map you've never been that are close to or within your highlighted area. Then systematically drive up and down the streets, imagining yourself living there. (The character of a neighborhood can change in the space of a city block, or right after a natural divider such as a freeway, park, or large housing complex.) Look beyond the houses and think about whether the local features fit your lifestyle—would you, in fact, walk to the bus stop, garden in the front yard, or jog at the local track? Focus on questions like:

- **How well are the homes maintained?** Neat homes and yards are signs that homeowners feel invested in their properties.

- **Who's around?** You can tell a lot about a neighborhood by who's out and about, whether it's children on bicycles or post partiers walking to breakfast joints on Saturday morning.

- **How's the traffic?** Are people driving sanely or zooming around with music blasting? Does the major street leading to the neighborhood become a noisy parking lot during rush hour?

- **What types of local businesses are there?** Franchise chains, funky coffee shops, and upscale restaurants could become your favorite hangouts—or you could be in for frustration if your favorite cuisine is nowhere to be found or there's no dry cleaner nearby.

- **Check the signs.** Literally. If you see lots of "For Sale" signs, it *could* mean people are moving out, and you'd want to know why—a new factory or mini-mall being built nearby? A surge in crime? You'll either have a greater chance of snagging a bargain, or you may decide to look elsewhere. On the other hand, a lot of homes for sale could also mean the neighborhood is hot, hot, hot!

If you like what you see, you might even add another color highlighter to the map, showing your favorite streets (useful for cross-referencing with later home sale ads). You're guaranteed to find a surprise or two.

Lesson learned the hard way **The grill's going every night!** Barry is a vegetarian, while his girlfriend Ann is not. After a long search, the couple found an adorable house near a commercial street dominated by Korean restaurants. Barry says, "We carefully had the house inspected and talked to the neighbors about safety. But we'd visited the house only in daylight. Our first evening after we moved in, we noticed a cloud of aromatic smoke coming from a nearby Korean barbecue. I was horrified, and Ann started mischievously suggesting sneaking out for a bite. We love the house, but it took awhile to get used to the permanently barbecue-scented night air."

On Foot: Talking to the Natives

There's probably no better way to find out what a certain neighborhood is like than talking to people who already live there. Pick a day when you're feeling relaxed (preferably not open-house day). Then walk around, paying attention to smells and sounds. (Cocooned in your car, you might not notice odors coming from a nearby brewery, airplane or freeway noise, the buzzing from a local generator, or rowdiness at a nearby commercial strip.)

Talking to people in neighborhoods still under construction is obviously harder—but it may be possible if you're not the first to buy. Or, you can look in surrounding developments to get a general feel.

Look for people out gardening, or walking their dogs. It might feel funny to strike up a conversation with a stranger, but complimenting said garden or dog is a pretty reliable conversation starter. Explain that you're thinking of buying, and ask questions like:

- What do you like most and least about this area?
- Which streets are considered the best to live on?
- Do you feel okay about walking outside at night?
- Do you have kids? Do they go to public school here?

- Are there any changes planned that will make the neighborhood better or worse (such as a new development, changed policing system, or pending school initiative)?
- What kind of person would be happiest living here?

CD-ROM
Use the "Questions for Talking With Locals" worksheet in the Homebuyer's Toolkit on the CD-ROM, which includes questions and space for your notes.

Coffee shops and local restaurants are also good places to meet people, including the business owners. And even on open-house days, you can meet a lot of locals and talk to real estate agents about community issues (though the agents won't be offering up much negative information).

Sunrise, Sunset:
Getting Day and Night Perspectives

There's a reason open houses are usually scheduled on Sunday afternoons: The sun is high in the sky, the neighborhood is quiet, and no one's working. Life couldn't be better! To plug back into reality, though, try visiting a neighborhood at different times of the day or week. In neighborhoods with lots of local schools, it can sound like a parade is passing weekdays around 3:00—and then the insanely bright floodlights at the football field click on after dark. Neighborhoods located in lovely little gulches or valleys may seem dull by early afternoon, when they lose their daily dose of sunshine. And late at night, if you see more tough-looking characters hanging out on street corners than dog walkers, you might want to recheck those crime stats.

Best thing we ever did

Drive through the neighborhood at night. Sam and Kari were looking to buy a place at a time when the market was crazy and their options limited. According to Sam, "When we saw a nice, affordable house right on the border of a good neighborhood, we were so excited! On a whim, we drove back later that night. There was a whole other side to that neighborhood: Cars slowly cruised by blaring music, and loud groups loitered around, drinking and smoking. Seeing our bewildered looks, an elderly neighbor asked whether we were lost, then advised us, 'Don't buy here; it's not safe. I'd get out if I could.' We took her advice and are so glad we took that evening drive."

Got Houses? Finding Out What's Locally Available

By now, you've probably narrowed down your search to specific neighborhoods. But can you afford anything more than a tiny patch of grass there? To find out, look at what's for sale right this minute. It's the easiest research task you'll ever take on, thanks to widely available advertisements, in:

- **The Multiple Listing Service (MLS).** This is the granddaddy: a database of homes for sale kept by Realtors® nationwide, and once guarded as closely as the Coca-Cola™ recipe. Now you can usually access it—or selected portions of it—for free on the websites of local Realtor® associations or newspapers. Start with the NAR's website, www.realtor.com. Or, try searching for "MLS" and the name of your state or city. (The homes won't change much, but the formatting will.)

- **Trulia.com.** This well-designed search engine offers attractive features like the ability to search by type of home (such as single-family or condo), to limit your search to houses where the seller has already reduced the price, and (under "Stats & Trends"), colorful maps that show you average list prices by zip code.

- **Real estate sections of city or community newspapers.** City papers often have online classifieds, but don't forget tiny community papers—they sometimes have the best classifieds, because they're devoted to a limited geographical area.

CD-ROM

Wondering what FB, HDWD, or S.S. Kit means? You must be reading a paid-by-the-word ad. For some deciphering help, check out the "Common Real Estate Abbreviations" list in the Homebuyer's Toolkit on the CD-ROM.

- **The Owners Network at www.owners.com.** These homes (so-called "FSBOs") are being sold without help from real estate agents, so they may not appear in the MLS. Also try www.forsalebyowner.com. For more on buying a FSBO, see Chapter 9.

- **Websites sponsored by local real estate brokers.** Some brokers provide photos, neighborhood information, and advice. Try local Re/Max Realtor®'s websites, for example. The downside to broker sites is that sometimes you'll have to enter personal information to access the listings and could get a call from an agent looking for your business.

- **Looking for a newly built home?** Check out www.move.com (by the National Association of Home Builders), where you can refine your search with criteria such as "Green Features" or "Pool." Also worth checking are www.newhomesource.com (with extensive information on custom, "build-on-your lot" builders) and www.americanhomeguides.com. It's best to search all three sites; each gives different results.

How Much Did That One Go For? Researching "Comparable" Sales

All the houses you see advertised come with a price tag—but the price may have little to do with reality. How much a buyer actually pays will probably vary from the list price, up or down, by thousands or even tens of thousands of dollars. In a softening market, many sellers have an inflated idea of what their house is worth, and it eventually sells for less. In hot markets, some sellers set an artificially low list price in hopes of attracting a large pool of potential buyers, which results in outrageously high bids.

There's no sense in choosing—or eliminating—a neighborhood or area based on price until you find out how much houses there are *really* selling for. (Later, such knowledge will ensure you don't pay too much or offer too little for a particular house.) Look at sale prices of houses comparable to the type you're interested in, or "comps." The most accurate comps come from houses that sold recently (preferably within the last six months) within the same general area (around six blocks) and with the same basic features as the house you hope to buy (like number of bedrooms, square footage, garage, neighborhood, lot size, general condition and construction quality, and landscaping).

You'll never find two exactly comparable houses, so do your best to take a sort of average. Your agent, once you're working with one, will also be able to give you this type of information. And when you're ready to bid on a particular house, the agent may draft up a report on the comps. But for quick and dirty comparable sales data, use the websites listed below.

CHECK IT OUT

Here's where to get comparable sales data. Two cautions apply, however: One, the listings may be out of date, or just plain out of whack, since they're generated by a computer, not a person. Two, beware of signing up to be contacted by an agent.

- www.zillow.com
- www.domania.com
- http://realestate.yahoo.com (click "Home Values").

EXAMPLE: Paul and Leslie want to buy a three-bedroom house in Ardmore, Pennsylvania. They take the address of one such local home and pop it into one of the websites above. The closest matches are a three-bedroom, one-bath house that sold for $250,000 three months ago; a three-bedroom, 1½-bath house that sold for $275,000 five months ago; and a three-bedroom, one-bath that sold for $228,000 six months ago. Without looking at the actual houses, they project that they'll need to pay somewhere in the mid- to high-$200,000s for the house they want. They might also posit that prices are rising, that the house currently for sale may be overpriced, or that adding a one-half bath can measurably raise the value of a house. Unfortunately, websites don't tell you about details such as house style, condition, landscaping, or charm. As Paul and Leslie start visiting actual houses and working with a knowledgeable agent, they'll have a chance to sharpen their understanding of local house values.

Eventually, your knowledge of sale prices will turn you into a sort of amateur appraiser and help you decide on the appropriate price for houses you're looking at. Don't discount the value of your own research and intuition: House values depend partly on buyers' subjective responses to them, and you're a buyer. Placing an exact market value on a house is an inexact science, though appraisers, real estate agents, and sellers do their best to come close.

Hot or Cold? Take the Market's Temp

To figure out home values, you also need to know whether you're in a market that's primarily hot or cold (or balanced somewhere in between). At local open houses, do you have to wait in line just to squeeze up the stairs, or do you find yourself all alone with a chatty seller's agent? When talking with friends about homebuying, do they tell stories of how being outbid on houses drove them to couples' counseling, or how they're plotting how to get a bargain from a seller whose house has languished on the market for weeks? These are just a few of the more extreme indicators of whether the local housing market is hot or cold.

A hot market means there are more buyers than sellers, or not enough houses on the market to satisfy demand. As soon as a house is listed for sale, it's snapped up, and sellers can be inflexible about the price and buyers' other negotiating requests. In the hottest markets, sellers may pit you against other buyers competing to offer the highest price, the shortest closing period, and the smoothest transaction.

A cold market means there are more sellers than buyers, and houses may remain on the market for months at a time, waiting for a buyer. If, as happened recently, this is coupled with a major economic downturn, foreclosures can flood the market and bring down prices. This gives the buyer leverage when negotiating, because the longer a seller has waited, the more desperate he or she may be to unload the place. Meanwhile, sellers know that you have other options.

TIP

Markets can be lukewarm or mixed, too. As Realtor® Mark Nash notes, "Hot and cold is a generalization. For example, in some markets, starter single-family homes could be hot, and penthouse condos could be cold."

The urgency of your house search, and your approach to sellers, will all be shaped by knowing whether you're in a market that's hot, cold, transitional, or balanced in the middle. It's not hard to figure out the basic "hot or cold?" question—as long as you focus in at the neighborhood level and aren't fooled by general headlines. The more difficult part is to gauge where the market is going—a market can move up or down in a matter of weeks.

The housing market can be affected by the local and national economy, mortgage interest rates, the availability and cost of housing (including rentals), the supply of and demand for homes, and more. Scads of real estate commentators make their living trying to predict what's next, but none know for sure. Nor do they specialize in the corner of the world you're looking at, which might have its own mini hot and cold regions.

You'll develop a sense of where your local market is going once you start seriously househunting. If, after several weeks, you find yourself able to predict the asking prices of newly offered homes, the market is probably pretty stable. If, on the other hand, you notice open house or "price reduced" signs on houses you looked at a few weeks ago, the market is probably plateauing or cooling. A real estate agent can also tell you about cooling trends, based on an increasing number of listings in their MLS database and a longer average time that houses stay on the market. And if you've been outbid on a house or two and notice that the list prices of similar houses seem to be inching out of your range, the market is heating up and you'll need to act quickly.

> ## TIP
>
> **Don't put your life on hold trying to predict the future.** For every person who waited for the market to drop further and got a good price, there's another one who watched it pass them by. Just find a house you want at a price that's fair and affordable at the time. If you're planning to stay there for more than a few years, you'll weather any downturns.

Lesson learned the hard way **Waiting for the downturn that never came.** Eva, an artist, says, "At one point, I thought I'd never marry and decided to buy my own house. I began looking, accompanied by my dad, who'd offered to pitch in on the down payment. But every time I found a place I liked, my dad said, 'That's way too much, prices will come down soon.' He said that first about houses in the $200,000 range. Then I watched as similar houses started selling for $300,000, then $400,000. I bought a tiny place soon after, which fortunately has since risen in value. But it kills me that I could have had it for much less a couple years earlier—or could have had a bigger house that would fit my, guess what, husband and new baby!"

Just Looking: The Open House Tour

Visiting open houses—where sellers throw the doors open to just about any interested party—is educational, free, and fun. For now, don't look only at houses that are smack dab in your price range. By looking at too-expensive and too-cheap houses, you'll get a feel for what various house features—like another bedroom or an updated kitchen—are worth. As you visit open houses, compare their features to your Dream List, to get a sense of which items will or won't be easy to find. Now's a good time to refine your list, too, if you realize that "a fenced yard would be great," or "I can't live next to an apartment complex."

Remember, unless you're ready to read the rest of the chapters and ramp up your activities in a hurry, don't fall in love with a house yet. You're still getting to know what's out there. In later chapters, we'll discuss how to take a hard look at a particular house—evaluate its physical condition, whether it's priced appropriately, and whether it meets your long- and short-term needs—as well as how to prepare an appropriate offer.

If a house really does look perfect, and you can't resist, at least heed this final warning: Don't sign anything on the spot. You may meet an oh-so-friendly agent who says, "I can write up your offer, no problem!" That agent represents the seller, whose interests, including getting the highest price and the most advantageous terms, will be put first. Go home, take a deep breath, look at later chapters of this book, and do some quick shopping for a buyer's agent—if you really want to buy that house.

Best thing we ever did

Just start looking. Fiona was more convinced than her girlfriend that they could handle the financial commitment of a house. Fiona says, "Even after we'd done our research, had a mortgage broker evaluate our finances, and asked our parents to pitch in on a down payment, she resisted going to open houses. According to her stressed-out logic, we weren't *really* ready, so it was a waste of everyone's time. Finally I got her out looking, and it was great—seeing open houses suddenly made the process fun. Of course, it was also a reality check, since we realized we could afford less than we'd thought. But we ended up finding a wonderful house, with great neighbors."

Nothing to Look at Yet?
Finding Your Dream Development

If you're thinking of buying a newly built home, your community-to-be may look like a large sandbox. But that doesn't mean you can't do advance research. Your most important task will be to choose the best-quality developer before you go any further. Why? Well, as with any other product, different house manufacturers make different quality products, or have different track records for reliability. You don't even want to go near a house built by a developer at the low end of the quality spectrum, or who's teetering on the edge of bankruptcy, no matter how affordable it seems.

Figure out which developers are working in your area, which are worth buying from, and whether they offer the types of houses you want. To find developers, use the websites listed under "Got Houses? Finding Out What's Locally Available," above. Then use the following tips to research them:

- **Talk to people.** This includes others who have purchased from a particular developer, local contractors, real estate professionals, and city planning staff. Don't stop until you've gathered information about each local builder's reputation from a variety of sources.

- **Ask tough questions of the developer and others.** You'll want to find out how long the developer has been in business; how well funded the business is; whether it's ever been sued and for what; and the credentials of the developer, its employees, and contractors. Don't just take the developer's word for it—double-check with your state's licensing board and the local building office.

- **Search online.** The National Association of Home Builders (www.nahb. org) is a good starting point. To hear feedback from other consumers, try searching Internet blogs, local newspaper websites, and homeowner-run websites such as HomeOwners for Better Building (www.hobb.org).

- **Call your local Better Business Bureau.** It's often the first place that people turn to with complaints about local developers.

What's Next?

You've hopefully gotten a sense of which neighborhoods not only have a character you like, but offer the safety, schools, or other amenities you need. You've also gotten a sense of the local market and whether it offers houses you might want at a price you can afford. You're almost ready to do some serious house shopping. But first, let's figure out who's going to help you do it.

Select Your Players: Your Real Estate Team

Meet Your Adviser

Nancy Atwood, with ZipRealty, based in Framingham, Massachusetts. Nancy is a Designated Broker, responsible for the legal compliance and mentoring of real estate agents who directly serve buyers and sellers. ZipRealty is a full-service brokerage offering rebates on agent commissions (see www.ziprealty.com).

What she does

Nancy started with ZipRealty as an agent, where she helped countless homebuyers and sellers. She moved up to her current position as a broker and is now responsible for 175 full-service buyer and seller agents statewide. She was named a ZipRealty outstanding employee of the year in 2006. Nancy's pre-real-estate experience includes 25 years in the hi-tech industry doing customer service, sales, and marketing.

First house

"It was a three-bedroom ranch-style home in Harvard, Massachusetts (not the college—Harvard is a rural town, 32 miles west of Boston). Finding it took a little work—I wasn't in real estate then, and our agent kept showing us places that cost $30,000 more than our absolute limit or needed more work than we were then capable of handling. But eventually we found this place and were so excited to be moving out of the city and into an area with good schools and more open space. Still, the house itself was so small that our kids would sit on the washing machine to talk to me while I made dinner."

Likes best about her work

"I really like training and helping agents, especially those new to the business—I'm so excited when one of my agents makes his or her first deal. I tell them that it's not a sales job, but a support job, in which customers need to trust you with the largest purchase in their lives. I'm also particularly interested in ethical issues around real estate. Because it's a commission-based job, agents sometimes forget that our fiduciary responsibility is to the clients, not the commission. I tell them you can't control other people's ethics, but you can control your own. My agents like to hear that, they get it, and I'm proud of the fact that we've never had one ethics complaint filed against us here in Massachusetts."

Fantasy house

"The house I live in now. Around 1984, my husband and I bought four acres of land, designed a house, and had it built in Harvard, one quarter mile from the center of town. It's contemporary in style, very open and sunny, with passive solar energy. I know some couples fight over home construction, but for my husband and I it turned out to be an incredible bonding experience. We spent every weekend at Lowe's or Home Depot, choosing fixtures, lighting, and hardware. He did such tasks as the wiring, while I focused on designing the kitchen. It's the biggest room in the house, with granite countertops so I can just roll out my homemade pizza dough, and windows that overlook our neighbors' horse farm."

Top tip for first-time homebuyers

"Choose an agent you can trust. Interview your agent, and ask lots of questions—not only about the agent's experience, but about their level of caring and consistency of customer referrals. For example, when interviewing, I ask agents what they're most proud of. If they say something like, 'I'm still invited to so-and-so's home every December during the holidays,' that's wonderful. There are really a lot of agents like that out there, and not just at ZipRealty. Don't let the negative things you may have heard about some agents make you settle for one who isn't both caring and professional."

Buying a first home is a complex process, and there's no reason to do it alone. You can bring together a team of experts who've seen it all before (many times!). They'll not only help you understand what you need to do but also perform key tasks themselves, like negotiating with the seller, finding the best deal on a mortgage and helping fill out the paperwork, and making sure a property doesn't have hidden defects. Your real estate team will usually include:

- a real estate agent, who will help you find, negotiate for, and complete the purchase of your home
- a mortgage broker or banker, who will help locate the best financing
- a real estate attorney (in several but not all states), who will make sure the deal is properly and fairly drafted and that the seller has good title
- a home inspector, who will examine the property's condition, and
- a closing or escrow agent, who will help ensure that the transfer happens smoothly and on time.

Unlike a sports team, these players may not work together directly. But even if they never meet, they share a common goal: to help you purchase your house on the best possible terms. Still, you're the boss (and the checkbook), so you'll want to be confident about your players and their abilities. In this chapter, we'll explain each person's role and how to select top players.

Your Team Captain: The Real Estate Agent

Your real estate agent has the broadest role of any team member: You'll work together from start to finish.

Who Real Estate Agents Are

You've probably heard different names—broker, agent, or Realtor®—used to describe real estate agents. These convey different levels of experience, training, and knowledge.

- **Agents.** A "real estate agent" is the most generic of the choices. Agents must be licensed in the state where they work. This usually means completing 30 to 90 hours of classroom instruction, passing an exam, and renewing their licenses every one or two years.

- **Brokers.** A real estate broker is one step up from an agent. Brokers have more real-estate-related education and experience. In many real estate agencies (also referred to as "brokerages"), the buyer works with an agent on a daily basis, but the agent is supervised by a broker. If the buyer has problems the agent can't resolve, the broker will handle them. In smaller, independent agencies, the buyer may work directly with a broker. When we use the term "real estate agent," we're referring to both agents and brokers.

> *Real Estate Agents on the Silver Screen*
>
> - Annette Bening plays Carolyn Burnham in *American Beauty*.
> - Jack Lemmon, Kevin Spacey, Alan Arkin, and Ed Harris play competing agents in *Glengarry Glen Ross*.
> - Julianne Moore plays Marlene Craven in *The Hand That Rocks the Cradle*.
> - Craig T. Nelson plays Steven Freeling in *Poltergeist*.

- **Realtors®.** Over half of all licensed agents are members of the National Association of Realtors® (NAR), a trade association. NAR members can use the designation "Realtor®." They must comply with the NAR's standards of practice and Code of Ethics. Membership also suggests that the agent is up-to-date on real estate issues (because NAR provides training, member newsletters, and other resources) and has a network of contacts through the organization.

Realtors® may also have advanced designations/certifications through the NAR and its affiliate organizations. You're particularly interested in the Accredited Buyer Representative (ABR) or Accredited Buyer Representative Manager (ABRM) designations, given to Realtors® or brokers specializing in representing buyers.

What Your Agent Does for You

Your real estate agent is your team captain, answering to you but coordinating other players and handling multiple tasks. Expect your agent to:

- **Suggest neighborhoods.** Although this book helps you look for the right neighborhood, your agent should be able to pinpoint possible locations. Ideally, your agent will live in or around the area you're interested in and give you an insider's perspective.

- **Show you comparable sales data.** To help you gauge the market value of any house you're interested in, your agent should compile a written report (called a competitive market analysis, or CMA) of comparable properties ("comps") that sold in the last six months.

CHECK IT OUT

You can get some MLS data on your own. Although real estate agents get access to the full details, anyone can view portions of the MLS at www.realtor.com, the NAR's consumer website. You may be able to get more-detailed MLS listings on your local paper's website, from a local agent's site, or by working with an agency like ZipRealty (discussed below).

- **Find prospective homes that meet your needs.** You'll tell your agent how much you want to spend, what physical characteristics are important to you, and what type of neighborhood you're looking for. A good agent will search for properties that meet your criteria and show them to you as soon as they're available. Any competent agent knows that this task may take one day or one year—in either case, the agent will patiently help you find what you're looking for.

- **Walk through prospective properties with you.** Your agent will actually take you to look at properties, too. Your agent acts as another set of eyes, helping you think about practicalities (like whether the house provides enough storage space or has an impractical floor plan), and spotting potential problems (like a water stain on the ceiling indicating a possible leaky roof, or an old plumbing system in a sparkling new kitchen). The agent might also suggest easy-to-make improvements, such as converting an unused nook into a home office space. The agent will coordinate a second and even third showing, if needed.

> **TIP**
>
> **Don't hire an agent who'll push you off onto an assistant.** Illinois Realtor® Mark Nash says, "Choosing a high-producing agent isn't always your best bet, because such agents might not be available to work with you until you're ready to write an offer. In the meantime, they'll have a less-experienced, licensed assistant take you to look at properties. But an agent learns a lot about a client—and the client's needs and preferences—from walking through properties together. Make sure your agent is going to take you around personally before you hire him or her."

- **Draft a written offer and negotiate the sale.** In the majority of states, your agent will help you draft an offer or other written statement that includes your offer price and terms. The offer process will be discussed in detail in Chapter 10. The agent will also ensure you receive any legally required disclosures about the physical condition of the property.

- **Explain the process.** Your agent should (beginning at your first meeting) be able to summarize the process of and timeline for searching for homes, writing an offer, finding and applying for financing, opening escrow, checking title, obtaining insurance, removing contingencies, and closing the deal.

- **Open escrow.** Your agent should open escrow for you (help begin the process of finalizing your purchase) or give you recommendations for a reputable escrow or closing company or real estate attorney (depending on which state you're buying in).

- **Manage day-to-day activities leading up to the closing.** Once your offer is accepted, you have a lot to accomplish before the deal is finalized, such as scheduling home inspections, lining up financing, and getting insurance. Your agent should guide you through each step, either handling the tasks directly or working with the appropriate professionals. Your agent should also be present for major events like inspections, the appraisal, the final walk-through, and the closing.

Make Sure Your Real Estate Agent Plays for You

Real estate agents make a living representing one of two parties: the buyer or the seller. Since most agents have several clients at a time, they often represent both types in different transactions, sometimes selling houses for sellers, other times helping buyers purchase houses.

Usually, this isn't a problem. However, it can become one when the agent who is selling a house for one client has another client who wants to *buy* it. Then the agent could act as a "dual agent." This frequently results when a prospective buyer visits an open house, expresses interest, and the seller's listing agent says, "Don't worry that you don't have an agent yet, I'll write the deal up for you." In rare cases, the selling agent may even claim that you have to use that agent's services, because he or she found you first!

You can imagine the potential problems when one agent represents two parties with opposite interests: While the buyer wants to buy the place for as little as possible, the seller wants to sell for as much as possible. It used to be that the agent just worked it out as he or she saw fit. But many buyers who'd told their agents that they were willing to pay more for a house than they'd offered were appalled when their agents turned around and told the sellers that exact information.

Real-Estate Fiction

- *Death by Real Estate*, by Maggie MacLeod (Daybreak Publishing): Barb Parker is a mystery-solving real estate agent.
- *Closing Costs*, by Seth Margolis (St. Martin's Press): Five couples try to survive the cutthroat Manhattan real estate market.
- *Good Faith*, by Jane Smiley (Anchor): A divorced real estate agent is lured into a development deal by a newcomer to his small town.

These days, if an agent wants to represent both sides, most states require that the agent get written consent from both parties. But it's not a good idea to consent to this. You want someone who is on your team all the way. Your safest bet is to get your own, buyer's, agent—one contractually bound to represent only you (though your agent must still be fair and honest with the seller).

One good way to find out whether your agent will ever be a dual agent is to ask, before hiring, "Will you ever represent me in a dual agency?" Only work with agents who say "no." If you become interested in a property listed by that agent, he or she can help you find another agent to complete the deal.

In a similar situation called a designated agency, you're represented by one agent, and the seller is represented by another agent who works in the same brokerage. In states where designated agency is allowed, all parties must normally agree to it in writing. The risk of divided loyalties is much less than with a dual agency. Still, you'll want to be confident that your agent is trustworthy and be careful about what you disclose.

Some agents focus solely on buyers' needs. They're called exclusive buyer agents or "EBAs." An EBA will never represent a seller in any transaction. By default, this means you'll avoid any possibility of a dual or designated agency. But an experienced agent who won't act as a dual agent can serve your needs without being an EBA.

 **CHECK IT OUT**

To find an EBA in your area: Contact The National Association of Exclusive Buyer Agents, at 800-986-2322 or www.naeba.org.

Finally, on the other side of the table sits the seller's agent, sometimes called the "listing agent." The seller's agent is hired by the seller. While the seller's agent is ethically and even legally bound to be fair and honest toward you, this agent focuses on representing the seller's best interests. You want the seller's agent to remain where he or she belongs—on the other side of the table.

How Real Estate Agents Are Paid

After hearing about what a good agent can do for you, you may start mentally calculating whether you can fit one into your budget. The good news is, your agent is one person in this process you *won't* have to hand money to. The seller pays the entire commission (averaging 5% to 6%), which is split between the seller's agent and yours (usually, 2½% to 3% each). You do end up indirectly paying for your agent's services, though, because the seller will probably factor the cost of paying both agents into the purchase price of the home.

Some people will tell you that agents are mainly out to make buckets of money, by maximizing their commission and minimizing the amount of time they spend with you. They caution you that agents will show you only properties above your price range, push you to offer too much, or rush you into a purchase.

It's true that the more you spend, the higher the agent's commission goes. However, to say that agents are solely motivated by money is an overgeneralization—in fact, it's often not in the agent's own interests to behave this way. If, for example, you're pushed to offer an extra $10,000 on a home, and then don't qualify for the mortgage, the agent will have wasted a lot of time. Or what if you pay the extra $10,000, then feel the agent trapped you into it? You'll never use that agent again and will tell your friends not to, either. Neither prospect will appeal to the professional, experienced agent you'll be choosing—not to mention the fact that an extra $10,000 on the sales price adds up to only about $150 in increased commission.

Money-Saving Agent Agreements

As a first-time, cash-conscious homebuyer, you might consider hiring a full-service agent who'll give you a commission "rebate." For example, an agent whose commission is ordinarily 3% might return 20% of that to you when the deal closes. That's about $3,000 on a $500,000 purchase. There's no disadvantage for the seller's agent, who still gets paid the standard commission for the area.

In exchange for the rebate, you may need to share responsibility for finding prospective properties. For example, clients at ZipRealty (www.ziprealty.com) are given access to MLS information usually only available to real estate professionals, then select properties to visit.

You're best off choosing a full-service rebate agent rather than what's called a "discount agent." Discount agents don't ordinarily give you access to the MLS or help coordinate showings. They may require you to view properties alone or to pay extra for these services. You thus lose the benefit of the agent's experience.

Using an Agent When Buying a Newly Constructed House

When buying a new house from a developer, you can be represented by your own real estate agent. However, the agent usually needs to be with you on your very first visit or the developer won't allow the agent to collect the commission.

Developers usually have salespeople, paid by and loyal to the developer, who they'd prefer to have you use for the tasks your agent would normally handle, such as drawing up written agreements. Of course, these usually favor the developer, for example, limiting the developer's responsibility for shoddy work or late completion. It's worth bringing your own agent to advocate on your behalf and help you negotiate a fair deal.

However, if you're represented by an outside agent, the developer may, as a way of recouping part of the commission (particularly in a hot market), be less flexible about price or less willing to give special incentives or upgrades.

TIP

Consider adding an attorney-review contingency to your contract. If bringing your own real estate agent appears unnecessary or impossible, at least insist that an attorney review your agreement. You can make this a condition of the sale (a "contingency"), as discussed in Chapter 10.

Getting the Best Agent Out There

It's worth putting some effort into finding an experienced buyer's agent with whom you'll enjoy working. You could just walk into any real estate agency, but you'd probably end up with whoever had time to spare. Instead, start by getting recommendations from family members, friends, colleagues, or neighbors who've bought homes—particularly in the neighborhoods you're interested in.

If you come up dry, check out the NAR website at www.realtor.com, and enter your city and state under "Find a Realtor®." Your state association may also provide similar information. But keep in mind that this is a membership listing based on location and doesn't distinguish between good and bad agents.

CHECK IT OUT

Check their license. To make sure a prospective agent is currently licensed in your state, visit www.arello.com, the Association of Real Estate License Law Officials. The site can also link you to relevant laws and regulations.

Once you've got a few names, choose a few agents to meet in person. Look at the agents' websites, which may contain their photos and descriptions of their skills, services, or philosophies. You're looking for an agent who is knowledgeable about the area and the type of house you want to live in, experienced, easily reachable and responsive to your needs, ethical and honest, compatible, and loyal. At the interview, ask concrete questions about the agent's experience, certifications, and more, and how the agent's skills will be put to work for you. Also request the names of three references, and (assuming you're interested in the agent) follow up to make sure they had a positive working relationship.

CD-ROM

For a comprehensive set of questions for both the agent and his or her references: Use the "Real Estate Agent Interview Questionnaire" and the "Real Estate Agent Reference Questionnaire" in the Homebuyer's Toolkit on the CD-ROM. Samples of these forms are shown below.

Best thing we ever did

Got an agent who specialized in our neighborhood. Craig and Lorena had been looking for an affordable starter house in a much-desired neighborhood for months, with no luck. Lorena explains, "Although our agent specialized in our target neighborhood—she lived there—there just weren't many houses we liked at a price we could afford. We'd just about given up when she called us. A neighbor of hers was getting ready to sell and was willing to let us have first peek. We loved the place and immediately put in an offer, which was accepted. The place was never even advertised!"

Real Estate Agent Interview Questionnaire

Ask potential agents the following questions, as well as anything special to your transaction, like their experience helping buyers looking for fixer-uppers or newly constructed houses.

Name of real estate agent and contact information (phone, email, etc.):

Date of conversation:

1. Do you work full time as a real estate agent?

2. How long have you been in the real estate business?

3. Do you have additional certifications beyond your general real estate license? If so what are they?

4. Will you ever represent me as a dual agent?

5. How many residential real estate transactions have you been a part of in the past year?

6. In how many of those transactions have you represented the buyer?

7. What was the price range of homes you helped clients buy within the last year? What was the average price?

8. Do you specialize in a certain type of property?

9. Do you specialize in a certain geographic area?

10. Do you partner with other agents or use assistants?

11. How will I reach you? Are there days or times you're unavailable, or do you have any vacations planned?

12. Can you provide at least three names of recent clients who purchased first homes with you, who will serve as references?

NOTES:

Best Answers:

1. Yes.

2. The longer the better, but at least three years.

3. More certifications show a commitment by the agent. A Realtor ABR or ABRM designation indicates that the agent has significant experience working with buyers.

4. Only acceptable answer is "No."

5. Should be a minimum of ten.

6. Best answer is "all of them," but should be at least half.

7. Should be about your price range.

8. Should be the type of property you're interested in, like a single-family house, condo, or co-op.

9. Should be the geographic area where you're looking to buy.

10. If so, find out who you'll be working with, what their real estate experience is, and what they'll be doing.

11. Make sure you can reach the agent when you need to. If you plan to buy soon, make sure the agent will be readily available (not on vacation).

12. Only acceptable answer is "Yes."

Real Estate Agent Reference Questionnaire

Here's what to ask the agent's referrals. You can add any other questions that interest you, such as special issues if you're buying a new house in a development.

Name of real estate agent:

Name of reference:

Date:

1. How did you choose the agent? Did you know the agent before you worked together?

2. What kind of house did you buy?

3. Was the agent responsive? Did the agent return calls promptly, follow through on promises, and meet deadlines?

4. Did the agent take the time to find you the right property?

5. How long did you look?

6. How many houses did you look at before you bought?

7. Did the agent show you houses in your price range?

8. Are you happy with the house you bought, and the neighborhood it's in?

9. Did the agent help you coordinate other details of your purchase, like finding financing and working with the title company, inspectors, or insurance agents?

10. Did the agent keep you up to date, and explain everything in terms you understood?

11. Would you work with the agent again?

OTHER COMMENTS:

TIP

Don't spill your beans. Wait to tell the agent your own objectives (where you want to live, how much you want to spend, and what type of property you're looking for) until your questions have been answered. You don't want the agent to feed you the answers you want to hear.

If It Doesn't Work Out: Firing an Agent

One common misconception is that once you've chosen an agent, you can't fire that person. Whether you can extricate yourself from the relationship (and what it will cost you to do so) will probably be determined by the terms of your agreement. So try to insert a clause at the outset allowing you to release the agent with sufficient notice (usually, about 48 hours) if things aren't working out.

Even if you haven't done this, if an agent isn't showing you appropriate properties, or isn't responding to your calls or inquiries, or you just don't like working with that person, you may want to move on. Of course, if the problem can be resolved by a simple conversation, it's wiser to try that first. But if that's fruitless and the agent isn't willing to walk away, you may need to discuss the issue with the managing broker (the agent's boss).

If you decide to end a working relationship, do it *before* you find a house you want to buy. It would be totally unethical—and risk a lawsuit—to try to get out of the relationship just to avoid letting the agent claim the commission.

Who Does What	
It's your agent's job to ...	**But it's still your job to ...**
Talk to you about your needs.	Research and choose the right agent, and negotiate the terms of the agency.
Research houses and neighborhoods that meet your needs and give you data on comparable properties.	Clearly explain and describe to the agent what you're looking for.
Show you houses with features that you want, in your price range.	Choose the right neighborhood.
Help you write up offers (except in states where attorneys do this).	Choose the best house for you.
Deliver your offer to the seller.	Choose your professionals, like the mortgage broker, inspector, and closing agent.
Notify you of counteroffers and help you negotiate with the seller.	Secure your financing.
Recommend professionals like brokers, inspectors, and closing agents; help you coordinate working with these people.	Respond promptly to your agent's questions.
Attend important events like inspections, appraisals, the final walk-through, and (usually) the closing.	Avoid, or at least knowingly consent to a dual or designated agency relationship, if the situation arises.
Explain the process, timeline, and technical concepts.	Decide on the key terms of your offer.
Respond promptly to your phone calls and inquiries.	Speak up if there is a problem.
Help with any snafus you encounter during the process.	Read all documents carefully.
Disclose a dual or designated agency.	

Your Cash Cow: The Mortgage Broker or Banker

Even in inexpensive housing markets, you'll likely be taking out a mortgage to finance your purchase. In the next chapter, we'll talk about how to research options, select the best loan, and actually apply for it. Here, we're going to talk about the people you'll work with to do that.

As many as two-thirds of all buyers get their loans through a mortgage broker—a professional who's in the business of compiling and filtering through the options for you. Your other primary alternative is to go directly to a bank, credit union, or other commercial lender.

If you're buying a newly constructed home, the developer may line up financing for you—but it's worth checking out other options. While developers often form relationships with specific lenders, the terms offered sometimes favor the developer more than the buyer.

> **TIP**
> **A "mortgage broker" and a "mortgage banker" aren't the same thing.** A mortgage broker is the middleman who brings you and a lender together. A mortgage banker is a lender who actually lends you money.

Your Personal Shopper: The Mortgage Broker

A mortgage broker acts as your agent to "shop lenders" for the best possible loan terms, given your financial situation and goals. Many states require mortgage brokerages to be licensed, and individual mortgage brokers are sometimes certified by the National Association of Mortgage Brokers (NAMB). To be NAMB-certified, brokers must show a certain amount of work experience and other qualifications, pass a written exam, and attend continuing education training. There are two types of NAMB certification: Certified Residential Mortgage Specialist (CRMS) and Certified Mortgage Consultant (CMC).

As for compensation, mortgage brokers make most of their money by marking up the costs on the loan the wholesale lender is offering. This may get passed on to you in the form of points (one point is 1% of the loan value), processing fees, or a higher interest rate. Although the broker's commission ultimately comes out of your pocket, a savvy borrower can negotiate down a fee that seems excessively high. Of course, a good mortgage broker should be able to save you the equivalent of his or her earnings and then some, by finding you a more affordable mortgage than you could locate on your own.

TIP

Choose a mortgage broker before you find a house. If you wait to get a broker until you've found a property you want to buy, you'll have very little time to find the best professional.

What Your Mortgage Broker Does for You

To help you find the best loan possible, a good broker will:

- Talk with you about your financial situation and goals.
- Find and explain financing options available to you.
- Work with you to get preapproved for a mortgage.
- Help you complete and assemble the documentation the lender needs. This might include your loan application, confirmation of employment and wages, financial information, and credit report.
- Once approved, review loan documents before you sign them. If the lender refuses to approve your loan, your mortgage broker should explain what went wrong and help find alternative mortgage options.
- Coordinate the property appraisal.
- Continue to act as a liaison between you and the lender up through the closing day.

TIP

Run your own numbers. The mortgage broker's view of your finances will be much like the lender's—a measure of what you can qualify for based on your debt-to-income ratio. Don't look to the mortgage broker to tell you what you can comfortably afford: Conduct a personal evaluation of your finances, as explained Chapter 3.

Getting the Best Mortgage Broker Out There

Good mortgage brokers possess many of the same traits as good real estate agents—integrity, professionalism, and experience. They should also be skilled (and patient) at explaining complicated financing concepts. In addition, good mortgage brokers stay informed about the policies, requirements, and products of various mortgage lenders, so as to provide you with up-to-date and accurate advice.

Get recommendations from friends, coworkers, and other homeowners. Your real estate agent, if you have one, is another good resource. A less reliable option is the "search for a mortgage broker" feature on the NAMB website, www.namb.org. NAMB membership is just a starting point: You'll want to learn more about each broker's education, experience, and philosophy. Ask whether the broker will tell you up front about every fee they'll charge you (you may want to negotiate these fees, as we'll discuss in Chapter 6).

Next, interview two or three prospective mortgage brokers. Ask about their experience and certifications, plus any questions special to your situation (like whether they can provide help getting an FHA or other government-backed loan). Also ask for the names of three references, and follow up to check whether these folks enjoyed working with the broker and are still happy with the loan they got.

CD-ROM

For a handy set of questions to use in your interview and when checking references: Use the "Mortgage Broker Interview Questionnaire" and the "Mortgage Broker Reference Questionnaire" in the Homebuyer's Toolkit on the CD-ROM. Samples of these forms are shown below.

Mortgage Broker Interview Questionnaire

To get the best mortgage broker on your team, ask the following questions, as well as any special to your situation (for example, concerning a credit history issue, your interest in an FHA or other government-backed loan, or the broker's experience with self-employed buyers).

Name of mortgage broker and contact information (phone, email, etc.):

Date of conversation:

1. Do you work full time as a residential mortgage broker?

2. How long have you been in the residential mortgage business?

3. Are you licensed (if applicable) and certified by the National Association of Mortgage Brokers?

4. How many residential mortgages have you brokered in the past year?

5. How many of those transactions were with first-time homebuyers?

6. Can you provide at least three names of recent clients who will serve as references, at least one of whom was a first-home buyer?

NOTES:

Best Answers:

1. Yes.
2. The longer the better, but at least two years.
3. Yes.
4. Should be a minimum of ten.
5. The more the better, but should be at least five.
6. Only acceptable answer is "Yes."

Mortgage Broker Reference Questionnaire

Here's what to ask the mortgage broker's references. You can add any other questions that interest you, for example, whether the person tried to negotiate the broker's fee down.

Name of mortgage broker:

Name of reference:

Date:

1. How did you choose the mortgage broker? Did you know the broker before you worked together?

2. What kind of loan did you get? Are you happy with it?

3. Was the broker responsive? Did the broker return calls and emails promptly, follow through on promises, and meet deadlines?

4. How long did you look?

5. Did the broker give you a variety of options?

6. Are you happy with the loan you got?

7. Did the broker help you coordinate other details of your purchase, like working with the title company or insurance agents?

8. Did the broker keep you up to date, and explain everything in terms you understood?

9. Would you work with the broker again?

OTHER COMMENTS:

Who Does What	
It's your mortgage broker's job to ...	**But it's still your job to ...**
Offer you loan products that meet your needs.	Give the mortgage broker all relevant information about your financial picture.
Explain financing concepts and loan products.	Provide personal financial documents.
	Decide which loan you want.
Coordinate loan approval with the lender.	Negotiate the terms of the loan if you think the broker's markup is too high.
Check your credit, help you fill out your application, arrange the appraisal, and verify your financial information.	Return your broker's calls and respond to inquiries.
Before the deal closes, make sure all of the lender's underwriting conditions are met, coordinating with you and the lender, appraiser, credit report company, title company, flood insurance certificate provider (if applicable), and mortgage insurance provider.	Read all documents.
Make sure all loan conditions are met and the cash is transferred for closing.	

Straight to the Source: Dealing With Lenders

Sometimes, a homebuyer goes directly to a lender, rather than dealing with a mortgage broker. The buyer may like the personal aspect of walking into a local bank branch or even have found a better deal than is available through a broker. You can often find a lender's advertised rates on the Web or in your local newspaper—we'll talk about searching for that in Chapter 6.

If you decide to work with a lender, you'll probably still be dealing primarily with a person within the institution called a "mortgage banker" or "loan officer." This person performs the same duties (more or less) as a mortgage broker, except that instead of scouring the entire loan market, the loan officer will help you identify which of the bank's own portfolio of loan products suits your needs. In other words, you'll be limited to the loan packages offered by that institution.

The loan officer should help you fill out your application and handle necessary paperwork like obtaining your credit report and getting an appraisal. However, once you've chosen a bank, you won't be able to choose your loan officer as you would a broker—or your available choices will be limited.

How much personal contact you have with a specific loan officer depends on the lender. Lenders come in all shapes and sizes, from the behemoth bank to the local credit union. Some operate almost entirely online, even having you apply online. These lenders may be keeping their overhead low by cutting out the operating costs of the local office, passing the savings on to you. If you work with online lenders, you'll have to rely more heavily on technology (email, fax machines, and scanners) to transmit documents. You may also have to accept that you'll never meet the loan officer face to face or that you'll be dealing with several different people during the transaction.

Your Fine Print Reader: The Real Estate Attorney

In some states, real estate attorneys are a regular part of the homebuying process. Even in states where this isn't the case, a complex transaction may need an attorney's assistance. After all, if you don't use an attorney and the transaction later goes awry, you'll still have to hire one, at much greater time and cost. Save yourself the headache by working with a lawyer to structure the deal, not salvage it.

> **TIP**
>
> **There's no substitute for your own attorney.** Don't expect the seller's attorney, the closing agent (who may be an attorney), the real estate agent, the mortgage broker, or anyone else in the transaction to look after your legal interests.

Who Real Estate Attorneys Are

A real estate attorney is, by definition, one who focuses on real estate trans-actions. This may sounds obvious, but you don't want to get stuck working with an attorney whose main expertise is estate planning or corporate mergers. Ideally, your attorney will have several years of real estate law experience, at least some of it working directly with other, more experienced attorneys. Additionally, in most cases, you'll want an attorney who specializes in helping buyers with their residential real estate transactions: drawing up contracts, researching title, and the like. An attorney who specializes in litigating disputes is a better fit if you think you'll need to sue or you might be sued—but when structuring your deal, you'll be trying to avoid that result.

CHECK IT OUT

Are attorneys always involved in real estate transactions in your state? Any experienced real estate agent should be able to tell you this right away, but you can also check with your state bar association. Find it through the American Bar Association's website at www.abanet.org/barserv (under "Find a local, state, or specialty bar association").

What Your Real Estate Attorney Does for You

Depending on your needs and which state you're in, your attorney may become involved in one or more of the following: negotiating, creating, or reviewing the sales contract; overseeing the homebuying process to check for compliance with all terms and conditions of the contract; performing a title search or reviewing the title abstract or title insurance commitment (to deter-mine whether there are any liens or encumbrances on the property); explain-ing the effect of any easements or use restrictions; negotiating or representing you in a contract dispute with the seller; and representing you at the closing.

TIP

Check your prepaid legal plan. Such plans—perhaps provided by your employer—may provide legal services for homebuyers, so if you have one, this may be the time to use it.

An attorney can also assist you in complex transactions, for example if:

- Legal claims have been made against your prospective house that must be satisfied by the time the property is sold.

- Problems show up with the title: for example, the driveway is shared by the house you want to buy and the neighboring house, but that isn't reflected in the title.

- You need help reviewing community interest development agreements and documents like CC&Rs, a co-op proprietary lease, or a new home contract drafted by the developer.

- You need to structure a private loan from a relative or friend to make the purchase.

- You purchase the house jointly with others and need to structure a cobuyer agreement and document how title will be held.

Getting the Best Attorney Out There

You may be tempted to get the cheapest attorney you can, but it's smarter to get one who's a real estate expert, even if it costs more. If you pay the attorney by the hour, the seasoned one will take less time than, for example, a criminal defense lawyer, who'll need to spend time just researching real estate laws.

Many, but not all, states require you to have a written fee agreement with your lawyer. It's worth doing, anyway. Your agreement establishes the terms of representation: what the lawyer is expected to do, how much you'll pay and on what basis (for example, hourly or a flat rate), and when the lawyer must be paid. Often you'll have to pay some advance money, called a retainer—but the rest of the lawyer's fee will be paid later.

TIP

Count the hours. If you have an hourly arrangement with your attorney, here's a way to keep costs in check: Ask that the attorney contact you before starting each discrete task (like reviewing condo CC&Rs) and give you an estimate of how long that task will take. If it sounds reasonable, say okay, but require the attorney to contact you if additional time is needed.

To find potential attorneys, get recommendations from friends, coworkers, and trusted real estate professionals. While you can check with professional organizations or use lawyer referral services, these systems suffer from the same problems as with other professions: Other than membership, you have no real way to gauge the person's effectiveness.

Then interview three or four attorneys. Clarify in advance whether you must pay for this interview time. Some attorneys offer free consultations, others don't. It may be worth paying, though, to start your case off with a highly regarded attorney. At the interview, ask about not only the attorney's general legal skills, but also how much time he or she spends on transactions similar to yours—especially if you're buying a condo, co-op, or newly built house.

If possible, get and check references for any attorney you plan to hire, especially if a substantial amount of legal work (and money) is involved. While some attorneys will be reluctant to provide names of clients (because of client confidentiality), it doesn't hurt to ask.

Who Does What	
It's your attorney's job to ...	**But it's still your job to ...**
Provide the services outlined in your agreement, such as drafting an offer or contract, reviewing the contract, or verifying title.	Give the attorney all relevant documents and information.
Tell you how much services will cost.	Return your attorney's calls and respond to inquiries.
Keep everything confidential.	Make all decisions affecting your transaction, such as whether to complete the sale if there is a cloud on title.
Explain problems, complications, and the meaning of legal documents or terms.	Decide how you want to take title.
Advocate on your behalf to make sure contract terms are legal, fair, and satisfactory to you.	
Explain your options for describing your method for taking ownership on the title, and the legal effect of each option.	

CD-ROM

For a handy set of questions to use in your interview and reference checks: Use the "Attorney Interview Questionnaire" and "Attorney Reference Questionnaire" in the Homebuyer's Toolkit on the CD-ROM. Samples of these forms are shown below.

TIP

You can look up an attorney's bar record. Attorneys who violate ethics rules may be disciplined by the state bar (the organization in charge of licensing and regulation). Many states have online tools that allow you to check records. Type "[*your state's name*] state bar" into a search engine.

Your Sharp Eye: The Property Inspector

Before you buy a property, you'll have it inspected at least once (per a contingency you'll put in your contract, as discussed in Chapter 10). The purpose is to make sure that you're getting what you pay for—namely, a house in as good a condition as it appears to be. Suppose you make an offer assuming a place is in tip-top shape, then discover that the bathroom needs to be redone because of a mold problem? The value of that property suddenly plummets—you might not even want to buy it at all.

The typical inspection contingency allows 14 days for inspections to be completed, and three days after that for you to approve them. That's not much time—and in some U.S. regions, the best inspectors have a waiting list. So it's good to choose your inspector before agreeing to buy a house.

Who Inspectors Are

A general home inspector visually examines your potential home, inside and out, for mechanical and structural flaws that could impact its value. Then the inspector prepares a written report summarizing the findings. General inspectors usually have a background in general contracting, residential

Attorney Interview Questionnaire

Ask the following questions, as well as any specific to your transaction—for example, regarding the attorney's experience with condo, co-op, or newly built house purchases.

Name of attorney and contact information (phone, email, etc.):

Date of conversation:

1. What percent of your time do you spend helping residential real estate buyers?

2. How many years have you been handling residential real estate legal matters?

3. Do you charge hourly rates (if so, at what rate) or flat fees for services?

4. Are you an active member of the state bar association?

5. Have you ever been subject to any bar association disciplinary proceedings?

6. Have you ever been sued for malpractice? What was the result?

7. How many individual homebuying clients have you represented in the past year?

8. Can you provide the names of three recent clients who will serve as references?

NOTES:

Best Answers:

1. More than 50%.
2. The longer the better, but at least two years.
3. No one right answer—you'll want to compare fees between attorneys. But try not to base your decision solely on how high or low the fees are.
4. Only acceptable answer is "Yes."
5. Only acceptable answer is "No."
6. Only acceptable answer is "No."
7. Should be a minimum of seven.
8. Not all attorneys will provide references, but if one does, it's worth your time to follow up.

Attorney Reference Questionnaire

Here's what to ask the attorney references. You can add any other questions that interest you—for example, if you're seeking a particular type of legal help, such as with buying a co-op.

Name of attorney:

Name of reference:

Date:

1. How did you choose the attorney?

2. Did you know the attorney before you worked together?

3. What kind of legal services did the attorney provide?

4. Was the attorney responsive? Did the attorney return calls and emails promptly, follow through on promises, and meet deadlines?

5. How long did you work together?

6. Are you happy with the attorney's services?

7. Did the attorney keep you up to date, and explain everything in terms you understood?

8. Would you work with the attorney again?

OTHER COMMENTS:

homebuilding, or engineering. Some states require home inspectors to pass a test and be licensed, while others do not. The more specialized inspectors have other areas of expertise and backgrounds and may need a state license (licensing is fairly common for pest inspectors, for example).

What Your Inspector Does for You

A general home inspection is usually limited to areas that can be seen during one visit without disturbing or damaging the property, such as viewing the condition of the roof, visually inspecting the electrical system, and examining the integrity of the house's foundation. This inspection may also reveal that other inspections are needed, for example, of the chimney or foundation.

A pest inspection, which most lenders require, is more limited in scope. The inspector looks for any damage-causing insects, such as termites or beetles, as well as dry rot.

Getting the Best Inspector Out There

When choosing a general home inspector, look for one who's been in the business for many years and is not only licensed (if that's available in your state), but affiliated with a professional or trade organization, most notably the American Society of Home Inspectors (ASHI). Ideally, you also want someone who has been a residential homebuilder or contractor.

Many buyers use a home inspector recommended by their real estate agent. Be careful: Inspectors who rely too much on agent referrals may be reluctant to find problems that could end up scuttling the deal, thus disappointing the agent. That's why it's worth getting independent recommendations from your friends, coworkers, and recent homebuyers.

TIP

The general inspector won't do the repairs. A general (not pest) inspector evaluates problems and recommends solutions. But no ethical inspector would say, "And guess what, I can fix that for you, at this price." That's a conflict of interest, violates the standards of the main industry trade groups such as ASHI, and is prohibited by law in many states.

When choosing a pest inspector, you can give greater credence to your agent's recommendations. Pest inspectors traditionally are the ones who do the extermination and fix-up work. Yes, it's a conflict, but that's the way the industry works, and the good news is that they actually have an interest in finding problems. For that reason, the remainder of this section will focus on general, not pest, inspectors.

To find a general inspector who will give the house a thorough going-over, interview two or three, asking questions about their experience, price, and scope of services. Also ask any questions specific to your situation, like whether the inspector has experience with historic remodeled properties. Then request the names of three recent references, and follow up to make sure they were impressed with the inspector's eye for defects and communication abilities—and haven't found subsequent problems!

CD-ROM

For a comprehensive set of questions for both the inspector and his or her references: Use the "Home Inspector Interview Questionnaire" and the "Home Inspector Reference Questionnaire" in the Homebuyer's Toolkit on the CD-ROM. Samples of these forms are shown below.

Who Does What	
It's your home inspector's job to ...	**But it's still your job to ...**
Inspect the house for defects.	Attend the inspection.
Write a summary report of the findings.	Read the inspector's report.
Recommend repairs or further inspections, if necessary.	Coordinate follow-up inspections.
	Negotiate with the seller over problems discovered during the inspection.

Home Inspector Interview Questionnaire

Ask potential inspectors the following questions, as well as anything specific to your situation, like whether the inspector has experience with historic or remodeled properties:

Name of inspector and contact information (phone, email, etc.):

Date of conversation:

1. Do you work full time as a home inspector?

2. How long have you been in the home inspection business?

3. Are you affiliated with ASHI?

4. How many home inspections have you done in the past year in this area?

5. What kind of inspection report do you provide? Can I see an example?

6. Do you have current, active liability insurance?

7. What did you do before you were a home inspector?

8. Can I accompany you on the inspection? Can I take photos or videos?

9. Can you provide at least three names of recent clients who'll serve as references?

NOTES:

Best Answers:

1. Yes.
2. The longer the better, but at least two years.
3. Only acceptable answer is "Yes." ASHI is the national organization with the most stringent professional standards.
4. Should be a minimum of 15.
5. Many inspectors have sample reports on their websites; you want as comprehensive a report as possible, versus a short checklist. And you definitely want to see a sample report if there isn't one on the inspector's website.
6. Only acceptable answer is "Yes." Be sure to ask for a certificate of this compliance.
7. Only acceptable answer is a building-related position, such as a contractor or building inspector.
8. Only acceptable answer is "Yes" to the question of whether you can accompany the inspector. But whether you'll be permitted to take photos or videos is a matter of the inspector's own preference.
9. Only acceptable answer is "Yes."

Home Inspector Reference Questionnaire

Here's what to ask the inspector's references:

Name of inspector:

Name of reference:

Date:

1. How did you choose the inspector?

2. Did you know the inspector before you worked together?

3. What kind of inspection did you get and how much did it cost?

4. Was the inspector responsive? Did the inspector return calls and emails promptly, follow through on promises, and meet deadlines?

5. Did the inspector take the time to explain everything to you?

6. Did you go along on the inspection?
   If not, why not?
   If so, how long did it take?

7. What kind of report did you get?

8. Are you happy with the home inspection services and report you got?

9. Did the inspector keep you up to date, and explain everything in terms you understood?

10. Would you work with the inspector again?

OTHER COMMENTS:

Your Big Picture Planner: The Closing Agent

A lot has to happen between signing the agreement to buy a house and closing the deal—it's a process that usually takes at least a few weeks. You want to make sure that the house is in good shape, your financing is squared away, and that the seller doesn't pull any surprises. And on the closing day, a number of documents need to be signed, and money transferred back and forth.

To take care of the many details, it makes sense to have a third party—in many states, a completely neutral third party—to make sure both of you are doing what you promised. That's where the closing agent (sometimes called the "escrow agent," "escrow officer," "closing officer," or "title agent") comes in. Every state's requirements for who can serve in this role are different. In states where attorneys handle the closing (such as Massachusetts and New York), you might not have one neutral intermediary, but instead two attorneys, yours and the seller's, sharing the tasks.

Who Closing Agents Are

Even though we call a closing agent a member of "your" team, the agent is really looking out for both you and the seller (unless you're each using your own attorney). The closing agent acts as a check on both of you, to make sure you complete the transaction according to the terms of the purchase agreement. The agent usually works for a title or escrow company.

What Your Closing Agent Does for You

Although you may not meet your closing agent until you're far into the purchase process—possibly until closing day—the agent will be working behind the scenes long prior to that. (You can meet your closing agent before then, if you want to—and if you have questions or envision some hairy complications, it's a good idea to get in touch.) Expect your closing agent to:

- **Arrange your title insurance.** The closing agent will order or perform (if he or she already works for a title company or is an attorney) a title search. The resulting report will show whether the seller is actually in a legal position to sell the property to you and whether any liens, easements, or other encumbrances affect ownership of the property (we'll translate that gobbledygook in later chapters). After the seller clears up any title defects, the closing agent will help make sure you're issued a title insurance policy.

- **Coordinate with lenders.** The closing agent is going to coordinate with two different sets of lenders: the seller's lender(s), assuming the seller hadn't already paid off the mortgage, and your mortgage lender(s). The closing agent will make sure the seller's lenders are paid in full when the property is sold.

- **Establish an escrow or trust account.** The closing agent will keep any money you deposit in a separate bank account, called an escrow or a trust account, until the closing date, when the money will be transferred to the seller. The seller may also agree to deposit money there, for repairs. In states where both parties are represented by attorneys, the seller's attorney opens this account.

- **Prorate expenses.** The closing agent will figure out who, between you and the seller, pays what proportion of any tax, interest, and insurance payments owing or paid during the time period around the sale.

- **Follow instructions.** The closing agent will follow written instructions prepared by you and the seller and make sure that all these tasks are accomplished by the date of closing.

- **Record the deed and pay the seller.** At the closing, the agent will transfer payment to the seller. Afterward, the closing agent will publicly record the new deed that transfers the property to you.

How You'll Pay the Closing Agent

The closing agent is paid a fee that's included in closing costs. In some locations, it's customary for the buyer to pay the fee; in other locations, the seller; and elsewhere the fees are split. Your real estate agent should know the local custom, though you and the seller can negotiate something different.

Getting the Best Closing Agent Out There

Who chooses the closing agent depends on local custom and how strongly you, as the buyer, feel about having a voice in the matter. The choice of a closing agent is usually made early on and spelled out in the purchase agreement. Often the closing agent is someone either the buyer's or seller's real estate agent knows, however. If you want to use a particular company or individual, mention it to your agent at the outset so it can be included in your offer.

Who Does What	
It's your closing agent's job to …	**But it's still your job to …**
Obtain a title report and coordinate issuance of a title insurance policy.	Understand and sign off on the instructions that guide the agent's activities.
Prorate costs like taxes, insurance, and loan interest.	Read the preliminary title report and, with the help of your real estate agent or attorney, resolve any disputes.
Hold deposits of money in a separate account and transfer them as appropriate.	Read all documents carefully before signing.
Pay recording fees and taxes.	Cough up the cash for whatever portion of the closing costs you agreed to pay (or arrange to have them paid through financing).
Collect and coordinate paperwork, including financing and required disclosures.	
Transfer and record the deed.	Coordinate directly with other parties— like the inspector, real estate agent, or mortgage broker—to make sure everything is in order.
Transfer your payments to the seller.	

TIP

Choose a closing agent who's conveniently located. You'll have to drive there at least once, for the closing, and maybe more often, for example, to sign a power of attorney or deliver an old divorce decree.

To make sure you're choosing the best closing agent, get referrals from not only your agent, attorney, or mortgage broker, but from trusted family members, friends, neighbors, or colleagues. Adviser Sandy Gadow, an experienced closing agent, suggests making sure your referral source had a good experience with the closing and found the closing agent to be efficient, accurate, and able to handle the closing according to schedule.

Strength in Numbers: Other Team Members

Although we've covered the key players for most homebuyers' teams, there are a few other professionals whom you'll either want to consider bringing in or probably interact with along the way. These include:

- **Tax professional.** You may want to consult an accountant or other tax pro to make sure you're taking advantage of all the tax benefits of buying a home. This is particularly important in the year you buy, when many of your expenses may be deductible.

- **Insurance agent or broker.** You're going to need to purchase homeowners' insurance for your house (the lender will require coverage of physical hazards, at a minimum, as described in Chapter 13). To do that, you'll probably work with an insurance broker. Your other option is to directly contact representatives of insurance agencies whose services come highly recommended.

- **Contractor.** If you're considering remodeling, it's worth getting recommendations for a good contractor early on. That way, you can have the contractor look at the house and tell you how much the remodel would cost, or whether it's worth buying in the first place.

What's Next?

With a team of professionals beside you, you're ready to really launch your home search. In the next chapter, we'll discuss one of the most important parts of homebuying: financing your mortgage.

Bring Home the Bacon: Getting a Mortgage

Meet Your Adviser

Fred S. Steingold, an attorney and author based in Ann Arbor, Michigan.

What he does   Fred's legal expertise includes real estate and business matters. He has helped hundreds of homebuyers with key tasks like drafting and reviewing sales contracts, checking title insurance commitments, and looking over closing documents. Fred is a coauthor of the Nolo book *Negotiate the Best Lease for Your Business* and the author of several other Nolo books.

. . . .

First house   "A 1,000-square-foot ranch house in an Ann Arbor subdivision, with just enough room for our two young children. I fondly remember sitting on the back porch during long summer evenings and walking to nearby University of Michigan football games. But I don't miss the small size of that house, and the crank-open windows with gears that were always getting stripped."

. . . .

Fantasy house   "Any house designed by Sarah Susanka would be fun to live in. She's an architect in Minnesota and the author of a series of books on not-so-big houses—they're sparkling gems with alcoves, woodwork, and interesting lighting. She knows how people want to live." (Note to readers: Check out Sarah's work at www.notsobighouse.com.)

Likes best about his work

"The range of people I get to work with. My first-time homebuyer clients are always so excited—and often more than a little nervous. I like walking them through the process and helping them overcome problems with the seller, the lender, and sometimes with their own real estate agent. Once in while, a purchase is about to fall apart over some knotty detail, and I can come up with a creative solution to save it. It's all part of helping these (usually) young buyers move up in the world."

* *

Top tip for first-time homebuyers

"You're probably expecting me to give law-related advice, but I'd say have a thorough inspection! Most us don't know how to spot a potentially leaky basement or roof, or other expensive problems. But an experienced inspector can give you a heads up so you can opt out of the deal or have repairs made on the seller's dime. And if you're having a house built for you, make sure to learn about the builder's reputation. You'll be extremely frustrated if the new house isn't ready until eight months after the promised date—or if you have to chase the builder to get postclosing warranty work done."

If you're like most homebuyers (over 90% of them, according to NAR statistics), you simply won't have the cash on hand to buy a home outright. Thankfully, in spite of the financial meltdown of 2008, there are still lenders willing to front you the money you'll probably need.

If you've already started researching mortgages, you may have been put off by all the numbers and fine print. People start out promising themselves, "I'm going to learn all about mortgages," and end up saying, "I'll take whatever's available; I just want to buy this house."

But you don't need to swing to either extreme—with a little buyer's savvy, you can avoid a mortgage that's just plain wrong for you or costs more than it should. We'll show you how by looking at:

- the basics of mortgage financing—interest rates, points, and more
- different loan options—fixed rates, adjustable rates, and everything in between
- how much to borrow versus how much to put down
- where to research mortgages, and
- the mechanics of applying for and getting a loan.

Let's Talk Terms: The Basics of Mortgage Financing

Before you start mortgage shopping, let's cover the basics: what a mortgage is and how it works. A mortgage is a loan to purchase property, with the property as collateral. That means that if you buy your dream home, and you don't make the payments, the mortgagor (the lender, in common parlance) can recover what it's owed by foreclosing on the property—that is, taking possession of and selling it.

The average home buyer spends double the time researching a car purchase as he or she does researching a mortgage.

—*Zillow*

Naturally, the lender gets into this risky business to make money. It does that primarily by charging interest and points (one-time fees when you take out the loan). The variety of mortgage options means you can borrow the same amount of money but with different terms and end up paying very different amounts back. While interest rates and points look like tiny numbers and percentages in the beginning, they add up to real dollars later.

EXAMPLE: Rob and Amy have found their dream house but don't have a mortgage yet. The local bank offers them a $350,000, 30-year, fixed-rate mortgage at 5.25% interest, with no points. The monthly principal and interest payment would be about $1,932, and they'd pay about $345,778 in interest over the life of the loan.

Meanwhile, Jimmy and Devon are interested in the same house. They go to a broker to discuss their options. She finds them a $350,000, 30-year, fixed rate mortgage at 4.5% interest, with one point. The point will cost them $3,500, but their monthly payment will be about $1,722, and they'll pay about $261,027 in interest over the life of the loan, $84,751 less than Rob and Amy.

All About Interest Rates

Most of us have been borrowing long enough—either to buy a car, go to college, or get this season's fashion must-haves—to understand what interest rates are and that we don't like them. An interest rate is an amount charged by a lender, calculated as a percentage of the loan amount. Interest rates are usually high on credit cards (sometimes above 20%), but thankfully lower on other forms of credit, like mortgages. And as we discussed in Chapter 1, interest paid on your mortgage is tax-deductible.

In the early 2000s, home mortgage interest rates hit record lows, dipping below 5% in 2010. When this book went to print, they looked unlikely to climb toward early 1980s levels (15% and up) anytime soon. Nevertheless, with the economy in flux, we should expect some volatility.

You're not stuck with your first mortgage for life. If you sell the house, you'll get a new mortgage when you buy your next one. And if you decide to stay put, you can refinance your mortgage (essentially, trade it in for a better one) if rates drop and the value of your house holds steady or climbs. Though you'll pay fees to refinance, it could be well worth it. (If the value of your house drops, however, refinancing may not be an option—the precise reaason that many homeowners, who were counting on refinancing, found themselves instead pushed into foreclosure in recent years.)

Monthly Payments for a $100,000 Fixed Rate Mortgage	
This chart shows the variation among monthly payments for a 30-year, $100,000 fixed rate mortgage at different interest rates.	
Interest Rate	**Monthly Payment**
4.0%	$477
4.5%	$507
5.0%	$537
5.5%	$568
6.0%	$600
6.5%	$632
7.0%	$665
7.5%	$699
8.0%	$734
8.5%	$769
9.0%	$805

What Those Percentages Really Mean

Unfortunately, mortgage interest rates aren't always as straightforward as they appear. For one thing, you may see them expressed two different ways: as a base rate and as an annual percentage rate ("APR"). Those two numbers aren't going to be the same. The base rate is the actual rate used to calculate your payment, while the APR is the total cost of taking out the loan, factored out over the life of the loan and taking into account any fees you pay, like appraisal fees and credit reports. Lenders provide the APR because they're legally required to.

The APR should be a good indicator of what a loan really costs, except that it factors the costs *over the life of the loan*—and the chances of living in the same place for the whole term of a mortgage, without refinancing, are pretty low. However, the APR can be informative—like when a loan is advertised at a very low interest rate, but a slew of additional fees increase the cost dramatically.

Why You Might Not Be Offered the Advertised Interest Rate

To complicate matters, the rates you see advertised aren't necessarily what you'll be offered personally. For starters, interest rates change daily, so if you're looking at the Sunday paper, by Monday the rates may be higher or lower. And the rates you're offered will depend on some factors unique to you, such as:

- **The type of mortgage you choose.** You'll typically be offered a lower initial interest rate on an adjustable rate mortgage (ARM) than on a fixed rate mortgage. Notice we said *initial*—stay tuned for more on that later in this chapter.

- **How risky you are as a borrower.** If you have a history of paying bills on time, a steady high salary or other significant income, low debt, plan to make a hefty down payment, and request a loan that doesn't break the bank, you'll probably be offered a comparatively low interest rate. If the opposite is true, your rate may be higher, to compensate the lender for the added risk.

- **The loan-to-value ratio.** A large down payment tells the lender that you're not likely to walk away from your investment. A small one, however, makes the lender nervous. If you default, the lender will spend time and money chasing you down and may have to initiate foreclosure proceedings. Also, the lender could lose money, if you owe more than the house is worth. It protects itself from such risks by charging you higher interest.

- **Whether the loan can be resold.** Lenders often resell loans on the secondary mortgage market, discussed below. That frees up the lender's capital to make more loans (meaning make more money). If your loan doesn't qualify for resale, it's less desirable for the lender. You'll pay a premium to make up for that.

The Secondary Mortgage Market and Jumbo Loans

A whole market exists in which original lenders sell loans to secondary lenders. Usually the original lender is paid a flat fee upon sale, and the new lender gets to collect the rest of your mortgage payments, including interest.

Why does this matter to you? Because the primary players in this secondary market, Fannie Mae (the Federal National Mortgage Association) and Freddie Mac (the Federal Home Loan Mortgage Corporation), buy only those loans that meet certain financial criteria, including that the mortgage doesn't exceed a certain amount (which varies by location and is regularly adjusted: for 2010, it was $417,000 in most places, but as high as $729,750 in high-cost areas such as Hawaii and New York City). If your loan won't qualify for sale to Fannie or Freddie (a given if it's a "jumbo" loan—over the monetary limit), you'll probably be offered a higher interest rate.

- **Whether the loan has points.** Loans with points (an optional up-front fee) will normally come with a lower interest rate.

You can't be certain of the interest rate and the exact terms of your mortgage until you've selected and applied for it. But knowing what affects the rate will help you view all options with a critical eye.

All About Points

No, this isn't some obscure score in the homebuying game. A point is a loan fee equal to 1% of the principal on the loan (so one point on a $100,000 mortgage is $1,000). Points are added to the cost of some mortgages in exchange for a lower interest rate. You probably won't be offered more than two or three points on a loan, because the lender would have to significantly reduce your interest rate to make it financially beneficial to you.

Since points are paid up front, they're a major source of immediate profit for the lender, and if your loan is resold on the secondary market, points are often the *main* source of the lender's profit. That doesn't mean they're bad for you—in fact, the lowered interest rate means it's often beneficial to get a loan with points, particularly if you have the cash, are planning to stay in your place for a while, and don't plan to refinance soon. (You may *need* the lower interest rate, because you don't qualify for a loan at the higher rate.) If you want to pay points but don't have the cash up front, you may be able to amortize the points into your loan. That means they'll be added to the principal and paid off over the life of your loan. Of course, that also means you'll be paying interest on that money.

EXAMPLE: Kelly and Brit need a $250,000 mortgage. They have two options, both 30-year fixed rates: one at 5% interest with no points, and one at 4.5% interest with two points.

If they take the first loan, their monthly principal and interest payments will be approximately $1,342. If they keep this house and loan for 30 years, they'll pay about $233,141 in interest, plus the $250,000 principal, for a total of about $483,141.

With the second loan, Kelly and Brit are going to have to cough up $5,000 right away, to pay the points. Their monthly payments will be $1,266—around $76 less per month. Over the life of the 30-year loan, they'll pay around $206,018 in interest and points, which, plus the $250,000 principal, comes to about $456,018. The second loan offers them a long-term savings of almost $27,123.

But what if they don't keep the house for the full 30 years? If they decide to take the loan with points but a lower interest rate, it will take Kelly and Brit a long time before their lowered interest makes up for the $5,000 they paid. To figure out how long, they divide the $5,000 in points by the $76 in monthly savings. The answer is 65 months, or five and a half years.

As you can see in the example, if Kelly and Brit choose the loan with two points and then stay in their place for more than five years, they'll start to see some serious savings. On the other hand, if two years after choosing the loan with points, they decide that the cottage that seemed so charming is actually too small for their two dogs and three cats, they will, upon selling, say goodbye to the extra money that they spent by taking the loan with points ($3,176, because they've recouped $1,824 of the original $5,000 in the first two years, when their monthly mortgage payments were $150 less). It sort of makes that loan … pointless. Not exactly, but you get our bad joke. The longer you plan to stay, the more seriously you should consider a loan with points.

To do this calculation with your own numbers, use the table below or an online mortgage calculator.

When to Pay Additional Points for a Lower Interest Rate													
Use this chart to determine how many years you should stay in a house to recoup the cost of points.													
Interest Rate Reduction	Additional Points												
	0.25	0.5	0.75	1.0	1.25	1.5	1.75	2.0	2.25	2.5	2.75	3.0	3.25	3.5
⅛%	2.3 yrs.	5.3	10.0	23.5	No matter how long you plan to have the loan, don't pay the extra points.								
¼%	1.1	2.3	3.7	5.3	7.2	10.0	13.5	21.0						
⅜%	0.7	1.5	2.2	3.1	4.2	5.3	6.5	8.0	9.8	12.0	15.0	21.0		
½%	0.5	1.1	1.6	2.3	2.9	3.6	4.4	5.3	6.2	7.2	8.5	9.8	11.4	13.5
⅝%	0.4	0.8	1.3	1.8	2.3	2.8	3.3	3.9	4.6	5.3	6.0	6.8	7.7	8.7
¾%	0.3	0.7	1.1	1.4	1.8	2.3	2.7	3.2	3.6	4.1	4.7	5.2	5.9	6.5
⅞%	0.3	0.6	0.9	1.2	1.6	1.9	2.3	2.6	3.0	3.4	3.8	4.3	4.7	5.2
1%	0.3	0.5	0.8	1.1	1.3	1.6	2.0	2.3	2.6	2.9	3.3	3.6	4.0	4.4

CHECK IT OUT

Ready to run some numbers? These websites have calculators that allow you to figure out whether a points or no-points loan works best for you:

- www.nolo.com/legal-calculators
- www.mtgprofessor.com
- www.dinkytown.net.

If you're not sure how long you'll stay in a place, you may just have to guesstimate. If you want flexibility and think it's possible you'll move in the next few years, get a no-points loan. But if you expect to stay put for awhile, a loan with points might be worth it. And if you hate guessing, you can also compromise—points aren't all or nothing. There are many choices between zero points and several (broken down by eighths of a percentage point, even).

A final advantage to points it that they're tax-deductible in the year you pay them. In slow markets, sellers sometimes pay for points as an incentive to the buyer, and you can even deduct those. In the first year, when money is tight, this might be a significant advantage.

Watch Out for Prepayment Penalties

Many loans come with prepayment penalties, which don't permit you to pay your debt off early without paying a fee. Read loan terms carefully—this may be buried in the fine print. (It will also be included on your Truth in Lending (TIL) disclosure statement, a form your lender is required to give you.) Prepayment penalties can limit your flexibility to refinance or sell your home— a particular drag if interest rates drop.

Many loans with prepayment penalties limit the length of time you're bound by this restriction (usually five years or less), limit the amount of the penalty (state laws often impose these limits), or make exceptions for refinancing or selling the property. Still, prepayment penalties are usually worth avoiding altogether.

Who's Got the Cash? Where to Get a Mortgage

There are two major players in the mortgage game, both of whom can help you get the loan you need. You may work with a mortgage broker, who will help you find the best available mortgage from among a variety of lenders. Or you may go straight to a lender (sometimes called a mortgage banker), which will probably mean fewer options, but possibly a better deal. For more information on choosing a mortgage broker or lender, look back at Chapter 5.

Narrowing the Field: Which Type of Mortgage Is Best for You?

Mortgages come in two basic flavors: fixed rate mortgages and adjustable rate mortgages (also called ARMs). There are variations on these two types, and some are better for certain kinds of buyers than others. Though you'll discuss your unique situation with your broker or lender, you can first educate yourself about the options.

CHECK IT OUT

Mortgages have their own lingo—use the following glossaries if you need help decoding:

- www.mtgprofessor.com (click "Glossary")
- www.bankrate.com (click "Glossary")
- www.fanniemae.com (under "Homebuyers," click "Glossary of Terms").

Fixed Rate Mortgages

If you like predictability and stability, you'll probably like fixed rate mortgages. The interest rate is set when you get the loan and never changes. If you borrow $250,000 at 4.65% interest, you'll continue to pay 4.65% interest until you've paid off the loan.

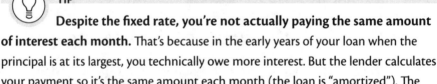

TIP

Despite the fixed rate, you're not actually paying the same amount of interest each month. That's because in the early years of your loan when the principal is at its largest, you technically owe more interest. But the lender calculates your payment so it's the same amount each month (the loan is "amortized"). The way amortization shakes out, the interest you owe makes up a greater portion of your early monthly payments. As you gradually start to reduce the principal, less interest accrues, and so more of your payment goes to reducing principal.

Beyond buyers who crave predictability, fixed rate mortgages are good for those who want to stay put long term, particularly if interest rates are low. Even if interest rates go sky-high, you'll have a fixed rate you can live with. You pay a premium for this stability, because fixed rate mortgages usually have higher starting interest rates than ARMs. That protects lenders who are stuck giving you a nice low rate for the full term of the loan, even when interest rates increase and other buyers are paying them more.

The Gold Standard: 30-Year Fixed

The ultimate in predictability and stability tends to be the 30-year fixed rate loan. It allows borrowers to finance their home purchase at a preset interest rate and pay it off over a full 30 years. These loans make sense for people who plan to live in their homes for several years. (Of course, you don't have to stay in your house that long.)

The Saver's Special: 15-Year Fixed

If you're extremely disciplined and can afford it, you might consider a shorter-term fixed loan, most typically a 15-year mortgage. Like any fixed rate mortgage, these have stable interest rates and predictable terms. By paying more each month, you ultimately pay less interest overall. As an added plus, you probably get a relatively low interest rate.

You can see why they're not as popular, however: Paying money back faster means committing yourself to relatively high monthly payments.

EXAMPLE: Adina wants to take out a loan for $150,000 to buy a new condo. She can choose between a 30-year, fixed rate mortgage with a 5% interest rate, and a 15-year fixed rate mortgage with a 4% interest rate.

With the first loan, Adina will have a monthly principal and interest payment of around $805. After 30 years, she'll have paid about $139,888 in interest. If Adina takes the second loan, she'll have a significantly higher principal and interest payment, approximately $1,110 each month. However, at the end of 15 years, she'll have paid off her mortgage and spent about $49,716 on interest ($90,172 less than with the 30-year mortgage).

Shorter-term fixed rate loans free your income for other purposes earlier than longer-term mortgages do. If you know you're going to want money for something else—for example, to pay college tuition, purchase a second home, or retire—such a loan can act as a serious forced savings plan.

That doesn't necessarily make it the most financially savvy option, however—especially not if you can make money by investing elsewhere or reducing your higher-interest debt (like on credit cards). For example, if you commit to a 15-year mortgage instead of contributing your money to a retirement plan, you could end up house-rich but cash-poor—with a place to retire in, but not enough money to do so. A better way to accomplish your savings goals might be to take out a longer-term loan and contribute the cash you've freed up to a 401(k) or IRA.

As a compromise, some people take out a 30-year fixed rate loan but then make higher-than-required monthly payments to the loan principal. The more principal you pay, the less interest accrues, so if you make early payments, you also end up paying less interest overall. While this strategy won't save you quite as much money as a shorter-term fixed rate loan would (since your interest rate will probably be a little higher), you face less future risk. If someday you can't afford to make more than the minimum payment, you're not locked in.

> **TIP**
>
> **Put it to principal.** If you decide to make a prepayment, write on the check that the payment is to be applied toward principal. Otherwise, the lender might apply it toward the next payment that's due, which will defeat your purpose.

The Endless Loan: 40-Year Fixed

If you're interested in the stability of a fixed rate loan but won't qualify for a 30-year term, you may be drawn to another option: the 40-year loan. These loans have become less available in recent years, but if you're able to find one, it can offer a tempting combination of relatively low monthly payments and a stable interest rate.

However, the 40-year fixed is expensive over the long term. Since you're borrowing the money for a longer period of time, you're going to pay a lot more total interest, so you won't see a huge reduction in your monthly payment.

EXAMPLE: Sarah and Jorge plan to borrow $300,000 to buy a home. They're considering two options: a 30-year, fixed rate mortgage at 6.5% and a 40-year fixed rate mortgage, also at 6.5%.

If Sarah and Jorge get the 30-year loan, their monthly principal and interest payments will be about $1,896 and they'll pay $382,637 in interest over the life of the loan. If they get the 40-year loan, they'll pay $1,756 per month ($140 less) in principal and interest—but their total interest payments after 40 years will be $543,058—a whopping $160,421 more in total interest.

Another drawback of 40-year fixed rate loans is that most have a higher interest rate than would be offered on a 30-year loan, so the difference in monthly payments is even less. Finally, remember that taking out a 40-year loan means that you'll have debt hanging over your head for 40 years (assuming you stay put and don't refinance or prepay). Depending on your age, that could take you well into retirement.

CHECK IT OUT

Tally up how your 401(k) contributions will grow between now and retirement: Go to www.bankrate.com, click "Calculators," then under "Investment Calculators," click "How much money can I save in my 401(k) plan."

The Poser: Balloon Loans

At first glance, balloon loans look pretty attractive. Their interest rate usually starts below the market rate on a 30-year fixed rate mortgage. You make payments for a fixed period of time—usually somewhere between three and ten years. However, your monthly payments are calculated as if you were paying the same amount each month for 30 years, which keeps them low. (The technical way to say this is that the loan is amortized over a 30-year period.)

However, at the end of the fixed period, you owe the entire loan balance, then and there. This isn't necessarily a problem, since you may be able to refinance with another lender, assuming interest rates are favorable at the time and that you have sufficient equity.

But it's difficult to bank on that happening, which is one reason these loans aren't as readily available as they were a few years ago. The balloon payment could become a problem if you find yourself unable to qualify for another loan because the value of your house has dropped (hopefully temporarily), your financial circumstances change, or you have some credit snafus in the meantime. Unlike an ARM, you won't even have the option of continuing to make payments at a higher rate. A better alternative is to get a hybrid loan, discussed below.

Adjustable Rate Mortgages

As the name implies, the interest rate on an adjustable rate mortgage ("ARM") can fluctuate during the loan term—and no one can predict with certainty where interest rates will go. For buyers who aren't put off by this risk, or see buying their first home as a short-term stepping stone, the ARM may be an attractive option.

The relatively low initial interest rates are certainly eye-catching and have made ARMs a favorite among new buyers.

But what about those fluctuating interest rates? They're definitely the main risk factor in an ARM. After the starter rate runs out, the rate adjusts periodically at an agreed-upon term. This term (called the *adjustment period*) may vary from one month to several years. Buyers in the last several years were lured by lenders offering ridiculously low initial interest rates, only to find their payments completely unaffordable once the rate adjusted (sometimes, as quickly as a month later). This contributed to the very problems in the mortgage market that make lenders more careful about offering ARMs today.

When you're looking at the loan description for an ARM, check out a number called an *index*: The lender will adjust your rate to equal the index plus an extra amount, so that it makes a profit. That bit of profit, calculated as either a set amount or percentage, is called a *margin*.

Luckily, your lender doesn't get to invent the index. It will draw on a particular published, market-driven number. Common indexes include the London Interbank Offered Rate (LIBOR), the 11th Federal Home Loan Bank District Cost of Funds (COFI), U.S. Treasury Bills, or Certificates of Deposit (CDs). The LIBOR is usually the most volatile, meaning it jumps up or down quickly and dramatically, while the COFI is less volatile. Also, an index that averages rates over the long term (a year or every six months) is preferable to one that moves up and down based on the weekly "spot" rate.

Another number to seek out when comparing ARMs is the *life-of-the-loan cap*. This is a maximum on the ARM's total interest rate, no matter how high the index rises. The lender usually allows a well-padded 5%–6% above the starting interest rate, which can affect your monthly payment by hundreds or even thousands of dollars. Still, it's far better than getting an ARM without a life-of-the-loan cap—that's downright dangerous.

In addition to a life-of-the-loan cap, most ARMs limit how much your interest rate can increase at any adjustment period. This number is called the *periodic cap*. It's also a floor, limiting the amount the rate can decrease at one time. Look for an ARM that doesn't change by more than 2%–3% at each adjustment period. Otherwise, your monthly payment could shoot up very rapidly.

EXAMPLE: On a $200,000 loan, you're choosing between a 30-year, fixed rate mortgage with a 5.85% interest rate and an ARM with an initial 5.5% rate. The life-of-the-loan cap on the ARM is 11.5%. Your monthly principal and interest payment on the fixed rate loan would be approximately $1,180 and never increase above that. Your monthly payment on the ARM would start at approximately $1,136. However, if your interest rate adjusts to the maximum 11.5%, your payment could go as high as $1,980—about $700 more.

Traditional ARMs

The traditional ARM works like this: The loan starts out at a below-market interest rate, called a *teaser rate*. This rate adjusts frequently, as frequently as every month in some cases. As we've seen, that adjustment can make a big difference in your monthly payment.

A traditional ARM is rarely a good financing strategy. Many people who choose it can't really afford the home that they're hoping to buy. If you can only afford the monthly payment in the first few months when the interest rate is artificially low, what are you going to do when it goes up?

The exception is if you expect a significant increase in your income very soon, or you're in line for some other form of income, such as an inheritance or gift. If so, a traditional ARM might be a bridge until you can qualify for a loan with better terms or pay off your property entirely.

> **◉ CHECK IT OUT**
>
> **Interested in a traditional ARM?** You'll need to know what maximum amounts you could owe each month. Your mortgage broker should be able to calculate this for you, or you can use an online ARM payment calculator, like the ones at www.nolo.com/legal-calculators, www.interest.com, or www.dinkytown.net.

Interest-Only ARMs

Another type of ARM is the interest-only variety: once very common, but increasingly difficult to find. (Although interest-only loans don't *have* to be ARMs, they usually are.) This is, at least at the beginning, just what it sounds like: You start out paying only the interest that accrues on the loan principal, making for very low monthly payments. The downside is that you don't reduce the amount you borrowed (there's no "P" in your PITI). And of course, you have to start paying off the principal some day—usually between three and ten years later. At that time, you'll either have to pay much higher monthly payments or, with a balloon loan, pay the whole thing off.

Interest-only loans are attractive when home prices are going up fast, with first-time buyers squeezing into the market. These buyers hope to make the low monthly payments long enough for their house to rise in value, then either sell without having to pay off the loan principal or refinance on better terms.

But as the recent turn in most real estate markets shows us, this can be a dangerous strategy. Such buyers pin all their hopes on the value of the property increasing, especially because interest-only payments don't increase their equity. If the value of the property drops, the buyer could face a serious loss, particularly if forced to sell (maybe due to a job transfer) or after a change in the terms of the loan (an adjustment to the interest rate). And the buyer would remain responsible for paying the difference between the amount the house can be sold for and the remaining loan balance.

Buyers who pay down principal are in a much better position to weather unexpected drops in home prices. Even if forced to sell, they'll owe less than their interest-only counterparts, because they'll have built up some equity by reducing principal.

Judging an ARM Beauty Contest

If you decide to get an ARM, here's a summary of the features to examine:

- **Initial interest rate.** This should be significantly less than is available on a fixed rate mortgage, to balance the added risk of rate increases.

- **Adjustment period.** Look for annual or biannual (not monthly) adjustment periods.

- **Index.** A slow-changing index (such as the COFI) is preferable to a rapidly changing, volatile one.

- **Life-of-the-loan cap.** Don't agree to pay a maximum interest rate greater than 6% above the initial rate.

- **Periodic cap.** The interest rate should change only a reasonable amount at each adjustment period; 2% is about right on a one-year ARM.

- **Low margin.** The margin should be as low as possible; around 2.5% on a six-month ARM or 2.75% on a one-year ARM.

- **No prepayment penalty.** You don't want to be charged extra for making early payments or refinancing.

- **Assumability.** ARMs are sometimes assumable, which means that when you sell the house, the next buyer can take over your loan. If interest rates are high then, this can be an incentive to prospective buyers.

Hybrid Loans

Hybrid loans, like hybrid cars, can save you money. While hybrid cars do it by eating less gas, hybrid loans do it through lower interest rates. They're a safer and more realistic option for many first-time buyers who want to break into the market but don't plan to be in their first homes forever.

Hybrids work like this: For a set period of time, you pay interest at a fixed rate—usually, below the market rate on a regular fixed mortgage—and after that, the rate becomes adjustable. The fixed-rate term is usually three, five, seven, or ten years. The frequency of the adjustment varies, but it's usually every six months or one year. (A "5/1," for example, means that the rate is fixed for five years, then adjusts every year.)

That means you want to know how long you'll be in your home before signing up for a hybrid ARM. If you're not sure or you want to maximize flexibility and reduce risk, select a hybrid with a longer fixed-rate term (such as ten years). You might have to pay a slightly higher interest rate, but you'll save the cost of a refinance, if you realize at the end of the shorter term that you're not ready to go. And you'll save yourself the stress of trying to predict where you—and interest rates—are going to be in ten years.

Two-Step Loans

A two-step loan is essentially a hybrid loan with only one adjustment. During the first "step" of the mortgage—typically a period of five or seven years—the loan has a fixed rate that's usually below comparable fixed rate mortgages. Then the rate adjusts to a newer fixed rate, but unlike a hybrid, it doesn't keep changing every six months or year. The second step's interest rate will be set based on the index at the time of the adjustment plus a margin.

If you see a loan referred to as 5/25 or 7/23, that may indicate that it's a two-step loan. The first number is the number of years of the first "step," and the second number indicates the length in years of the second "step." Look closely, though, as some balloon mortgages are similarly labeled.

Of course, if you get a two-step mortgage (and they're hard to find these days), make sure you'll be able to afford the second step. Since it's impossible to know future interest rates, you may find that it makes more sense to refinance when the first step ends.

Getting Your Cash Together: Common Down Payment and Financing Strategies

Talk to anyone who bought their first home in the last few years, and you may hear, "We put zero down!" or "We got two mortgages so we could avoid private mortgage insurance!" Many buyers employed some creative down-payment strategies to help get into their first homes, and lenders obliged.

But with the market having done a huge turnaround, these methods have nearly dropped off the map. To make sure you understand the full range of possibilities, however, we'll explain all the strategies here, from the traditional to the more creative.

The Traditional: 80/20

Lenders feel safe with buyers who pay 20% down and finance the rest. If you're willing to pay that much up front, the lender is relatively confident that you're not going to default: You've already shown you're a serious saver, and you'll have a lot on the line, too. Even if you default, the lender has a good chance of collecting what it's owed if it sells the house through foreclosure, because you have more equity in the property. In turn, the advantage to you of putting 20% down is that you avoid paying for private mortgage insurance (PMI), and you'll pay less interest overall.

> ### Not a Recommended Strategy
>
> **Homer:** *Homer Simpson does not lie twice on the same form. He never has and he never will.*
>
> **Marge:** *You lied dozens of times on our mortgage application.*
>
> **Homer:** *Yeah, but they were all part of a single ball of lies.*
>
> —The Simpsons

Of course, if you're in a very hot market, you may not want to wait until you've scraped together a 20% down payment. That's especially true if increasing prices mean you'll later have to pay even more for a house (uh oh, that 20% amount just became a moving target). You could end up being priced right out of the market. What's more, if values are rising while you're saving, you won't reap the benefits of the increased value—instead, you'll pay for it down the road, when you're finally able to afford a place.

The Risky: Little or Nothing Down

Almost nonexistent today, 100% financing was all the rage just a few years ago, when up to one third of first-time buyers purchased this way. Today, lenders almost universally don't allow borrowers to do it. If the value of the property drops and you haven't paid off a significant portion of the mortgage, the lender stands to lose everything; and with the downturn in the housing market, lenders simply aren't willing to risk that.

> **TIP**
>
> **If you want to make a low down payment,** check out FHA mortgages, which allow you to purchase with as little as 3% down. For more information, see Chapter 7.

If you are able to find one of these loans, you'll usually have to show fabulous credit and pay higher interest rates and more fees, including PMI. So while the out-of-pocket expenses will be relatively low (pared down to your remaining closing costs), your monthly costs will be significantly higher.

While we won't prophesy heartache, putting nothing down is still risky. If the value of the property falls below what you owe, you're either stuck paying your way out of the hole or selling the house for less than you paid and finding cash elsewhere to pay off the mortgage balance.

The risk is even greater when you combine low-cost financing tools like interest-only mortgages. In those cases, if you can't afford to pay down the loan principal and your property value doesn't rise, you could go deep into debt and even lose your home.

Where Do I Look? Researching Mortgages

Once you understand your loan options, you can start researching where to get the best deals. We advise exploring several research avenues, from a mortgage broker to online. Then you'll have plenty to choose from, or at least know what to ask a mortgage broker about.

As you research, organize your findings in one folder or file. It's easier to do this if you get printed information about different loan options, so ask for that whenever possible. You might also want to create a worksheet or spreadsheet to compare different mortgage features like interest rates, fees, or other terms or requirements. You can create this worksheet yourself or use one available online, like on the Federal Trade Commission website (www. ftc.gov, search for "Mortgage Shopping Worksheet"). No need to fill out your worksheet for every mortgage, just the few you're seriously considering.

Online Mortgage-Related Sites

The quickest way to get information about mortgages is on the Internet. In addition to sites operated by individual lenders, various sites aggregate lender information and allow you to compare different loan options. At bankrate. com, for example, you can compare rates based on your geographic location, the amount you want to borrow, and the terms you're seeking. Then you can contact the prospective lenders directly to get more information.

 CHECK IT OUT

Check out these sites to compare different lenders:

- www.bankrate.com
- www.hsh.com
- www.compareinterestrates.com.

Be careful, however, about any websites that require you to enter personal information like your name, Social Security Number, or address. In the worst case, you can actually agree to purchase a mortgage online—not the smartest impulse buy. More likely, you'll be contacted by potential lenders, or they'll check your credit history (and multiple inquiries can affect your credit score, though all checks within a 14-day window are treated as one).

Newspaper Ads

The real estate sections of newspapers often advertise interest rates. Usually, lenders will list the different loan products they offer, with their base interest rate, APR, any points, and sometimes fees charged. These are probably the lowest rates offered to the very best borrowers—not necessarily the rate you'll get. Also, because interest rates change daily, these numbers may not be an accurate reflection of what actual rates are. Use them only to ballpark what's available.

Banks and Other Direct Lenders

You can also research rates through banks and other direct lenders (such as savings and loans, credit unions, and investment firms). You can do this online, pick up printed information that's available in bank lobbies or sent in the mail, or talk to a loan officer. Your options range from large national lenders to small local ones: Don't assume a bigger bank means a better loan.

Mortgage Brokers

A mortgage broker is an obvious resource and should be able to give you detailed information and help you get preapproved when you find a good loan. For more information on choosing a broker, refer back to Chapter 5.

I'll Take That One! Applying for Your Loan

Assuming you get preapproved for a loan (described in Chapter 3), you'll have already dealt with most of the necessary loan paperwork and given a lender a laundry list of your relevant financial information. (Even if you decide to work with another lender, you'll still have all the documents in one place.) If you don't get preapproved, you'll probably get a loan after you've made an offer on a house and may be pressed for time. Usually, your contract will give you a few days to find financing on terms laid out in the contract. The lender is still going to want the documents listed in Chapter 3, as well as those below.

Assembling Your Documents

After preapproval, and after you've chosen a house, but before the loan is finalized, your lender will need:

- **A copy of the house purchase contract.** Your real estate agent should be able to provide this directly to the broker or lender.

- **A preliminary title report.** The title company should give this directly to the lender or broker. The report tells the lender whether the seller owns the property free and clear and whether there are any financial or other encumbrances on the property.

- **A property appraisal.** The appraisal report tells the lender whether you're asking to borrow more than the house is worth. The lender will probably schedule the appraisal and just ask you to show up for the appraiser's house visit. The appraiser will normally give a copy of the report directly to your broker or lender.

It's also typical for the lender to ask permission to get more financial information about you by contacting different entities that have that data. This can include getting not only your credit history, but also your employment and bank records, and possibly even IRS tax records.

CD-ROM

The **"Financial Information for Lenders" worksheet** in the Homebuyer's Toolkit on the CD-ROM includes a complete list of the documents you need to apply for a loan.

Filling Out the Application

Many lenders use a standard mortgage application form called the Uniform Residential Loan Application (sometimes called "Form 1003"), mainly because it's used by Fannie Mae and Freddie Mac. You might want to take a peek at the form before it's given to you, at www.efanniemae.com. Although the form is quite long, a lot of the information is stuff you already know. The rest, the loan officer or mortgage broker should be able to help you with.

If you're lucky, your mortgage broker or loan officer will actually offer to fill out the form for you (sometimes after asking you to fill out a mini-version). At a minimum, they should be willing to explain how certain items should be filled out. Ultimately, however, you're responsible for making sure the information is accurate, truthful, and complete, so review the form carefully before signing.

You May Want to Lock in a Rate

Interest rates change frequently. If you apply for a loan and rates go up before the sale is complete, the lender will require you to pay the higher rate.

To avoid that, you can ask for a "lock in" or "rate lock." It ensures you get the interest rate quoted to you. If interest rates are on the rise, this is a great thing, especially if you can't afford a higher rate.

There are some downsides: Lock ins are usually tied to a specific property, and they're usually short term. Typically, you can get a lock for 30 to 60 days without much trouble, but you may have to pay for it, often in the form of extra points or a slightly elevated interest rate.

If you get a lock in, make sure it's in writing and specifies the interest rate and points you'll pay on the mortgage. For more information, see www.federalreserve.gov/pubs/lockins.

TIP

Play it straight. Think a little fib on your application is no big deal? Watch out: It's known as mortgage fraud, and as mortgage broker Russell Straub explains, "It's rarely prosecuted on the front end, but if a mortgage goes bad and ends up in foreclosure, a scapegoat is usually looked for. The original application is scrutinized, and in the worse cases—which I've seen—borrowers go to jail."

Getting an Appraisal

The final step in your loan application process is allowing the property to be appraised. Usually, you literally stand back while the lender chooses the appraiser and tells you what day to be at the house to meet him or her. You also pay the appraiser's fee, around $400.

The appraiser's job is to determine the value of the house, and thus make sure you're not borrowing more than it's worth. The appraiser will take a good look at the property, inside and out, floor to ceiling. Any flaws that make the property less marketable will be noted. The appraiser will also consider how the local real estate market is doing and comparable sales data from nearby homes.

If the appraiser says your house is worth as much as or more than the amount you're paying for it, and everything else in your application looks good, your loan should be approved. If—as is increasingly common—the appraisal report says you overpaid, however, you may be in for trouble. The lender won't want to approve the loan, and you may have to dispute the appraisal or ask for a second one. But think twice: What if you really did overpay? Unless the property is uniquely valuable to you, you may not want to buy it at that price after all—or should at least commission an independent appraisal. (And you should be able to back out, based on your contract's "financing contingency," to be discussed in Chapter 10.)

Monitoring Your Loan Once You're Approved

After you're approved for the loan, you can focus your energy on other things. Trust us, plenty of other tasks will be competing for your attention. But realize that the loan isn't actually made until the day you close on the house. It's worth staying in touch with your broker or lender, particularly if you have continuing concerns about the terms of your loan or approval. Also be mindful of any date restrictions (for example, lock-in deadlines) as you finish the purchase process.

But before you forget about the details of your loan entirely, make sure you get a Good Faith Estimate (GFE) from the lender. You're entitled to receive this document within three days of applying for your loan.

Beginning January 1, 2010, lenders are required to give you a standard GFE that looks like the sample below. Read it carefully. It spells out some very important details about the loan you're getting—for example, the initial interest rate, the initial payment amount, whether the amount can rise, and whether the loan has a prepayment penalty or balloon payment.

The new GFE is important in another respect too: it prohibits lenders from raising certain costs at closing, and it locks the amount other costs can go up. For example, lenders cannot increase the origination fee (the up-front fee paid to the broker, usually a percentage of the loan amount), and can only increase title insurance costs by up to 10% over the estimate on the GFE. This prevents lenders from tacking on "junk fees" at closing. The U.S. Department of Housing and Urban Development (HUD) estimates the use of the new GFE will save borrowers an average of $700 at closing.

 CD-ROM

The Homebuyer's Tool Kit on the CD-ROM contains a blank "Good Faith Estimate." A partial sample is shown below.

Sample From Good Faith Estimate (page 1)

OMB Approval No. 2502-0265

Good Faith Estimate (GFE)

Name of Originator	Borrower
Originator Address	Property Address
Originator Phone Number	
Originator Email	Date of GFE

Purpose

This GFE gives you an estimate of your settlement charges and loan terms if you are approved for this loan. For more information, see HUD's *Special Information Booklet* on settlement charges, your *Truth-in-Lending Disclosures*, and other consumer information at www.hud.gov/respa. If you decide you would like to proceed with this loan, contact us.

Shopping for your loan

Only you can shop for the best loan for you. Compare this GFE with other loan offers, so you can find the best loan. Use the shopping chart on page 3 to compare all the offers you receive.

Important dates

1. The interest rate for this GFE is available through _____. After this time, the interest rate, some of your loan Origination Charges, and the monthly payment shown below can change until you lock your interest rate.

2. This estimate for all other settlement charges is available through _____.

3. After you lock your interest rate, you must go to settlement within ___ days (your rate lock period) to receive the locked interest rate.

4. You must lock the interest rate at least ___ days before settlement.

Summary of your loan

Your initial loan amount is	$
Your loan term is	years
Your initial interest rate is	%
Your initial monthly amount owed for principal, interest, and any mortgage insurance is	$ per month
Can your interest rate rise?	☐ No ☐ Yes, it can rise to a maximum of %. The first change will be in .
Even if you make payments on time, can your loan balance rise?	☐ No ☐ Yes, it can rise to a maximum of $
Even if you make payments on time, can your monthly amount owed for principal, interest, and any mortgage insurance rise?	☐ No ☐ Yes, the first increase can be in and the monthly amount owed can rise to $. The maximum it can ever rise to is $.
Does your loan have a prepayment penalty?	☐ No ☐ Yes, your maximum prepayment penalty is $.
Does your loan have a balloon payment?	☐ No ☐ Yes, you have a balloon payment of $ due in years.

Escrow account information

Some lenders require an escrow account to hold funds for paying property taxes or other property-related charges in addition to your monthly amount owed of $ _____.

Do we require you to have an escrow account for your loan?

☐ No, you do not have an escrow account. You must pay these charges directly when due.

☐ Yes, you have an escrow account. It may or may not cover all of these charges. Ask us.

Summary of your settlement charges

A	Your Adjusted Origination Charges (See page 2.)	$
B	Your Charges for All Other Settlement Services (See page 2.)	$
A + B	Total Estimated Settlement Charges	$

Good Faith Estimate (HUD-GFE) 1

Unique Financial Considerations for Co-op Buyers

Much of the standard financial advice regarding homeownership doesn't apply to co-ops. Here's a summary of what's different:

- **Two-tiered financing.** Two loans are often involved with co-ops. First, the cooperative will take out a mortgage for its purchase of the property (which you'll probably help pay for, as part of your regular maintenance fees). Later, you'll probably need a loan to purchase your shares.

- **Higher down payment.** Co-op boards frequently require buyers to make large down payments—often upwards of 25% of the purchase price. Your co-owners have good reason for this: They want to make sure you're in sound financial shape and can afford your monthly maintenance payments.

- **Higher interest rates.** Some lenders are reluctant to finance co-op purchases, because if a buyer fails to pay on time, there's no house to foreclose on, only intangible shares in a corporation. Fewer willing lenders and greater risk translates into higher interest rates.

- **Tax deductions.** Tax deductions for co-op mortgage and maintenance payments are more complicated than with condos or single-family homes. While the co-op management will help you calculate how much of the maintenance payment can be deducted, you may need to consult a tax professional.

- **Flip taxes.** A "flip tax" is a misnomer—it's really a transfer fee levied by the co-op when a member sells. It can be calculated different ways: for example, based on the number of shares the seller holds, a flat amount, or the sale price. Usually the seller is responsible for this fee, but the seller may pass it off to the buyer.

What's Next?

You've probably got a good idea of which traditional method for financing your home works, if any. Still, you might want to consider alternatives. In Chapter 7, we'll discuss such methods as borrowing from family or friends or getting government-assisted or seller-backed financing.

Mom and Dad? The Seller? Uncle Sam?
Loan Alternatives

Meet Your Adviser

Marjo Diehl, Mortgage Adviser at RPM Mortgage in Alamo, California (www.rpm-mtg.com), NMLS #280959, DRE License #00896740.

What she does   Discusses alternatives with people buying or refinancing their homes, to help them determine the best available financing options depending on their specific financial and personal goals. She then works the mortgage transaction all the way to completion, including assisting the borrowers with preparing the loan application and gathering the documentation, dealing with the underwriters to get the loan approved, ordering loan documents, making sure the loan closes successfully, and communicating with all parties—buyers and real estate agents—the whole way through. Diehl's work has recently included handling an increasing number of FHA loans, as first-time homebuyers get into the market with minimal down payments.

First house   "It was a condominium in San Leandro, California, that I bought at age 24, while I was working as a flight attendant. It was all I could afford, but it was a dream to be able to stop renting and have a place of my own! Buying as a single woman wasn't as popular then, and some people were surprised. But it worked great for me. It was close to my job at Oakland airport. I probably spent 40% of my time away from home, traveling. It was also nice to have the homeowners' association looking after the exterior maintenance. I stayed in my condo for two years, until I got married and bought a single-family home with my husband."

Fantasy house   "The house I live in now is my fantasy house! It's in a beautiful neighborhood, with views overlooking a canyon with lots of trees. We've upgraded it completely, with granite countertops, hardwood flooring, and big windows that take advantage of all the views. We also re-landscaped the backyard, with lots of flowers and color. Our kitchen, which we're in all the time, overlooks our yard, and sometimes we just stand there and gaze out the window, enjoying the scenery and peacefulness that surrounds us."

- -

Likes best about her work   "Working with the variety of people that I do, and helping them make financial choices that are truly best for them. I particularly like working with first-time buyers, helping them reach financial goals that a lot of times they didn't think were possible. For example, I did an FHA loan recently for a couple who were just finishing a bankruptcy. I was actually surprised that we were able to complete the transaction without a hitch, given that their bankruptcy had not yet been released. They were so thrilled when the house closed."

- -

Top tip for first-time homebuyers   "I think it's so important to live where you want to live—don't just buy in order to buy, but pick a location where you know you're going to feel safe and be happy, within the range of your own affordability. Some people seem to just settle; they get anxious and want to get the home purchase done and over with, now, instead of being patient and waiting for the right home or the right situation to present itself."

With competing payment pressures from student loans and other bills, and the high cost of housing, it's hard—if not impossible— to come up with all the cash needed to buy a house. You may be struggling to get a down payment together or to qualify for a mortgage. And most traditional loans don't provide much flexibility, especially if down the road you want to make an adjustment to your payment schedule.

If this sounds familiar, we suggest you look into alternative, more flexible or affordable forms of financing. (Yes, this could mean your mother—but keep reading; it may be worth it.) We'll cover:

- gifts or loans from family members and friends
- financing directly from your house's seller
- low-down-payment loan programs available through federal, state, and local agencies, and
- special financing options available for new homes, such as direct financing from developers (buydowns).

No Wrapping Required: Gift Money From Relatives or Friends

Don't be shy: Many first-time homebuyers (nearly one-quarter) get some gift money from a relative (usually their parents) or a friend, according to the National Association of Realtors®. If used for the down payment, such gifts help buyers reduce their monthly mortgage payments or increase the amount of house they can afford. Large gifts may even be used to finance the entire purchase. Some buyers also use gifts for moving costs, home furnishings, and remodeling.

By making your home purchase possible, the giver gets not only emotional satisfaction, but financial and tax benefits. If someone is planning on leaving you money by inheritance anyway, a gift is a way to reduce the size of their taxable estate (large enough gifts can be taxed, though the laws on this are continually in flux). And better yet, your parents or other gift givers can watch you enjoy the money during their lifetime, rather than watch you pay extra interest to a bank.

For advice on approaching your parents or others for a cash gift, see the discussion below on borrowing money from family or friends.

How Gift Givers Can Avoid Owing Gift Tax

Believe it or not, the IRS attempts to keep track of cash gifts—and if someone makes total gifts over a certain amount during his or her lifetime, that person's estate can end up owing "gift tax," even though the recipients of the money don't! Fortunately, not every gift counts toward this total, and the gift giver has to give away quite a bit of money for it to apply. Anyone can give a tax-free gift up to $13,000 per year to another person (2010 figure, it's indexed to go up with inflation) without any tax implications. That means, for example, that every year, your mother and father can give you $26,000 (plus $26,000 to your spouse or partner, if you have one), without it counting against the lifetime tax-free limit.

EXAMPLE: Leslie and Howard would like to buy a house for $260,000 and hope to raise a 20% down payment, or $52,000. If each set of parents gives Leslie and Howard $26,000, the couple have reached the needed amount, with no tax liability for anyone.

If a relative or friend wishes to give you more than $13,000 during a single year, that person will need to file a gift tax return (Form 709) with the IRS. This doesn't mean the gift giver will have to pay gift taxes, because computing the gift tax debt is (as of recent years) put off until the giver's death. At that time, the first $1 million of all the gifts made over the person's lifetime will be exempt from the tax. For more information, see IRS Publication 950, *Introduction to Estate and Gift Taxes*, available at www.irs.gov. If a sizable amount of money is involved, your relative or other gift giver should consult an estate planning or tax attorney.

Why You Need—And How to Get—A Gift Letter

If you use gift money to buy your house (not just furniture), your bank or mortgage lender will require written documentation from the gift giver stating that the money is in fact a gift, not a loan. Remember, the lender is carefully evaluating how heavy a debt load you'll have. It wants to make sure it's not competing with another creditor for your monthly payments.

The "gift letter" should specify the amount of the gift, your relationship to the gift giver, and the type of property (the exact address, if you know it) for which the money will be used. Most important, it should state that the money need not be repaid. Ask the gift giver for a letter or prepare your own for the giver's signature. Your lender may also have a gift letter form.

 CD-ROM

The Homebuyer's Toolkit on the CD-ROM includes a "Gift Letter" you can tailor to your situation. A sample is shown below.

If the gift money hasn't been transferred to your account yet, the lender may want verification that the money is available, including the name of the financial institution where the money is kept, the account number, and a signed statement giving the mortgage lender authority to verify the information.

Preventing Emotional Fallout From Gift Money or Family Loans

To avoid family blow-ups, it's usually best if parents or relatives discuss the gift or loan with other close relatives (like your siblings). They might do well to make similar loans on the same terms to all children and document the transactions. Preferential treatment, or lack of documentation of intentions, are known to cause jealousy and conflict, especially if loans remain outstanding at the time of death and the children have differing recollections of the parents' intentions.

Gift Letter

A relative or friend should prepare this gift letter for your bank or other lender. Before finalizing the letter, check with your lender to make sure that it includes all required information, such as evidence of the donor's ability to provide these gift funds.

Date: _____

To: _[name and address of bank or lender]_____:

I/We __[name of gift-giver(s)]__ intend to make a GIFT of $ __[dollar amount of gift]__ to __[name(s) of recipient(s)]__, my/our __[relationship, such as daughter]__, to be applied toward the purchase of property located at: __[address of the house you're buying, if known]__.

There is no repayment expected or implied in this gift, either in the form of cash or by future services, and no lien will be filed by me/us against the property.

The SOURCE of this GIFT is: __[the account the gift is coming from]_____.

Signature of Donor(s):

_____

_____

Print or Type Name of Donor(s):

_____

_____

Address of Donor(s): Street, City, State, Zip:

_____

Telephone Number of Donor(s):

_____

All in the Family: Loans From Relatives or Friends

Private loans are an increasingly popular way to finance a home: About 6% of first-time homebuyers borrow money from family or friends, according to the 2009 NAR "Profile of Home Buyers and Sellers." (And that's just for their down payment. It doesn't include those lucky buyers whose parents lend them the entire purchase amount.) Before you say, "Oh no, not my family," consider that the numbers probably wouldn't be this high unless there was something in it for the family member or friend, too. Take a look at the total amount of interest you're likely to pay before your mortgage is paid off—wouldn't it be better to keep that amount within the family?

This section will explore private (also called intrafamily) loans, including:

- different ways to structure a loan from family or friends
- the benefits for borrower and lender
- how to raise the issue with your family member or friend, and
- dealing with the legal and tax issues concerning private financing.

Structuring the Loan

You can use a loan from family or friends for your:

- **Down payment.** An intrafamily loan can be helpful if you're short on cash and want to avoid paying for private mortgage insurance (PMI), but can save up to pay back your private lender over time or when the house is sold.

- **First mortgage.** You could sidestep the traditional lending industry and finance your entire purchase price with a mortgage loan from your relatives, friends, or others.

- **Second mortgage.** A private loan may also be used to supplement a bank mortgage. How is that different from a down payment loan? Your private lender records the mortgage publicly, putting themselves in line behind the bank for repayment if the house is foreclosed on—a good way to protect the private lender. It's unwise to forgo this step unless the loan is relatively small (less than $10,000), for the reasons discussed below.

If you're borrowing part of the house's purchase price from an institutional lender, check whether it requires you to structure your private loan in a certain way or limits the amount you can privately borrow. For example, if you're borrowing down payment money, many institutional lenders require that at least 5% of the purchase price comes from your own funds.

Especially if a sizable amount of money is involved, you should get some advice on how to structure the loan from a real estate attorney.

Benefits of Intrafamily Loans to the Borrower

Some of the reasons that first-time homebuyers turn to family and friends for help financing their houses include:

- **Interest savings and tax deductions.** Family and friends often charge 1½% to 2% interest points less than conventional lenders, resulting in thousands of dollars in interest savings over the life of the loan. And if you document the loan properly (as we describe below), you can usually deduct the mortgage interest charged on your taxes, just as with a traditional mortgage.

- **Flexible repayment structures.** While a bank is probably going to require an unchanging monthly payment schedule, a private mortgage holder might be more flexible. For example, you may mutually agree that you'll make quarterly (not monthly) payments or delay all payments for the first few years. And if down the road you want to temporarily pause payments (perhaps to take unpaid leave from work after the birth of your first child), your parents or other private lender may agree to that. Good luck finding such a flexible institutional lender.

- **No points or loan fees.** Institutional lenders often charge thousands of dollars in loan application and other fees. Family and friends don't.

- **Easier qualifying.** Your relatives or friends probably won't require that you have a great credit score. You qualify as long as your lender trusts that you'll pay back the loan.

- **Saving on private mortgage insurance.** If you borrow more than 80% of the house purchase price from an institutional lender, you'll have to pay PMI. By borrowing privately, you can avoid this cost.

- **Minimal red tape.** To borrow from an institutional lender, you must fill out an application form and provide documentation verifying every item on the form, then wait for approval. Friends and family don't usually adopt this level of scrutiny.

- **Better deal on the house.** If you've arranged private financing in advance and can close quickly, sellers who are time pressured may accept a slightly lower offer.

- **No lender-required approval of house's physical condition.** Private lenders don't usually require that a house's major defects be repaired before closing, as institutional lenders do. That would let you buy a fixer-upper and take care of its defects later. (Of course, you should still have the house professionally inspected.)

Benefits of Intrafamily Loans to the Lender

Here are a few ways that making a private loan can also benefit your family members or friends:

- **Competitive investment return.** You can offer to pay an interest rate that's higher than your lender could get on a comparable low-risk investment like a money-market account or certificate of deposit (CD). (And you're still likely to pay less than you would to a bank.)

- **Ongoing source of income.** Some investments just sit there and gain in value or pay occasional dividends. With your private loan, your lender will receive regular payments from you, which can be reinvested.

- **A financially liquid asset.** Some investments, such as long-term CDs, are hard to cash out in an emergency. Don't worry; we're not saying your family lender can change his or her mind. But he or she can potentially sell your mortgage to someone else. (There is a secondary market for the purchase and sale of existing mortgages, or you may be able to refinance if your lender wants out.)

- **Low risk.** Your parents or other private lender can count on two things: first, your commitment to repay the loan, somehow, someday, even if the original repayment schedule needs to be rejiggered; and second, that your house offers collateral. If worse comes to worst, you can sell it and repay the loan. (Or your lender can foreclose on you, though few would ever do that.)

- **Emotional satisfaction.** Don't underestimate the sense of achievement that your loved ones get by watching you gain a foothold in the world, with their help.

Best thing I ever did

Borrow from Mom and Dad. When Amy decided to buy a 1904 farmhouse in Northampton, Massachusetts, she assumed she'd get her mortgage from a bank. Then, her mother made her an offer she couldn't refuse: Borrow $180,000 from Mom and Dad, at a competitive 5.75% interest rate. Her mother notes, "I figured, 'Why is my daughter paying the bank when she could be paying me?'" In addition to helping their daughter, Amy's parents earn a decent yield on a low-risk investment, not easy in these days of low interest rates. "It's a little bit scary borrowing from your parents, but this is an official thing," says Amy. And her mother jokes, "The mortgage was actually $173,000, but she wanted a little extra for shoes."

Will Private Financing Work for You?

Still feeling hesitant? The following questions will help you decide whether private financing will work for part or all of your home financing:

- **How much money do you need?** If it's $5,000 or $10,000 to help with the down payment, that will probably be a lot easier to come by than $50,000 or $100,000.

- **How long do you need to borrow the money for?** Some private lenders may be fine with a ten- or 20-year repayment period (and for tax reasons, may actually prefer a longer term). But if your relative or friend wants the money completely repaid in a few years, make sure such an arrangement is financially feasible for you.

- **Do you have any other options?** Is your credit so bad that no bank will approve the loan (or you'll only qualify at really unfavorable terms)?

- **Does a close relative or friend have the money to lend for the amount and term you need?** If your parents are well-off but are going to need money soon for retirement or to pay your brother's college tuition, they may not be in a position to help.

- **What are the personal costs to you?** If you risk hurt or jealous feelings of siblings, cousins, or others; a sense of perpetual debt or guilt; or similar hazards, the loan may not be worth it.

- **What are the costs to set up a private loan?** Getting specialized help from an attorney and accountant to structure your private mortgage may run in the thousands. Consider companies like Virgin Money that can set up and manage the loan for much less or just go back to your conventional lender, especially if the private loan would be fairly small (say, less than $10,000).

- **Does your family member or friend trust you?** Your lender wants assurance that you'll eventually pay the money back, so not only love, but trust, will be key. If you have a history of credit problems and debts, you'll need to show concrete evidence—to your lender and yourself— that you've learned how to responsibly handle debt.

How to Approach Mom, Dad, or Another Private Lender

Even people who are convinced that private loans are a win-win proposition may blanch at the thought of asking for one. But if you approach it like a business proposition, it's not so hard. You're offering a loan at a fair rate of interest, secured by a promissory note and a mortgage.

To present it this way, of course, you'll need to find the appropriate time and place. Never surprise a potential lender by blurting out a request at a social event or informal occasion, such as on the way back from shopping. Make an appointment, even if you see your parents (or brother or old roommate) regularly and the formality seems odd. Give them a general idea of what you want to talk about, but save the details. For example, you might say, "As you know, I'm actively house hunting now and looking for various ways to finance this. Rather than go into all the details now, I'd like to sit down and talk with you about this." If you sense resistance, back off gracefully.

If you get a positive response, schedule a specific time to meet. Be prepared to discuss your proposition logically and honestly. Ideally, you will have done a lot of homework trying to arrange a loan from a traditional lender, so you'll have all the numbers at your fingertips. Bring along photocopies of all relevant documents, such as the financial materials you pulled together for your bank or other lender.

Prepare a separate one-page list of key terms and issues you want to discuss with a relative or friend, including:

- the amount you want to borrow, at what interest rate and repayment schedule (see below for advice)

- the amount of money you have available for the down payment (the higher it is, the lower the lender's risk of loss)

- your financial ability to make monthly payments (even without setting rigid qualification rules, your lender will want to know)

- the financial protections you'll offer the lender (a promissory note and mortgage, as described below), and

- the financial benefits to the lender (how your proposed interest rate compares to money-market and CD rates).

When you meet, give the potential lender ample time to ask questions, and don't expect a decision on the spot.

The Loan Amount and House Purchase Price

How much you'll ask for depends on how much you expect to pay for your house and how much you think your parents or other private lender can spare. Your intrafamily loan will most likely be a second mortgage, to supplement financing from a bank or other traditional lender. The terms "first" and "second" literally refer to who gets paid first if there's a foreclosure. Your bank or institutional lender will no doubt insist on being the first in line, regardless of the size of its loan.

Your house purchase price won't be exact unless you've already made an offer and had it accepted. If you're still looking, be prepared to show the potential lender a close estimate, based on the price range you're looking in. If your private lender wants to make sure the house you find will be worth what you plan to pay, offer to get it appraised prior to purchase (if you're not already doing that for an institutional lender).

The Interest Rate You Propose to Pay

For a private loan, the interest rate you and your lender pick can in theory be anything between 0% and the limit set by usury law in your state. But for practical as well as tax reasons, it's best to charge a rate that's higher than the Applicable Federal Rate (or AFR; more on that below) but lower than what you'd pay to an institutional lender. Propose paying a little less than half the difference between these two. For example, if fixed rate mortgages cost 6% and the AFR is at 4%, you might propose paying 5% interest. (In this example, banks would probably be paying around 3% on CDs, but that figure becomes irrelevant given the minimum 4% AFR.)

Websites such as www.compareinterestrates.com, www.bankrate.com, and www.hsh.com will give you a sense of current interest rates. By the way, although the AFR and interest rates change month by month, your loan doesn't have to follow suit—it's fine to stick with the rate you settle on in the month you sign the loan.

CD-ROM
Use the **"Private Loan Terms Worksheet"** in the Homebuyer's Toolkit on the CD-ROM to organize your presentation to a parent or other private lender.

TIP
Is your family member reluctant to charge you that much? Tell them they can always decide later to "forgive" you some or all of your payments, of not only interest but principal. For tax reasons, they should write you a letter referencing the loan and stating the amount they're forgiving. They'll also have to factor this decision into their gift tax obligations—forgiven loan payments are considered gifts. And it's best not to structure the whole loan with the assumption you'll never repay—the IRS sees this as a fraudulent way of avoiding gift tax, by stretching a one-time gift out over several years.

Check the AFR: Too-Low Interest May Cause Your Lender Tax Problems

The IRS sets a minimum rate for private loans, called the "Applicable Federal Rate" (AFR), each month. The exact percentage varies but is usually less than bank mortgage rates and higher than money-market account or CD rates. In mid-2010, the AFR averaged a little less than 4% for long-term loans (those lasting longer than nine years). For the current rate, visit the "Tips & Tools" section of www.virginmoneyus.com (within the "Social Loans" section); it updates the AFR monthly. You can also search the IRS website at www.irs.gov for the latest AFR.

What's the big deal if your private lender charges you less than the AFR—or even no interest at all? No problem for you (who wouldn't want a low interest rate?), but there may be tax ramifications for the lender. This is mainly an issue if you're borrowing a substantial amount of money from a relative or friend, or receiving a loan on top of a gift that exceeded the $13,000 exclusion. If the interest rate doesn't meet the AFR, the IRS will "impute" the interest to your lender—meaning it will act as though your lender really received the AFR-level interest on the loan. The question then becomes, where did the interest money go? Aha, reasons the IRS, your lender gave it right back to you, as a gift. Then the IRS can demand that the private lender file a gift tax return for any amount over the annual gift tax exclusion.

Also, even if your private lender charges you less than the "imputed" interest rate, the IRS requires him or her to report interest income at the imputed rate. If the lender doesn't and is audited, and the IRS discovers the omission (unlikely), the IRS will readjust his or her income using the imputed interest rate and charge the tax owed on the readjusted income plus a penalty. Theoretically, the IRS could zap the giver under both income and gift tax rules.

Other Proposed Loan Terms

You don't need to go into your discussion with a completely drafted loan agreement—after all, part of your objective will be to negotiate those details with the lender. Still, you can show that you've thought carefully about how to structure the loan profitably for both of you, by suggesting a:

- repayment schedule (such as monthly or quarterly)
- mortgage term (length)
- payment amount, and
- plan if things go wrong, such as late payments and fees, what constitutes loan default, and loan restructuring options.

Again, be sure to run these by your institutional lender, if any, before finalizing your loan agreement with a relative or friend, to make sure you won't be undermining your qualification for institutional financing.

Gracias, Arigato, Merci

Find a way to show your thanks for a gift or loan—a card, lunch at your new house, and maybe more. In case you're stuck for gift ideas, check at www.redenvelope.com. But be aware that, depending on your relationship with your relatives, they may also expect frequent stays in your new guest room, want you to follow their decorating advice, or feel that they can comment on your spending habits. Then again, some may act like this without having contributed to your house purchase!

Creating Your Loan Documents

If your relative or friend agrees to lend you money, you'll need to finalize the loan with the proper legal paperwork. A handshake isn't good enough for anyone. For one thing, it's easy to misunderstand something you've only talked about. Clarifying and writing your agreement down now avoids disputes, as well as memory lapses down the line. For another, failing to record your lender's mortgage on the property leaves that person out in the cold if some other lender or creditor forecloses on your house—they wouldn't be entitled to any of the proceeds, some of which might go to a creditor who came along later (like a contractor who worked on your house, whom you haven't yet repaid and who files a lien). And finally, written proof that you're paying mortgage interest allows you to deduct it at tax time.

To make your agreement legally binding, you'll need these two documents:

- **Promissory note.** You'll need to sign a note for the amount of the loan, including the rate of interest, repayment schedule, and other terms, such as penalties for late payments. You can find several promissory notes for sale on Nolo's website (www.nolo.com). If you're borrowing only a few thousand dollars or less, a promissory note may be all you need. But for most intrafamily loans, it makes legal and financial sense to also prepare a mortgage.

- **Mortgage (or "deed of trust," in some states).** A mortgage gives your lender an interest in your property to secure repayment of your debt (per the promissory note). It needs to be recorded with a public authority, such as the registry of deeds.

Unless you're experienced in real estate transactions, we recommend you get an expert's help with preparing and recording a mortgage and related legal documents. Ask your lender or closing agent for advice.

A One-Person Bank: Seller Financing

Surprisingly, the seller can be one of the most flexible sources of financing for your new house. Seem counterintuitive? There are several ways that sellers can help—admittedly not that common, but keep your eyes open for situations where:

- The seller is having difficulty finding a qualified buyer or is anxious to move a house that's been on the market a long time.

- The seller would prefer to be paid over time at a favorable interest rate rather than receive all the equity at the time of sale, perhaps to supply a regular income for upcoming retirement.

- The seller can justify a higher price by helping with the financing.
- The seller's house has substantially appreciated in value over the years, so that the seller will owe a high amount of capital gains tax when it's sold. By in effect selling the house to you over time, the seller can reduce the tax hit.

Here's a brief overview of the various forms of seller financing. As with loans from family and friends, be sure to consult with your primary lender to find out how seller financing will affect your eligibility, and get expert help for documenting and recording the mortgage.

Getting a Mortgage From the Seller

A form of seller financing often called a "seller carryback" allows the seller to essentially sell you the house on an installment plan. The seller transfers ownership of the house to you at the closing, but in return receives a promissory note entitling him or her to scheduled payments and a mortgage, providing a lien on the property until the loan is repaid. It's often structured so that the buyer has a balloon payment after a few years, at which point you'd either refinance or move out of the house. This kind of arrangement works best for a seller who already owns the house free and clear and won't have to turn around and pay off a bank loan upon sale.

You can also use seller financing to cover a second mortgage, when the amount you've saved for a down payment plus your bank loan doesn't quite add up to the sales price. Experts say you can save 1% or 2% by offering to accept a seller-finance arrangement rather than taking out a second bank loan.

If seller financing looks like an option, approach the seller in an organized way (see our suggestions, above, for approaching family and friends). Be prepared to provide detailed information about your income, credit, and employment history, plus references—more information than you'd need for a close relative. As with other private loans, seller financing can be flexible and creative. You might ask the seller for:

- a competitive interest rate (less than you'd pay for a fixed-rate mortgage)
- low initial payments (unless you can easily afford high ones)

- a mortgage rate buydown (as described below)
- no prepayment penalty
- no large balloon payment for at least five years, plus the right to extend the loan at a reasonable interest rate if market conditions make it impossible to refinance or pay the balloon payment in full, and
- the right to have a creditworthy buyer assume the second mortgage if you sell the house.

This is a hard bargain, so be prepared to give up on the less important terms.

Assuming the Seller's Mortgage

Another option is to assume the seller's mortgage: Essentially, you take the seller's place with the seller's mortgage holder, subject to all the conditions the seller agreed to. This type of financing makes most sense when the interest rate on the seller's mortgage is lower than the current market rate. It's all aboveboard, done with the lender's consent (unlike something called a "wraparound," where you pay the seller and the seller pays the unwitting bank—not recommended).

One problem with assumable mortgages is that you'll probably have to pay much more for the property than the seller owes on his or her mortgage and will either need a very large down payment or a second mortgage to cover the difference. Since second mortgages are usually at a higher interest rate, you won't want to assume a seller's mortgage if the savings on the assumed mortgage will be cancelled out by the higher rate on the second mortgage.

Another potential problem is that usually, only adjustable rate mortgages (plus FHA and VA loans, with some conditions) are assumable, so the interest rate probably won't stay where it is. Examine how high it might go using the suggestions in Chapter 6.

Finally, the seller usually wants something out of the deal, too: often, a higher asking price. That's because the seller is still on the hook for the mortgage if you default.

> **CAUTION**
>
> **Seller-funded down payment assistance programs are illegal.** The Housing and Economic Recovery Act of 2008 prohibits the use of down payment assistance programs funded by those who have a financial interest in the sale, such as Nehemia and AmeriDream. This new federal law does not prohibit other assistance programs provided by nonprofits funded by other sources, churches, employers, or family members. And the law does not prohibit the type of seller financing we discuss above. Check with your lender or local government housing agency if you have questions on the legality of a particular program.

New-Home Financing

If you're buying a newly constructed home, the developer is likely to offer you some unique financing alternatives. The usual possibilities include closing costs paid by the developer, mortgage subsidies (buydowns), or allowances for upgrades like higher-quality fixtures. All are more common when developers have large numbers of unsold properties and there's a large supply of new homes on the market. (And in particularly slow markets, developers may offer packages featuring everything from cruises to free fireplaces!)

Mortgage Rate Buydowns

To make its houses more affordable, a developer may offer to "buy down" your mortgage. That means subsidizing the interest rate you pay for the first two or three years by prepaying part of the mortgage interest. In a 2-1 buydown, for example, you pay a below-market interest rate (and make reduced mortgage payments) the first year of the loan, and a slightly higher (but still below-market) rate the second year, with the developer filling in the gaps. The two-year period is meant to cover the time when money is usually tightest for first-time homebuyers.

EXAMPLE:

Year	Interest rate you pay	Mortgage payment on a $300,000 fixed-rate, 30-year mortgage
1	4.25%	$1,476
2	5.25%	$1,657
3–30	6.25%	$1,847

Depending on the particular developer, you may be able to apply a buydown to a mortgage you find yourself or you may be limited to mortgages offered through a developer's preferred lender. You usually need good credit to qualify for this type of program.

And as with any loan package, make sure the buydown works for you—will you really be able to pay the increased mortgage payments after the initial reduced-rate period? If there are any strings attached, such as high initial points or above-market interest rates after the buydown period ends, also consider how much you'll end up paying over the life of that loan. If you can afford higher monthly payments from the start, you may find a more competitive mortgage elsewhere. Use one of the mortgage calculators recommended in Chapter 6 to compare mortgage options.

Other Developer Financing Incentives

Many developers offer special financing deals to new homebuyers who use the developer's in-house or preferred lender. In some cases, the lender has done a blanket appraisal of all houses in the particular development, so you don't have to pay for a new appraisal. The lender will probably also offer special mortgage programs, often with faster or easier approval for creditworthy purchasers and simpler closing procedures. To seal the deal, developers may offer to pay closing costs or points; provide upgrades, such as better-quality carpet or countertops; even offer gift certificates for home design stores.

Although the developer may present its in-house financing as the world's greatest deal or even the only possible deal, don't cave to the pressure without doing your research. It might seem easier (time- and paper-wise) to go with the developer's recommendation, but that convenience may come at a price—

namely, above-market interest rates. Particularly if the developer is anxious to sell, you might instead get a loan from another lender but negotiate with the developer for another benefit like a lower purchase price (a better deal than most financial incentives); a mortgage buydown; extra features, such as more closets or built-in bookshelves; or upgrades such as higher-quality lighting.

Backed by Uncle Sam: Government-Assisted Loans

The government thinks homeownership is a good thing—in fact, the federal Department of Housing and Urban Development (HUD) declares that its mission is "to create … quality affordable, homes for all." That may translate into some financial help for you, depending on where you live and whether you meet the eligibility requirements for programs administered by the:

- Federal Housing Administration (FHA)
- U.S. Department of Veterans Affairs (VA), or
- state and local housing finance programs.

We provide a brief overview of government low-down-payment and insured mortgage programs below, with contact information so you can check the latest offerings and eligibility requirements. New programs spring up all the time.

The application process for many government loan programs is similar to applying for a conventional loan. Your mortgage broker or lender can tell you what's available, which lenders participate, and whether or not you qualify based on your income and other eligibility requirements (such as your veteran status) and the price of the house you want to buy.

TIP

All types of homes qualify. Government loans are often available for loans for new houses, condominiums, co-ops, and manufactured homes—although there will be a few more hoops to jump through in terms of inspections, warranties, and other requirements.

> **CHECK IT OUT**
> **Looking for a list of all government housing loan programs?** Check out the "Housing" and "Veteran" loans sections at www.govloans.gov. In addition, be sure to see the sites mentioned below for FHA, VA, and state and local housing finance programs.

FHA Financing

The Federal Housing Administration, or FHA (an agency of HUD), helps people get into a home using a low down payment. The FHA itself doesn't provide financing, but it does provide government insurance for a variety of fixed- and adjustable-rate mortgages. The insurance means that if you default and the lender forecloses, the FHA reimburses the lender for its losses. This reduces the lender's risk and increases the lender's willingness to offer low-down-payment plans.

The FHA's most popular program (Section 203(b)) requires a low down payment—usually a minimum 3.5% of the sales price (an attractive alternative to the 5%–10% down payment most lenders require). This low down payment, coupled with higher loan limits, makes FHA financing more popular with homebuyers now than in previous years. (Maximum loan limits vary by area, but are generally between $271,050 and $729,750 for single-family homes in 2010.) FHA loans are assumable by qualified buyers, which may make your house easier to sell when the time comes. Also, there is no prepayment penalty, should you decide to refinance or pay off your loan early. FHA loans are a particularly good option for buyers with less than stellar credit histories (including bankruptcy), because they're generally easier to qualify for than conventional loans.

Another important benefit to FHA loans, according to adviser Marjo Diehl, is that, "Unlike with other loans, you're allowed to get the entire down payment, as well as the closing costs, gifted to you. And family members are allowed to cosign on the loan to assist you in qualifying."

Sound good? Unfortunately, FHA loans don't work for all buyers, because of:

- **Fees.** Like all loans FHA loans might include a loan origination fee (though some have dropped them) that you must pay at closing, plus a higher-than-normal mortgage insurance premium (the up-front portion of which can be added to the amount of the mortgage loan—but not the ongoing premium payments).

- **Appraisals.** The lender must have an appraisal of the house you want to buy done by an FHA-approved appraiser. If the appraised value is less than what you pay for the house, you must make up the difference in cash (not with the FHA loan).

- **Ineligibility of major fixer-uppers.** Standard FHA loan programs won't help you buy properties needing significant repairs; any work recommended by the appraisers must be done before the sale closes. (If you're buying a fixer-upper, check out the FHA's Rehabilitation Mortgage Program, known as Section 203(k).)

If you're planning to buy a condominium, stringent new FHA requirements passed in early 2010 may affect you. Lenders will be able to obtain FHA backing only if all the following are true:

- In the case of new projects, the developer has applied for and received preapproval of the entire project before individual buyers apply for their loans.

- The development maintains a reserve fund of 10% of the amount of its annual budget.

- No single investor (whether a person or a company) owns more than 10% of the units.

- No more than 15% of the condo owners are behind on paying their dues.

CHECK IT OUT

Looking for current information on local loan limits and approved lenders? Check out www.hud.gov (under "Buying" in the "Homes" section). HUD's website includes information on all kinds of FHA and other government loan programs, including special programs for Native Americans, homebuyers in rural areas, and more. You can also call the FHA at 800-225-5342.

VA Loans

The VA provides access to competitive loans, usually with no down payment and no PMI, for men and women currently in military service and to veterans with an honorable discharge. There are specific eligibility rules that primarily relate to the length of service. For example, service personnel now on active duty are eligible after serving 181 days of continuous duty, regardless of when the service began.

Eligible veterans must have a good credit history, proof of employment during the past two years, enough cash to cover any down payment plus the closing costs, and enough income to meet monthly mortgage payments.

The VA doesn't actually make these loans but, similar to the FHA, guarantees repayment to the lender of certain loans (available from participating private lenders, such as mortgage companies, banks, and savings and loans). The most common offerings are 30-year fixed rate mortgages or ARMs.

The VA itself doesn't set a maximum loan amount, but its rules effectively set limits:

- The amount of the loan the VA will repay is based on the size of the loan—for example, the VA will guarantee 50% of loans of $45,000 or less, and 25% of loans between $144,000 and $417,000. For loans over $417,000, the VA's maximum guaranty amount in most areas for 2010 is the greater of 25% of $417,000 or 125% of the area median price for a single-family home (as long as this doesn't exceed 175% of the Freddie Mac loan limit for a single-family home in the county in which the property securing the loan is located). In a few high-cost areas, the maximum guarantee could be close to $1 million. VA maximum guaranty amounts are adjusted annually.

- The loan amount may not exceed the property's "reasonable value," based on the VA's appraisal of the property.

You must pay the VA an administrative ("funding") fee for the loan, typically ranging from 1% to 3% of the total borrowed (depending on the amount of the down payment). Also, the VA places certain limits on what closing costs you may be charged for.

To avoid making a cash down payment, your loan must be at or below the VA's appraised value for the house. Of course, despite the VA providing back-up, you're still expected to repay the whole loan.

CHECK IT OUT

To apply for the VA's "Certificate of Eligibility" (which may take several weeks) and see lists of participating lenders, contact the VA. See its website, www.homeloans.va.gov, or call 800-827-1000. Check out VA publications such as *VA-Guaranteed Home Loans for Veterans*. Regional VA offices (listed on the main VA site) may also provide loan information.

State and Local Programs

Your state or local housing financing agency may sponsor special home financing programs at competitive rates and with low-down-payment options for first-time homebuyers. Also look for other local benefits, such as down payment assistance or local tax credits.

CHECK IT OUT

Looking for more information on state and local homebuyer programs? See the HUD website, at www.hud.gov/buying/localbuying.cfm.

What's Next?

Now that you understand all your financing options, you're ready to get out there and buy a house. Chapter 8 shows how to make the most of your house search.

I Love It! It's Perfect!
Looking for the Right House

Meet Your Adviser

Mark Nash, an Associate Broker with Coldwell Banker, who serves the Chicago, Evanston, Skokie, and Wilmette areas of Illinois (www. marknashrealtor.com).

What he does When Mark's not working with homebuyers (or sellers), he shares his expertise through books, articles, and media interviews. Among his many books, you'll want to check out *1001 Tips for Buying and Selling a Home*, about which the Library of Congress invited him to come to Washington, DC, and make a presentation. For the past ten years, Mark has helped hundreds of people buy their first home in Chicago and its suburbs. He's toured thousands of homes as a Realtor® and as a real estate investor.

First house "It was an 800-square-foot place across from Wonder Lake in Illinois, in a community then mostly used by vacation owners. The view was beautiful, with an empty lot between me and the lake. But the house itself was pretty tired—my mother, who was quite the suburban type, stood in the tiny kitchen (7' x 7'), leaned out over the sink, and said, 'Mark, this is the craziest thing you've ever done.' But by the time I sold it, the area was in greater demand by full-time owners, and it went for three times what I paid for it."

Fantasy house "The older I get, the less space I want. How a house is finished is more interesting—I like high-quality flooring, cabinetry, and trimwork. As for location, I'd take either Gualala, California (I rented a house on the Pacific there once), or the beach in Naples, Florida."

Likes best about his work

"The people part. For me, real estate is more about people than houses. I've worked with some homebuyers for ten years, from their first home on up. For example, I helped one couple now in their 50s buy a series of homes, then I worked with the wife's brother, and most recently her parents, who are downsizing into a condo. I'm not exactly part of the family, but I've sure gotten to know them well. There's a lesson in that for first-time homebuyers—make sure your agent is the type who attracts return business."

• •

Top tip for first-time homebuyers

"Don't overspend. The first house is for you to get into the market. You don't want to spend all your disposable monthly income. Have a life, go out to dinner, go hiking, kayaking, or whatever. I've seen people spend so much on a house they were unable to personalize it or even buy furniture. I could show you 4,000-square-foot houses where the buyer has been able to furnish only one room—sure, they can brag about their square footage, but they can't even invite anyone in!"

CD-ROM

For more tips from Mark Nash, check out his audio interview on the CD-ROM at the back of this book.

The brakes are off, and you're ready to visit houses that seem to match your Dream List, and choose one. "Whatever you do, don't settle," says Realtor® Maxine Mackle (after nearly 20 years of experience in the Connecticut market). "You should be really enthusiastic about a house before you make an offer on it."

But first, breathe deeply and cultivate some nonattachment. Sellers of beautiful houses usually know they've got a gem and price it accordingly. Meanwhile, the market contains its share of duds: houses with dark rooms, weird layouts, and repair nightmares. This doesn't mean your perfect house isn't out there, just that you're unlikely to find it on day one. So to make your search productive, we'll show you how to:

> **Survey Says:**
>
> The average homeowner looks at 10–15 houses before buying one. Some must be looking at a lot more than 15, so don't sweat it if you're among them! One of this book's coauthors looked at over 200 houses before buying (she had a *very* patient agent).

- get help from your real estate agent, friends, and neighbors
- compare each house with your Dream List, looking past the fancy furniture or staging, the need for fixing up, or the shininess of a recent remodel
- see whether you can live with the layout
- review disclosure and other information you receive from the seller
- do your own, informal inspection for repair issues, and
- understand how to approach buying a not-yet-constructed house, or one in a common interest development (CID).

How Your Agent Can Help

While you should take an active role in househunting, your agent's expertise will be invaluable in several ways.

Identifying appropriate houses. Using the Multiple Listing Service (MLS) database, your agent can access far more information than the general public (unless you work with a brokerage like ZipRealty, which gives its clients full access). Illinois Realtor® Mark Nash explains, "The MLS helps me tell buyers things like how long the house has been on the market, its current status ('active,' 'under contract,' 'sale pending,' or 'closed'), what its existing mortgage is, and more. I've had clients say, 'Don't call me unless something comes up within this one city block,' so I keep tabs on such things through the MLS. And when there's a glut of available houses during a down market, many of which may have been sitting unsold for a while, I can help buyers sift through to find the gems."

TIP

No need for embarrassment, your agent has heard it all. Some agent's stories might as easily have come from a therapist: homebuyers they've counseled about whether to have children, couples whose divorces they predicted. Get used to your agent knowing your private concerns, but try to work out any disagreements on your own. A house visit isn't the place to argue about whether you need an extra bedroom for your mother-in-law to live in.

Apart from the MLS, the agent has been watching the market for longer than you and may hear about houses coming up for sale long before they're advertised—valuable even in a down market, where the most desirable houses become the focus of buyers' interest. You'll be driving along and hear your agent say, "If you can wait another week, that house will be on the market."

Identifying reasonable sellers. Especially when the market is changing, some sellers may be stuck in the past, or bent on getting a certain price. Your agent may be able to find out which houses' sellers are worth negotiating with or are ready to drop their price.

Arranging showings. Your agent should take you to tour homes you're interested in—more than once per house, if need be.

Helping evaluate houses. Another set of eyes can be a great help when visiting houses. Your agent may point out defects that you missed or possibilities you hadn't imagined. Just don't let your agent's judgment overtake your own. And don't be shy about visiting houses without your agent—you can always bring the agent back for a second look. (And you absolutely *should* bring your agent back into the process when it's time to prepare an offer.)

And more. Some agents find creative ways to help. For example, home-buyers visiting from out of town may find their agent is willing to pick them up at the airport and make hotel reservations. Mark Nash keeps five umbrellas in his car for rainy days. And agents regularly work evenings and weekends, showing you houses, reporting back on houses they've previewed, and more.

Best thing we ever did

Visit open houses without our Realtor®. Although Pat and her husband loved their Realtor® (their second one, after they'd fired the first), she was extremely busy. And, says Pat, "We knew finding an affordable house in a good school district, with yard space for our children, wasn't going to be easy—so we spent Sundays looking at every open house we could. By a stroke of luck, an agent at an open house told us that a nearby house would be up for sale soon. Its owner lived out of state and needed to sell in a hurry. Our Realtor® made some calls, and we put in a bid. On Christmas Eve, we found out that our bid had been accepted, and we got the house!"

What's Better? Open House or Individual Appointment?

The answer may actually be "both." Open houses are great for scoping out the possibilities quickly and anonymously, particularly on an action-packed Sunday. Visiting open houses unaccompanied by your agent can be nice for gauging your own reactions with no outside influence. But a quick visit is never enough—if a house looks promising, it's worth revisiting, with your agent.

The Rumor Mill: Getting House Tips From Friends

People planning to sell their house don't usually make a big secret out of it—they tell friends and neighbors, long before they formally list the house. If you can tap into the same network (most likely if you already live nearby), you may find out about a house before it's up for sale.

Tell friends, neighbors, your hair stylist, the florist, your dentist, and more. Some home seekers even print up letters explaining exactly what they're looking for and promising a treat or reward to anyone who helps them find a house.

Planning Ahead for House Visits

Don't get too ambitious—most buyers find that visiting between four and eight houses per day is all they can handle before their brains fry. To make the most of your visits, do some prep work. Make sure you've got not only the complete list of houses you want to visit and a map, but all the items on the House Visit Checklist shown below.

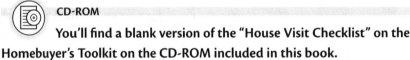

CD-ROM

You'll find a blank version of the "House Visit Checklist" on the Homebuyer's Toolkit on the CD-ROM included in this book.

Luke: *Maybe one place wasn't so bad.*

Lorelai: *Oh good, describe it to me.*

Luke: *I don't know. It had walls with a kind of a floor with a light.*

Lorelai: *Okay, hold on there, mister. If you tell me it's got a roof, I'm stealing that baby out from under you.*

—From the TV series *Gilmore Girls*, 2000

While you're looking at a house, the seller's agent (and the seller if present) are evaluating you. Dress comfortably but professionally, without overdoing it. As Realtor® Mark Nash puts it, "A lot of bling or overdress means the seller or agent will think you can afford full price. You want to be well groomed, understated, and home-price-range appropriate. This is a business transaction—don't give them a negotiating edge by allowing them to overread you."

💡 **TIP**

If the house has a rental unit, never tell existing tenants what you will or won't do as owner. For instance, saying "I'll keep the rent low" could create false expectations, leading to later arguments. But be friendly, and ask tenants for information concerning roof leaks, sewer backups, break-ins, and more. Tenants may reveal things you'd never learn any other way.

Unless your child is small enough to carry in a sling or backpack, leave the kids at home for the first visit. Most parents can focus better without chasing a toddler or hearing choruses of "This will be *my* bedroom"/"No, *mine!*" You can (and should) get your kids' okay later. And this should go without saying, but don't bring your pets.

House Visit Checklist

Tuck the following into your bag:

- ☐ your Dream List (from Chapter 2)

- ☐ your list of Questions for the Seller or Condo/Co-op Checklist (from later in this chapter)

- ☐ your First-Look Home Inspection Checklist (from later in this chapter)

- ☐ a pen and paper, for taking notes

- ☐ binoculars (handy for examining the roof)

- ☐ a camera or camcorder, preferably digital, to remind yourself of what you saw

- ☐ a tape measure and notes on the type and size of your furniture.

Come on In: What to Expect as You Enter

Okay, your feet are crossing the welcome mat, and you're getting your first peek inside. The agent is probably in one of the front rooms, happy to greet you and to answer questions. If you've made an appointment, either the seller's agent will let you and your agent in, or the agent will get a key from a lockbox. In rare cases (and with FSBOs), the seller will be there as well.

> **TIP**
>
> **If it's *really* awful, you can leave!** No need to be polite and do the full tour. While some aspects of a house can be changed, such as filthy blinds or old cabinets, trust your instincts and don't waste your time.

Picking Up the Paperwork

Your first task is to see what paperwork the sellers have made available to you. This might include a property fact sheet, with basic information like the house's size and amenities; a disclosure form that details what the seller personally knows about the condition of the house's features, appliances, and environment; and/or a pest report and possibly a general inspection report, including details discovered by a professional.

You probably won't get all three of these—you may get none, or only the basic fact sheet or a flyer. How much information a seller is *legally* required to give potential buyers varies from state to state (though they may give more).

> *Got Homing Pigeons?*
>
> Yes, there are still people who keep them, usually to race. There's just one problem—homing pigeons can't be trained to return to a new address! See "Little Wing," in *The New Yorker*, February 13 and 20, 2006.

> **TIP**
>
> **"As-is" on a fact sheet equals red flag.** It normally means the seller wants you to buy the house without requesting payment for any repairs, perhaps without even doing a home inspection. Ask what it means to *this* seller.

First Questions to Ask

If the house looks promising, you and your agent should ask some basic questions concerning repair needs, utility costs, neighbors, and more. You'll most likely ask these of the seller's agent, but if the seller is there, or is selling without an agent, ask the seller directly.

CD-ROM

Use the "Questions for Seller Worksheet" in the Homebuyer's Toolkit on the CD-ROM. A sample is shown below. Tailor this worksheet to your interests, for example, adding a question on whether there's hardwood flooring under any carpets. (Also, if you're buying a condo or co-op, the Toolkit contains a separate checklist for you.)

Do We Have a Match? Using Your Dream List

Even the "right" house probably won't be just as you imagined. Carrying your Dream List (with the first two columns filled out) will help you stay organized and avoid getting distracted—for example, being so impressed with stainless steel appliances that you forget that one bathroom won't be enough. Fill out your Dream List before leaving each house. At the end of a day's househunting, when you can barely remember your own name, it will answer questions like, "Was it the brick house that had the patio?"

TIP

Get organized. Keep a file for each house that seems like a possible match. Include your filled-out Dream List, property fact sheet, and other paperwork.

Questions for Seller Worksheet

Here are some basic questions you and your agent will want to ask about a particular house, in terms of repair needs, utility costs, and neighbors. Add anything else to this list of interest—for example, if you have specific questions about the garden. You'll most likely ask the seller's agent these questions, but if the seller is there, or is selling without an agent, ask the seller directly.

1. How long has the house been on the market? _____

2. What repairs have been done in the last few years? _____
   _____

   What are the house's major or most immediate repair needs?
   _____

3. Does the seller use a particular repairperson, plumber, electrician, or pest control person? If so, please provide their names: _____
   _____.

4. How much money does the owner pay for monthly utilities (gas, garbage, electricity, water) and, if applicable, for association fees?
   $ _____
   $ _____
   $ _____
   Are there any other ongoing costs? $ _____

5. Has the owner had any problems with water or dampness in the basement or any other part of the house?

6. Is there a furnace and a central A/C system, and if so, when was it installed?

7. How are the neighbors? Are there issues regarding fences, trees, or property lines?

Questions for Seller Worksheet, continued

NOTES:

How to evaluate the answers:

1. If it's more than a few weeks (depending on how fast houses are moving in your market), ask whether there's been a price drop and whether any offers have fallen through and why. Maybe it's overpriced and ripe for you to make a lower bid on.

2. Some of these repair problems may be stated in the pest or other inspection report, but it's helpful to have the agent summarize them for you. Don't hesitate to be direct and ask things like "Have there been any roof leaks?"

3. Any use of repairpeople can reveal repair issues the seller didn't mention when answering Question #2. The information will also be useful if and when you move in!

4. If you're stretching just to buy the house, make sure it doesn't come with unusually high ongoing costs.

5. The basement and attic are likely suspects here. Moisture problems are hard to repair and hard to insure.

6. Installing a new furnace or A/C can be another major expense—and one that's important to deal with soon, for the sake of your personal comfort.

7. Difficult neighbors can't be repaired. Specifically ask about their level of noise; cooperation regarding fence, tree, or parking issues; and any behavioral problems or oddities.

All the World's Been Staged: Looking Past the Glitter

In the old days, you'd see houses for sale pretty much as the sellers lived in them—with their furniture, dishes, and clutter. But the real estate industry has learned that by emptying out and then gussying up a place, with rented furniture, flowers, curtains, artwork, and more, buyers will be wowed into paying more—often tens of thousands more—for a home.

The resulting makeover job goes by the trade name "staging." And it's your job to look past it, to see whether the house has good bones or is just wearing a lot of cosmetics and concealer. To avoid being hypnotized:

- **Figure out whether each room has all the furniture it needs.** Stagers usually remove most of the owner's furniture and then bring in a select few pieces—some smaller than normal. As you look at a bedroom, for example, picture it with your queen-sized bed, nightstands, and bureau, not the twin bed and delicate side table.

- **Notice where flowers and knickknacks have replaced functional objects.** In a normal laundry room, you'd expect to find detergent, laundry baskets, and a drying rack. Not in a staged house—you're more likely to see a wicker basket filled with fluffy, lavender-scented towels.

- **Observe what your eyes are being led toward—and therefore away from.** If the entry hallway is small and dark, you can bet you'll see a glorious display of flowers on a nearby table.

- **See whether your stuff will fit into the closets and cabinets.** With the owners having moved out their clutter, you might not immediately notice that there's no hall closet, linen closet, medicine cabinet, basement, or attic.

- **Figure out what style the house is without the staging.** Stagers can make a ranch house look like a Victorian, or a 1950s drab home look like an Arts and Crafts bungalow.

- **Turn on all the lights, including table lamps.** Stagers often set lamps next to beds or couches, even though there's no electrical outlet. A lack of outlets is a common defect in older homes. Also, check that kitchen and laundry appliances actually have a source of power and other connections needed for operation.

- **And smell that apple pie.** If the house smells dreamy or the music sounds divine—well, someone made it that way. And they don't come with the house.

Staging isn't all trickery—if it's well done, you might pick up some ideas for how you'd do up the place yourself. Just don't pay more than the house is worth simply because it looked gorgeous after the staging job.

Recent Remodels: What to Watch Out For

If you can afford a house that someone else has fixed up, great—you can save a lot of effort and ongoing maintenance. But not all sellers have good motives, judgment, or taste. In particular, watch out for houses where the seller has:

- **Never lived there, but fixed it up to make a profit.** This is called "flipping." Unfortunately, since the seller had no personal stake in the house, you can't count on good materials or workmanship. If you get as far as making an offer, you'll of course hire an inspector. But before things get that serious, save yourself a heap of trouble by making sure the necessary permits were issued and getting an independent appraisal before relying on appraisal reports the seller shows you. Fraud cases involving flipping are surprisingly common, where the appraiser is in cahoots with a seller and overvalues the house based on superficial or low-quality improvements.

> **Donkey:** *Whoa. Look at that. Who'd wanna live in a place like that?*
>
> **Shrek:** *That would be my home.*
>
> **Donkey:** *Oh and it is LOVELY. You know, you're really quite a decorator. It's amazing what you've done with such a modest budget. I like that boulder. That is a NICE boulder.*
>
> From the movie *Shrek*, 2001.

- **Made fix-ups to suit unique tastes.** Overcustomizing can be detrimental to a house's value, like if the seller was a sports fan who did the whole house in team colors. If you and the seller are kindred spirits, great—but good luck finding the next buyer.

- **Overimproved the house.** A property can actually be made so fabulous that it's no longer comparable to surrounding homes. Unfortunately, surrounding homes set the standard for home values in that area. You might enjoy the house while you live there, but be prepared for slow rises in value and difficulty reselling.

Feng Shui Tips

The Chinese practice of feng shui is based on a simple truth: Your exterior and interior surroundings can influence your life. Even if you don't believe it, a house with good feng shui may appeal to later buyers. According to feng shui consultant and author Kartar Diamond (www.fengshuisolutions.net), "Every house has what I call an energetic blueprint. This can either enhance or undermine your health, well-being, and career." Though some feng shui issues can be fixed, Diamond recommends homebuyers avoid the following problems:

Exteriors

- lots of cracks in the outdoor pavement
- a triangular-shaped lot or one that narrows in the back
- a corner house on a busy street
- a house at the bottom of a cul-de-sac or below street level
- trees that appear to be leaning away from the property (like they're trying to escape!)
- a house within view of a cemetery, church, hospital, fire station, ugly eyesore, or place that makes a lot of noise, like an auto repair shop or bar.

Interiors

- chronically dark rooms or tight, congestive spaces
- uneven floors
- big exposed beams in the bedrooms
- front door aligned directly with back door or window
- toilet or kitchen in center of house
- stairs right behind entrance door.

Walk the Walk: Layout and Floorplan

The physical layout of a house can make a huge difference in whether you're comfortable living there. When visiting a house, imagine going through your daily activities. For example, "I'm opening the refrigerator—it bumps the oven door, and I'll have to chop vegetables on this tiny countertop across from the sink."

⭐ **B**est thing I ever did — **Not buy the house with the weirdly placed bathroom.** Kurt, an avid gardener, was close to bidding on a two-bedroom Victorian. He says, "It was on a corner, with a lot of garden space around it. I was already visualizing planting roses. The problem was, the one and only bathroom was stuck right between one bedroom and the kitchen. It just had a door on each side. Imagine being a guest and having to worry about locking both doors! I'm hugely relieved I held off."

What Do They Know? Reviewing Seller Disclosure Reports

One of the most important pieces of paper in this process is the disclosure report, which most—but not all—states require sellers to give prospective buyers. (Exceptions are sometimes made for certain properties, such as those in probate, where the original owner has died.)

Most state-required disclosures are made using a standard form, upon which the seller will check off features of the property and rate or describe their condition. If the house hasn't yet been built, the developer obviously won't have much to disclose—but may still need to tell you about things like the type of soil; previous uses of the property; possible future uses of surrounding land; and the developer's intentions regarding existing trees, streams, and natural areas.

What you read may affect your decision whether to make an offer. To find out more about a topic mentioned in the form, ask for it in writing. And if you receive the disclosure form *after* making an offer, you can cancel the sale if you don't like what you read. Even after the sale has closed, if a problem pops up that you believe the seller knew about and didn't disclose, you can sue the seller on that basis.

Exactly *when* you're given the seller's disclosures varies by state. In a few states, such as Alaska, Kentucky, and New Hampshire, sellers must give you disclosures before you've made an offer. But most states don't require the seller to do this until *after* you've made an offer, often just before the two of you sign the purchase agreement.

What's in a Typical Disclosure Report

The typical disclosure form is a few pages long and describes features like appliances; the roof, foundation, and other structural components; electrical, water, sewer, heating, and other mechanical systems; trees, natural hazards (earthquakes, flooding, hurricanes); environmental hazards (lead, asbestos, mold, radon, or contamination by use as a meth lab); and zoning.

Some disclosure forms also cover legal issues, such as ownership problems, legal disputes concerning the property, or community association fees. Strange but true, the forms might also require information about suicides, murders, and other deaths on the property; nearby criminal activity; or other factors, such as excessive neighborhood noise.

CD-ROM

See the sample disclosure forms in the Homebuyer's Toolkit on the CD-ROM. They're from Indiana and California, representing a range between short and long versions of the form. (California's disclosure laws are among the most demanding in the country and require sellers to also fill out a Natural Hazard Disclosure Statement, also included.) A page from the California dislosure form is shown below.

California Real Estate Transfer Disclosure Statement

(CALIFORNIA CIVIL CODE § 1102.6)

THIS DISCLOSURE STATEMENT CONCERNS THE REAL PROPERTY SITUATED IN THE CITY OF _____ ,
COUNTY OF _____ , STATE OF CALIFORNIA, DESCRIBED AS _____
_____

THIS STATEMENT IS A DISCLOSURE OF THE CONDITION OF THE ABOVE-DESCRIBED PROPERTY IN COMPLIANCE WITH
SECTION 1102 OF THE CIVIL CODE AS OF _____ , _____ . IT IS NOT A WARRANTY OF ANY
KIND BY THE SELLER(S) OR ANY AGENT(S) REPRESENTING ANY PRINCIPAL(S) IN THIS TRANSACTION, AND IT IS NOT A
SUBSTITUTE FOR ANY INSPECTIONS OR WARRANTIES THE PRINCIPAL(S) MAY WISH TO OBTAIN.

I
COORDINATION WITH OTHER DISCLOSURE FORMS

This Real Estate Transfer Disclosure Statement is made pursuant to Section 1102 of the Civil Code. Other statutes
require disclosures, depending upon the details of the particular real estate transaction (for example: special study
zone and purchase-money liens on residential property).

Substituted Disclosures: The following disclosures and other disclosures required by law, including the Natural
Hazard Disclosure Report/Statement that may include airport annoyances, earthquake, fire, flood, or special
assessment information, have been or will be made in connection with this real estate transfer, and are intended to
satisfy the disclosure obligations on this form, where the subject matter is the same:

☐ Inspection reports completed pursuant to the contract of sale or receipt for deposit.

☐ Additional inspection reports or disclosures: _____
_____
_____

II
SELLER'S INFORMATION

The Seller discloses the following information with the knowledge that even though this is not a warranty,
prospective Buyers may rely on this information in deciding whether and on what terms to purchase the subject
property. Seller hereby authorizes any agent(s) representing any principal(s) in this transaction to provide a copy of
this statement to any person or entity in connection with any actual or anticipated sale of the property.

THE FOLLOWING ARE REPRESENTATIONS MADE BY THE SELLER(S) AND ARE NOT THE REPRESENTATIONS OF THE AGENT(S),
IF ANY. THIS INFORMATION IS A DISCLOSURE AND IT IS NOT INTENDED TO BE PART OF ANY CONTRACT BETWEEN THE
BUYER AND SELLER.

Seller ☐ is ☐ is not occupying the property.

A. The subject property has the items checked below (read across):

☐ Range	☐ Oven	☐ Microwave
☐ Dishwasher	☐ Trash Compactor	☐ Garbage Disposal
☐ Washer/Dryer Hookups	☐ Rain Gutters	☐ Carbon Monoxide Device(s)
☐ Fire Alarm	☐ TV Antenna	☐ Satellite Dish
☐ Intercom	☐ Central Heating	☐ Central Air Conditioning
☐ Evaporator Cooler(s)	☐ Wall/Window Air Conditioning	☐ Sprinklers

Understanding Your State's Disclosure Requirements

Disclosure requirements vary among states, and some sellers try to wiggle out of the requirement altogether. Your agent should make sure the seller complies with the law—but the question will remain, how much did the law require the seller to tell you about in the first place? If the standard form doesn't mention past flooding, the seller doesn't have to, either (but shouldn't lie if asked). You might want to read your state's law, or at least the form, to look for holes.

As of this printing, the majority of states require sellers to either fill out a disclosure form or disclose material facts about the property.

But even in nondisclosure states, buyers can negotiate to make seller disclosures a part of their purchase—or may get them without asking. Law or no law, your state Realtor®'s association has probably created a standard disclosure form for sellers to use. In Massachusetts, adviser Nancy Atwood says, "Our MLS listings tell us whether the seller is providing a disclosure form. Most sellers know that if they don't, the buyers will think they've got something to hide." Beyond these possibilities, "It's buyer beware," says New York attorney Richard Leshnower.

And the Prize Goes to Arizona

... for the most interesting creatures listed on its seller's disclosure statement. The form asks sellers whether they've seen any scorpions, rabid animals, bee swarms, rodents, owls, or reptiles on their property.

To find your state's law, talk to your real estate agent or state regulatory agency. You can find yours at www.arello.com (click "Regulatory Information"). Or you can search online for "real estate disclosure," "disclosure form," or "disclosure statement" and the name of your state.

TIP

Buying a house built pre-1978? By federal law, the seller should, before you buy, give you a form disclosing whether there might be lead-based paint in the home and a pamphlet called "Protect Your Family From Lead in Your Home." For more on lead hazards, see the National Lead Info Clearinghouse at www.epa.gov/lead/pubs/nlic.htm.

Penalties for Failing to Disclose

Most states put some teeth into their disclosure laws, by allowing buyers to cancel the sale if the seller doesn't provide the disclosure form or doesn't fill it out completely and honestly. Some states also charge monetary penalties to sellers who violate the law, or punish sellers' real estate agents for failing to disclose problems that they observed or were told of by the sellers.

Can You Trust the Disclosures?

Now comes the question of how much to believe of what the seller discloses. There's no nice way to put it: Sellers are just people, and some of them lie. Even some upright citizens lie, after rationalizations like, "The basement hasn't flooded in years (never mind the drought)." And a less-than-honorable seller—for example, someone who's been running a methamphetamine lab within the home—is hardly going to admit it on the disclosure form. (The toxicity levels created by meth manufacturing are enough to make the home unsaleable.) If meth seems like a possible concern, ask the neighbors what they've observed, and get a separate inspection.

And lying isn't the only problem. Even honest sellers may be allowed to keep quiet about something they only suspect. Some state's forms may offer handy escape hatches, like a box saying "don't know," or "no representation." In Oregon, for example, sellers need only disclose problems of which they have "actual knowledge."

That can lead to situations like one described by Oregon real estate agent Debbie Stevens: "A buyer I represented moved into a house where, within

Will They Tell You If It's Haunted?

If plates fly around your prospective home's kitchen, a bloodstain reappears nightly on the staircase, or houseguests flee the back bedroom screaming, you want to know about it, right? But don't expect to see a "haunted" box on any state's disclosure form. Nevertheless, sellers are, in many states, obligated to disclose things that affect a house's marketability, which the oddities described above certainly could. Smart sellers would describe exactly what they've observed, without drawing conclusions.

one month, the water line from the street failed. Of course, we immediately wondered whether the seller had failed to disclose something. It turned out the seller's neighbors had had repairs done on their water line, and the repairperson had actually told our seller, 'Your water line is old, too; I can fix it while I'm in here.' But the repairperson couldn't predict when the seller's water line would fail, and the seller didn't want to pay for repairs. Unfortunately, we had to conclude that the seller wasn't necessarily wrong to say nothing, since he didn't know how close the water line was to failing."

Also, in most states, sellers aren't required to poke around for problems—just to tell you what they already know. A house's owners can remain blissfully unaware of many serious problems—a cracked foundation, termites deep in the walls, or a roof on the verge of leaking—and won't be held responsible.

Reviewing the Seller's Inspection Reports (If Any)

Some sellers voluntarily provide copies of inspection reports they've commissioned themselves, either pest reports (common in California) or general inspections. In theory, this is no mere subjective opinion—the report was drafted by a trained professional, right? The answer is a not-so-resounding "maybe." The quality of home inspectors varies widely, and are you going to gamble on the seller having chosen the most nitpicky one in town?

That's not to say the seller is trying to pull a fast one. But inspectors who are regularly hired by sellers describe feeling pressured not to be "deal-breakers," but rather to downplay problems they find. They tend to use fuzzy words in their reports like "worn" or "serviceable."

SEE AN EXPERT

Go to the source: Call the inspector directly. There's no law saying you have to rely solely on the inspector's written words. According to California inspector Paul A. Rude, "If you're seriously thinking about making an offer, call and ask the seller's inspector for details and for information about his or her background. Better yet, ask the inspector to come back and do a walk-through with you. Many will do this for a reduced fee."

So, if you've got a report in front of you, how do you evaluate its worth? Start by reading it carefully, following the advice on understanding inspection reports provided in Chapter 11. Also check whether the inspector is a member of ASHI (the American Society of Home Inspectors). And you can ask your real estate agent about the reputation of the inspection company—and of the seller's agent, who probably selected the company.

Best thing I ever did

Learn to decipher the pest report. Because Abby was looking for a fixer-upper, she knew it would have problems. But when the seller gave her the pest report, she says, "I almost called off the deal—the fix-up was going to cost almost half of what I'd be paying for the house. Then I took a closer look. The report said things like, 'cellulose fiber near foundation—$200 to repair.' It turned out that just meant there was a big piece of wood leaning on the foundation—all I had to do was brave the spiders and drag it away. I found a lot of items that weren't as major as they'd seemed."

Finally, no matter how reputable the seller's inspector, if the report was written more than a few months ago, it's too old. New problems can crop up in a day. And the seller might have already tried to repair some of the problems—for better or for worse. A professional inspection is important, but it's best to rely on the one you'll commission yourself, later.

Inspect This!

The largest Hollywood home, according to the *Guinness Book of World Records*, is "The Manor," in Bel Air, California. Built by (now deceased) TV producer Aaron Spelling, it covers about six acres, has 123 rooms, and includes a gym, bowling alley, tennis court, screening room, pool, and skating rink.

Poking Around: Doing Your Own Initial Inspection

From the first moment you look at a house, you should be taking stock of its physical condition. If there's a chance you might make an offer, you'll want a clear idea of how much the house is worth, based partly on its state of repair.

First-Look Home Inspection Checklist

Here's what to look for in your initial house visit, and why it's important to take a special look at these items. Jot down your findings on the little form that follows.

☐ **Examine the roof.** If the roofline is sagging, be prepared for foundation problems. Ask how old the roof is. A roof ten years old or older will probably need replacing soon, a $10,000-plus job. Loose, curling, or missing tiles or shingles also indicate a new roof is needed, as do shafts of light in the attic. Complex roofs with lots of gables, intersecting surfaces, and multiple roofing materials are difficult to maintain and expensive to replace.

☐ **Listen for squeaks when you walk.** Squeaks are caused by loose nails, often loosened by sagging or movement in the structure, which may mean settling problems.

☐ **Take cues from your feet.** They'll tell you whether the flooring feels unstable, or the house has started to settle unevenly. As you walk up stairs, make sure the heights feel uniform. And step close to the toilet and tub. If the floor feels soft, leakage may be occurring, possibly caused by the owner's failure to change the seals on the toilet or caulk the wall tiles.

☐ **Use your nose.** At worst, fusty odors or your sudden sniffling may mean a mold problem. Other odors, such as cat urine or cigarette smoke, are also a bother to get rid of and reduce the value of the house. (Or maybe you'll just smell a lot of air freshener, which should make you wonder what's being covered up.)

☐ **Turn on the faucets.** What does the water look like? If you see rust particles or discoloration, the pipes may be rusted, and need replacement. What do you hear? Knocking sounds may mean old, leak-prone pipes. Try turning the faucet to its maximum. If the underlying problem turns out to be low water pressure, this is tough to solve—but should be fixed if you plan on enjoying your showers. Also make sure the hot water arrives within a reasonable length of time.

☐ **Open windows and doors.** If you can't do so easily, that too may be a repair issue.

☐ **Look for signs of water damage.** Look for stains or puddles on the ceiling, around the window frames, by the water heater, under the sink, and all over the floor of the basement, if there is one. Not only are these repairs costly, but because of scares over toxic mold, they can make a house expensive to insure.

☐ **Find the electrical panel.** Is it an old style one, small, and with fuses rather than circuit breakers? That's a several-thousand-dollar upgrade. If you suspect old wiring, look at the plugs near the bathroom and kitchen sinks. If they've been modernized at all, you'll see special plugs with little rectangular "TEST" and "RESET" buttons (these help protect you from water-related electrocution).

☐ **Take note of peeling paint.** A paint job is an easy, cosmetic repair—but nevertheless can mean your paying someone several thousand dollars. And peeling paint can be especially problematic if it's old and lead-based or contains asbestos texturing material.

First-Look Home Inspection Checklist, continued

☐ **Turn light switches on and off, or try turning on many lights and appliances at once.** If the lights flicker, or the electricity goes, there may be a bad connection or a circuit overload. These aren't expensive fixes, but are safety priorities.

☐ **Examine the appliances.** Ask whether the refrigerator, stove, dishwasher, washer and dryer, and other appliances come with the house. Then look to see whether they add value or will require a trip to the dump. Test to make sure they're functional; open the refrigerator door, and light the stove's burners.

☐ **Ask whether the house has a furnace or air conditioner.** You'd be surprised at how many houses still operate on small units that work in only a few rooms. Ask that the furnace or A/C be turned on.

☐ **Look for unprofessional repairs or upgrades.** If the house has been in the hands of unqualified do-it-yourselfers, some work may have to be redone.

Item or Area	Okay	Problem
Roof		
Flooring		
Odors		
Water and plumbing		
Windows		
Doors		
Electrical		
Paint and walls		
Appliances		
Furnace		
Air conditioning		
Exterior		
Other		
Other		

NOTES:

CD-ROM

Bring along the "First-Look Home Inspection Checklist," found in the Homebuyer's Toolkit on the CD-ROM. A sample is shown above. It details both the easiest and most important issues to look for.

The checklist won't lead you through an in-depth inspection. But there's a lot you can look for on an ordinary open house visit, like sagging rooflines and leaking pipes. Wait for an individual appointment to do things like turning on heat and stove burners. And again, if you're really interested in the place, you should hire a professional inspector, normally after making an offer.

CHECK IT OUT

Eager to take on more-difficult inspection tasks? Get guidance from:

- The American Society of Home Inspectors website at www.ashi.org. Under "For Homebuyers/Sellers," click "Virtual Home Inspection" to get a fun visual tour of what your inspector will eventually examine.

- *The Complete Book of Home Inspection*, by Norman Becker (McGraw-Hill Professional). Written for the layperson, this book includes helpful checklists and photos.

- Local community colleges, adult schools, and home improvement stores, many of which offer excellent and inexpensive classes in home repair.

Hey, Nice Dirt Pile! Choosing a Not-Yet-Built House

If you're buying a new home from a developer, a number of choices lie before you: which lot you want, which type of model house you like, and which upgrades you'd like inside. All of this can require imagination if you're buying before the house is built (though some developments are nearly fully built in advance).

CAUTION

Don't forget to bring your agent along on the first visit! If you show up unrepresented, the developer may take the position that the agent should not be able to take credit for or be involved in the sale.

Choosing Which Lot Your House Will Be Built On

They may all look like squares on the map now, but walk around, and examine the map for the following:

- **Likely water flow.** Improper grading leads to poor drainage. It's a common complaint in new developments and difficult to fix, so avoid lots located at the neighborhood low spot or the bottom of a hill. A lot on a creek may sound nice but end up flooded by next year's "100-year storm." Also look for concrete-lined drain channels in hillsides above your lot, which are often poorly maintained, leading to flooding or even a landslide.

- **Roadways.** If your house will be next to a major roadway, expect extra noise and traffic.

- **Services.** While it's convenient to have services close by, being immediately adjacent to a grocery store, fire station, or school can raise levels of traffic, litter, and noise.

- **Lot size and position of neighbor's houses.** How big is the lot in relation to the size of your house-to-be? In many new communities, homes are built so tightly together that owners can hear their neighbors' television or see in their windows.

- **Location.** You'll pay more for a house that sits on a lakefront and less for one that backs up against the freeway. The more desirable the location, the less negotiable the price.

- **View.** If a view is an important asset on your lot, find out whether you have a right to prevent downhill neighbors from blocking it with new homes, additions, or trees. Many trees grow fast enough to block a scenic vista within five to ten years.

- **Remaining undeveloped land.** If there's a big, open field nearby, find out from the local zoning or planning department what it's zoned for and what kind of development is planned. Unless it's a park, you can be sure that something will be built there eventually.

Choosing Your House Design and Upgrades

For the house itself, you might be choosing which model type you want and whether you want upgrades. This is where that low, advertised price can change dramatically. The modest-sized model may look tiny compared to the model mansion next door, and the simple, standard kitchen may look shoddy next to the glossy custom cabinets. To help rein in your choices, consider:

> **TIP**
>
> **It's possible to negotiate for free upgrades, at least in slower markets.** Because it doesn't cost the developer nearly as much to make the upgrades as you'd probably be charged, they use them as incentives.

- **What the model home includes.** Some contain the upgrades, so that buyers mistakenly think that's what the final house will look like. Adviser Mark Nash says, "Ask how much the house you're looking at would cost with everything you see in it." Others contain cheap and tacky basics, to steer you toward the upgrades. Either way, look closely at the quality of woodwork, flooring, appliances, and more; decide which you're willing to pay to upgrade; and get the developer's promises in writing.

- **Your Dream List.** If you'd never thought about needing a wood-burning fireplace or an outdoor barbecue, why add them now?

- **What corners the developer will be cutting.** Watch out for so-called "value engineering," in which developers maintain the luxury look of a house without the actual quality—for example, by installing windows that don't actually open, or decorative beams that are made of foam, not wood. Examine the model home carefully, and ask lots of questions.

- **The retail cost of possible upgrades.** No need to pay a developer more to add high-quality materials than you'd pay for them yourself. Double-check the cost of big-ticket items like cabinetry or floor coverings at your local home improvement store. Then negotiate with the developer to bring the price down, or plan to hire a local contractor for upgrades.

- **What upgrades will add resale value.** If you ever sell your home, the less flashy, more practical upgrades will attract the most buyers. For example, swimming pools don't always add value to a house, while extra office or storage space will. Other practical, valuable upgrades include more electrical outlets, a fenced-in backyard, and wiring for high-speed Internet.

- **The tax impact of your house size and upgrades.** You may have seen a property tax estimate in the seller's written materials. If the house hasn't yet been built and assessed, however, that figure means nothing more than the value of the land. Call your local tax board for information.

Don't Fall for the Hype!

Watch out for these developer sales tactics, many designed to encourage an impulse buy on your first visit:

- **The luxury tour.** You may be whisked around lovely house models by an attractive professional, maybe even with tasty treats or drinks along the way.

- **The "now or never."** You may be told that a building or development is almost sold out—or is sold out. Whaddya know, you receive a call a few days later saying that a deal has fallen through, and a unit or house is now available.

- **The moment of silence.** If you're buying with someone else and find yourselves alone in an office, resist the temptation to do what the seller wants: Talk about what you just saw, and whether it's a good idea to buy it right that minute.

- **The "today and today only."** "Today only, upgraded granite countertops," or "We'll pay your closing costs." We can't say it's not true, but it's a favorite sales tactic.

- **The freebies.** As if buying a house weren't enough, some developers throw in motorbikes, cruise trips, and flatscreen TVs. Try to remember that these are minor extras compared to what you'll be paying to buy the property.

> **TIP**
>
> **If you back out, your upgrades won't be refunded—you pay for them up front.** "I've seen people lose $50,000 in upgrades because of a job transfer," says Realtor® Mark Nash. "The reason for this policy is that the property is less marketable with your personal choices stamped on it—it's more like a resale." Plan ahead!

Buying a New or Old Condo or Co-op? Research the Community

If you're buying in a community interest development, such as a condo, co-op, townhouse, or planned unit development ("PUD"), its physical state shouldn't be the only thing on your mind. You should also be asking, "How much power will the community association have over my life—and will it exercise that power?" Although the term "community association" may sound like a social club, the reality is that a few of your neighbors, whose personalities are up to chance, will serve in leadership roles. They'll make important decisions about your living environment. Some associations are responsible minigovernments, but many are like dysfunctional families. So, it's well worth your time to:

- read all the paperwork describing its governance and current situation, and
- ask questions of the sellers, the neighbors, and the governing body.

Read the Large and Fine Print

Community associations normally put their main rules into documents called the "bylaws" and "master deed" or "Declaration of Covenants, Conditions, and Restrictions" (CC&Rs). As soon as you're seriously interested, get a copy of these, as well as of this year's budget, and read them carefully (at the latest, you can make receiving these documents a contingency of your purchase offer, as described in Chapter 10). If you're buying a newly built home, the builder may include these as part of your disclosures.

You'll learn about things like the permission process if you want to add onto your house, what color you can paint it, limits on pets, types of allowable landscaping, how high the association dues are, when the association can decide to charge you special assessments for projects affecting the entire community (like the pool or common room), whether the builder will charge you a transfer fee when you sell (a new and noxious clause), and more. This isn't abstract stuff—it will have a real, direct impact on your daily life.

You may find that the association owners don't want to cough up these documents until you've made a purchase offer. For condos, however, anyone can go to the county recorder's office and get a copy of the CC&Rs. (They're part of the deed that's recorded to publicly show who owns the property.)

Unless you're buying into a completely new development, these documents are just the beginning. You'll also want to research what the association or board has been up to lately. Ask for minutes from recent meetings, and review these for signs of internal disputes, financial troubles, or planned new projects.

See whether they'll let you attend a meeting of the condo association or board. If the discussion is about what to do about recent lawsuits or the high vacancy rate, or whether it's time to foreclose on a certain member who hasn't paid his or her dues, proceed with caution.

 CAUTION

Signs of association money troubles: Ask further questions and think twice about buying if you spot evidence that:

- more than 15% of the units are in foreclosure or have been on the market for several weeks and remain unsold
- more than 15% of owners are overdue on their homeowners' fees
- the association's reserve account is almost empty, or
- major litigation is pending.

Also check on the ratio of units that are, or are allowed to be, rented out. The more units that are owner-occupied, the better the community usually is at attending to details like the budget and maintenance. Also, in a down market, investors are often the first to go into foreclosure.

Condo/Co-Op Worksheet

Here are some basic questions you'll want to ask the seller, seller's agent, and neighbors about a particular condo or co-op. Tailor this list according to the particular property (Hawaii homebuyers can delete the question about snow removal!), and add other questions of interest—for example, if you have specific questions about waste disposal or want more details about use of a pool.

1. Do you enjoy living here? What are the best and worst things about it?

2. What percentage of the properties are rented out to tenants?

3. Are you happy with the community association? Are there any particular problems? What do you wish it would do differently?

4. What exactly is included in your monthly association or maintenance fee? (Some might include heating, parking, storage facilities, and use of the clubhouse, while others charge separately for these services, if they're available at all.)

5. Where is your parking? Indoor? Outdoor? Reserved? Private garage?

6. What amenities are included in your membership (for example, a clubhouse or laundry room)? Are there any waiting lists?

7. Are any special assessments planned? When was the last one? What was it for?

8. What taxes can you expect—for example, local school taxes?

9. For co-ops: How much is the mortgage on the property itself? (This may affect your monthly maintenance fees and whether they are deductible because they pay the underlying mortgage.)

Condo/Co-Op Worksheet, continued

10. In the event of snow, by what time can you expect it to be shoveled or plowed? Does this include parking areas?

11. Are there any annual surcharges, such as for fuel?

12. How high is the reserve fund (of emergency money)?

13. Who determines how much is spent on various things?

14. Are meetings of the board or association open or closed? How do members or shareholders have input into decision making (for example, by submitting questions in advance of meetings)?

15. If people will be living above you, is there a rule saying the floor must be carpeted? Are the walls well insulated?

16. Are any of the neighbors difficult or inconsiderate?

17. How are package deliveries handled in the building if there's no doorman?

18. Do you have a right to sublet your unit?

19. Are there many vacancies in the building or development? How long does it take for the average unit to sell—are they in demand, or does it take a while?

20. When are workpeople allowed to enter and work on your unit? Saturdays, Sundays, evenings? Must they be licensed?

21. What kind of repair or construction work can be done without the approval of the association or board? What's the procedure for approval? How long does approval usually take?

Why so much research early on? First, if there are restrictions you can't stomach, you'll know the place isn't for you. Don't assume that the rules will change, or that an exception will be made for you! Second, you want to know how well funded the association is. If there isn't enough cash in reserve, your monthly dues may go up, you may have to pay special assessments, or you may find your property's value plummeting because neighboring homes are in foreclosure or sitting vacant.

Ask Lots of Questions

As with any neighborhood, it's worth finding out how people like living there, and who your neighbors will be. But you should also ask more-targeted questions, from your first interaction with the seller or seller's agent, and continuing on with people you meet within the community. Ask about everything from governance policies to package delivery to the neighbors' characters.

CD-ROM

Use the "Condo/Co-Op Question Worksheet" in the Homebuyer's Toolkit on the CD-ROM for suggested questions. A sample is shown above.

CHECK IT OUT

For more about meetings and other features of community living: See the resources offered by the Community Associations Institute (CAI, www.caionline.org). Your state's website should also link you to your community association law.

What's Next?

Still having a hard time finding the right house at the right price? Look to Chapter 9 for alternatives.

Plan B:
Fixer-Uppers, FSBOs, Foreclosures, and More

Meet Your Adviser

Steve Elias, an attorney who consults with homeowners and others dealing with foreclosure and bankruptcy, author of numerous Nolo books including *The Foreclosure Survival Guide* and *Chapter 13 Bankruptcy: Keep Your Property & Repay Debts Over Time*, and a programmer and volunteer at KPFZ 88.1 FM radio, in Lakeport, California.

What he does "My work as a lawyer is somewhat revolutionary, actually—I'm the only one I know of helping people who can't afford lawyers but want to do their own bankruptcy. For a flat rate, I'll interview the person and be available for questions afterward. I've worked with over 1,000 people so far. Because a number of the people I consult with were also homeowners, I've gotten into foreclosure advising as well. We discuss priorities—whether they're hoping to keep the kids at the same school, sell the property when it makes sense financially, or what?

"I've worked with Nolo for years on its bankruptcy and foreclosure books—and because the law keeps changing, so do the books. In fact, because the recent bankruptcy laws made the process so difficult and expensive, it's become more important than ever for readers to have access to useful, plain-English information.

"As for my radio work, I do three live programs every week, which include news and commentary.

· ·

First house "It was a brown-shingled place, with redwoods in the front and back yard, that we bought in Berkeley, in 1969. Both my wife and I were being paid as law students in legal assistance offices, but at $21,000, it didn't feel like too much of a stretch. Unlike many California houses, it had a basement, where friends would come and stay.

"We moved to Vermont a year later, and sold the house for a small profit. Now it's probably worth over a million."

Fantasy house

"Any house designed by Sarah Susanka would be fun to live in. She's an architect in Minnesota and the author of a series of books on not-so-big houses—they're sparkling gems with alcoves, woodwork, and interesting lighting. She knows how people want to live." (Note to readers: Check out Sarah's work at www.notsobighouse.com.)

Likes best about his work

"Whether it's working on my books or talking to people about their economic troubles, I like providing people with the information and perspectives they need to make their own decisions and handle their own legal affairs in the areas I cover."

Top tip for first-time homebuyers

"Think about the reason you're buying. People who choose a home because of the local schools, public transport, and liking the feel of the neighborhood—they're going to live there forever. But when it's your first home, there's a good probability you'll move on to other homes, so you also have to think about affordability and investment. In fact, you might want to buy in a place that isn't vulnerable to a lot of foreclosures—though there are good deals to be had in vulnerable areas, so it's hard to give general advice here.

"Another important tip I'd give is, don't overstate your income just to get into a house. It'll only lead to trouble later. People who didn't overstate their income are in most cases doing fine even in the midst of this foreclosure crisis.

"One last point: If you're happy where you are, your house's value shouldn't be a concern—you've got shelter, and would otherwise be paying rent."

You're already frequenting the open-house circuit, and you've got a good agent. But maybe the perfect house hasn't yet appeared, or at least not at a price you can afford. It's not hopeless! Check out some creative alternatives, including:

- houses that have stalled on the market
- starter houses
- potential remodels and fixer-uppers
- space that can be shared with a co-owner or renter
- FSBOs (houses "For Sale by Owner," without a seller's agent), and
- foreclosures and probate sales.

As Ira Serkes, a Berkeley Realtor® with Pacific Union, counsels, "The house you want, at the price you want to pay, may not actually exist. But it's important not to compromise on essential features such as neighborhood safety and number of bedrooms. Once you've gotten to know current market realities, and adjusted your expectations accordingly, finding a house you're happy with will happen much faster."

Castoffs: Searching for Overlooked Houses

In every market, some houses have been on sale for so long that buyers have moved on and lost interest—which gives you a chance to step in and offer a lower price. Houses get overlooked for a broad variety of reasons: Maybe they're priced too high, have cosmetic problems, or are unattractive to most buyers (because of a bad layout or a location on a busy street). They may even be "stigmatized properties," meaning they were the site of a crime, suicide or other death, rumored environmental dangers, haunting, or some other occurrence that gives buyers the creeps (and lowers the house's market value).

We haven't exactly made such houses sound appealing—but whether you should be interested at all comes down to two questions:

- If the house was simply overpriced, is the seller ready to sell it for what it's really worth?

• If the house has other problems, do they happen to be ones you can live with or feasibly change?

For example, when Realtor® Carol Neil was helping her daughter househunt in the always-competitive San Francisco market, she found they were getting outbid, and couldn't locate anything suitable for an acceptable price. So Carol went into the MLS and searched for listings tagged "expired" or "price reduction." Carol says, "It's wise to watch price reductions and visit the properties to see what the original 'flaw' was: cosmetics, price, or the property itself."

Carol's search led to a house with a view of the ocean and within walking distance of the elementary school that her grandsons attended. The problem? It was overpriced, because it smelled of cigarette smoke and was badly decorated, with tacky pink curtains and carpets—totally fixable, but hard for buyers to look beyond. The seller had rejected the only bid, expecting multiple, higher offers. When Carol's daughter came in four months later offering a price that accounted for the house's problems, the seller at last became realistic and accepted.

Your agent can help you with searches like Carol's and offer insights as to why a house hasn't yet sold. And you can also search for price-reduced houses on Trulia.com. If the problem is serious, or the seller appears extremely unrealistic, cross it off your list. But some houses may still remain prospects to pick up at an affordable price.

How'd They Sell That House?

After a famous murder in a house, it doesn't fare well on the real estate market:

• Nicole Brown Simpson's 3,400-square-foot condo languished on the market for two years before selling for $200,000 below the asking price. The buyers changed the address and remodeled.

• Jeffrey Dahmer's Milwaukee apartment building was so stigmatized by his series of gruesome murders that the entire neighborhood's occupancy rates went from 80% to 20%. The building itself was demolished by developers.

• In 2006, almost ten years after JonBenét Ramsey's body was found in the basement of her family's Boulder, Colorado, mansion, it was put on the market for $1.7 million—about $300,000 less than its estimated value. It brought in only $650,000, and has passed through several owners' hands since.

You may be a unique match for a particular property—for example, if you're unfazed by a house's criminal history. Also, some stigmas are more rumor than fact—maybe the former occupant actually died in the hospital, or an inspection turns up a logical reason for the spooky clanking noises.

One type of house that's worth steering well clear of, however, is a house that's been used as a meth lab. The highly toxic substances used to manufacture the illegal drugs known as methamphetamines can permeate various parts of the house, from carpets to drywall to countertops to air ducts. The health results haven't been fully studied yet, but may include respiratory illnesses, migraines, cancer, and more. Decontamination costs anywhere from $5,000 to $100,000, depending on the size of the home and other factors. If you hear any rumors that a house you're interested in used to be the local "drug house," have it checked for meth contamination. (And don't trust the seller's disclosures!) For more information, see www.methlabhomes.com.

 TIP

Newly constructed home seekers: You too can find castoffs. New-home discounts usually happen when a developer finishes an entire community, but some houses remain unsold or deals have fallen through. Meanwhile, the developer is eager to move on to the next project. You might see these advertised as "builder closeouts."

A Foot in the Door: Buying a Starter House

Every buyer's Dream List starts out ambitious—that's what dreams are for. Now that you've explored the market, you can decide whether to scale down your dreams concerning size, location, amenities, or something else. Perhaps you can get by without an office, or the kids can share for now (hey, the Cosby kids did it!). Or you might be able to identify a neighborhood that's up and coming. Watch where the artists go! As with New York's SoHo in the 1970s, artists are often the brave souls who turn a dicey neighborhood into a desirable one.

With a starter house you get your foot in the door of the real estate market, start building equity, and save enough to buy a bigger or better place in the not-too-distant future. It's a particularly solid strategy if you can expect increases in your income—for example, you or your partner will be graduating from school and getting a job soon. But even without saving, increases in the house's value and your equity can help launch you into the next house.

A few cautions apply to buying a starter house, however:

> ### Smallest House in the World
>
> According to Guinness World Records, this title is held by a fisherman's house in Conwy, a village in North Wales. Looking not unlike a British telephone booth (complete with red paint), the house contains just two tiny rooms atop one another, connected by a staircase. The house was built in the 19th century, which may explain why it has no toilet.

- **Buying ain't cheap.** You're going to have significant transaction costs each time you move: closing costs, agent commissions, and moving expenses.

- **Don't expect house price to drop proportionally to size.** Even if the house is matchbox-sized, you have to pay a reasonable amount for the land it sits on, particularly in a nice neighborhood.

- **Select the right mortgage.** Make sure your mortgage doesn't have prepayment penalties. Also avoid loans with points, because you might not recoup their cost.

- **Plan for any drop in value in the next few years.** If the value of your home drops, you won't be building much equity and might have to sell at a loss. That could make it tough for you to afford a bigger or better home.

Don't be scared by the number of cautions. Many homebuyers adopt this starter-home strategy. It allows you to start enjoying the benefits of homeownership right away, learn the ropes of being a homeowner, and develop a realistic sense of when and how you can move to your next place.

Have It Your Way:
Buying a Fixer-Upper or House You Can Add on To

Buying a house that needs a major overhaul, or will support an addition, is a great strategy for some buyers. The advantages are obvious: Pay less, and exercise your own excellent taste to produce a house you'll love living in and may sell at a profit. Plus, if the place is livable now, you can make these changes later, when you have more cash or equity (which you can borrow against).

Best thing we ever did **Buy a house we could add on to.** Erica and Carl had recently married and planned to have kids. But, says Erica, "All the houses in our price range were too small, too far from our offices, or had no usable backyard space—and we had an image of hanging out with family and friends on a back deck. After a year's searching, we decided to buy small and add on. We found a well-priced two-bedroom, to which we added a second bathroom and a deck soon after buying. That depleted our savings, but five years later, right before our second child, the house had gone up in value enough for us to qualify for a home equity loan and add another bedroom."

How Much Fixing-Up You Can Handle

Ideally, you'd like a house where the fix-ups are minor—like getting rid of the paisley wallpaper and mustard linoleum. Unfortunately, other homebuyers and investors are also looking for easy fixers, so huge bargains are sometimes hard to find. Nevertheless, a certain number of cosmetic fixers will remain overlooked, particularly if they look unappealing from the street (some potential buyers won't even get out of their car).

At the other end of the spectrum are major remodels,

How to Get on Extreme Makeover

Here's your backup plan for that fixer-upper: ABC's *Extreme Makeover Home Edition* is always looking for new contestants. Go to http://abc.go.com. Click "Shows," then "Extreme Makeover: Home Edition"; then click "Apply/Nominate" for application details. Also, HGTV's various series and specials are always looking for recruits (see www.HGTV.com).

requiring structural upgrades, adding or removing walls or rooms, and more. Unless you've got a contractor in the family, we suggest avoiding these—especially if they contain health hazards (such as mold) or are virtually unlivable (perhaps with big holes in the floor or roof). Here's why:

- The bank may refuse to approve your loan until a certain amount of repairs are done, and neither the seller nor you may be ready to pay for or complete these repairs.

- Major repairs can drain your bank account. You're looking for a fixer-upper because the perfect house doesn't seem to be in your price range, right? And don't forget that construction surprises are inevitable, and usually expensive.

- Dealing with large-scale improvements can disrupt your life and strain your personal relationships. If this is your first home, you might not be ready to hire contractors; take time off work to supervise the maelstrom of activity; and deal with delays, no-shows, or cost overruns—especially if you're living in the house.

The best bargain is usually a fixer-upper somewhere in the middle: one that can be made livable with a manageable amount of your own work or

Sisters Are Fixing It for Themselves

Who says home repairs are "man's work"? Anyone who's repair-challenged can take advantage of fix-it resources such as www.bejane.com, with tutorials, message boards, and a list of "Cool Tools." And Tupperware-partyesque Tomboy Tools workshops include hammers and demos (see www.tomboytools.com). Or try these books:

- *Dare to Repair: A Do-It-Herself Guide to Fixing (Almost) Anything in the Home,* by Julie Sussman and Stephanie Glakas-Tenet (Storey Publishing). With its Rosie the Riveter cover, it's easy to spot and teaches tasks from unclogging sinks to patching drywall.
- *Chix Can Fix: 100 Home-Improvement Projects and True Tales From the Diva of Do-It-Yourself,* by Norma Vally (Studio). Seen her on the Discovery Channel? Now you can read her lively instructions and stories on dealing with plumbing, electricity, walls, floors, doors, and windows.
- *The Tuff Chix Guide to Easy Home Improvement,* by Paige Hemmis (Plume). Another star author, from "Extreme Makeover." This book focuses on home repair advice for novices.

professional help. Think new paint, new flooring, and new windows rather than a new foundation and roof. When you find one that looks promising, be sure to:

- Make sure your plans are actually feasible. This almost certainly means checking with your city building department regarding height limits, requirements to bring old wiring and other systems up to code, setback rules, view ordinances, or parking restrictions.
- Ask architects, contractors, and engineers about the costs and feasibility of any major structural changes like adding a second story or a room.
- Have a serious conversation with anyone buying with you about the stress this project might cause. Discuss how you'll cope without a functional kitchen or bathroom, or who would deal with the many different contractors and workers.

Lesson learned the hard way **Expect the unexpected.** Noemi and Hugo bought a rundown house on a street where many young couples were buying and remodeling. Hugo explains, "Our plan was to live there through the remodel, stick around a few years, and then move into a bigger place. But almost immediately, we ran into complications. First, after the roof was torn off, we were told we'd need a special beam to get the raised ceiling we wanted. Meanwhile, rain poured in on our hardwood floors, which had to be replaced. This resulted in a trickle down effect (literally), with one delay after another. We ended up staying in our old apartment through the ten months of remodeling, paying both rent and a mortgage. We love our house, but we're no longer planning on moving soon!"

CHECK IT OUT

If tearing it down and starting over might be easier: Check out www. building-cost.net, which has a calculator to help you estimate the cost of replacing an entire house.

Will You Make Money When You Sell?

Although profiting on the sale of your remodeled or fixed-up house may not be your first priority, it's worth keeping an eye on. Not all upgrades excite buyers enough to pay more for—a new furnace, for example, rarely raises eyebrows. To check whether your planned changes will lead to profits, use the websites below.

CHECK IT OUT

Estimate your remodeling costs, see cost-to-value ratios, or get general remodeling advice at:

- www.contractors.com (with tips on various projects)
- www.nari.org (includes tips on how to select a good contractor)
- www.remodeling.hw.net (under "Facts & Figures," click "Cost vs. Value Report").

Share Your Space: Buying Jointly

Ask around: You're probably not the only person in your circle of friends or family who'd like to buy a house but can't quite make the finances work. You may find an interested, compatible cobuyer (or two). If you're living with roommates now, it won't be a big change.

You might want to look for a structure containing separate units, such as a duplex. You'd potentially each have your own entrance, kitchen, and more. But your lives wouldn't be completely separate—you'd still need to agree on major issues concerning your shared ownership, such as maintaining the roof and land.

Best thing I ever did **Buy a home with my sister.** Meggan and her sister had both finished college and were looking to rent apartments in Worcester, Massachusetts. "But," says Meggan, "the two of us got to talking. For the amount we'd each pay to rent separate apartments, why not just join forces and buy a multiunit house? Eventually we found a three-family home, built in the 1920s, with beautiful woodwork and built-ins. We split all the costs 50/50 (the mortgage, the expenses, right down to the lawnmower), and each took one floor. Some tenants were already living on the third floor—a dependable family—and they stayed on. Everything worked out great, and three years later, after my sister and I had both married, we sold the place for double what we'd paid for it."

The cheaper alternative is usually to buy a single dwelling and share the entire space jointly, meaning you'd have less autonomy. With some looking around, you may be able to find a place with a layout conducive to independent lives, such as bedrooms in opposite wings.

You'll have to make some major decisions in advance about the financial and other aspects of your shared ownership. The biggest financial question will be how you split the down payment and monthly expenses—an even split, or a percentage split based on the amount of money you each put in, the size of your bedrooms, or some other combination of factors? And remember that how you split ownership also dictates how you can claim the related tax benefits.

Another major question involves who gets the property if one of you dies: the other person, or someone named in the deceased owner's will? And in a less dire scenario, what if one of you wants to move out—can that person rent his or her portion of the place, sell to any buyer, force the whole property to be sold, or need to offer the remaining owner a chance to buy the "property interest" (that's legalese for an ownership share), either at its original or current value?

Think about these issues before buying, because the manner in which you describe your ownership on the property deed (in legalese, "take title")—for example, as tenants in common or as joint tenants with right of survivorship—will legally determine the answer to some of them. For example, joint tenancy almost always involves a 50/50 split (depending on state law; see Chapter 11).

Cobuying is a huge commitment, and it's crucial you choose the right person to share the responsibilities of homeownership and discuss issues like how often to mow the lawn or (unless you're in a duplex) do the dishes, clean the bathtub, and vacuum the living room. Sit down with your potential co-owner to discuss such issues, Then, no matter how compatible you two seem to be, put your agreement in writing, most likely with an attorney's help.

Cobuyer Discussion Worksheet

To make sure you will be compatible, discuss the following issues before buying a place with someone else. Add anything else important to this list—for example, whether or not you want a dog or cat. Jot down your notes and then draft a co-ownership agreement (with an attorney's help or with one of the contracts in Living Together: A Legal Guide for Unmarried Couples, *by Toni Ihara, Ralph Warner, and Frederick Hertz (Nolo)).*

1. How long you plan to stay in the house (and possible reasons that this may change, like moving to take care of an ill parent or getting married).

2. How you'll each be able to afford mortgage payments and carrying costs, and what happens if one of you falls on hard times.

3. Rules for sharing space (for example, cleaning up, dividing the costs of utilities and house supplies, limiting music volume levels, and overnight guests (short- or long-term)).

4. How nicely decorated the house should be, and how you'll budget for decorating.

5. How much of the property each of you will own, and how you will take title.

6. What will happen if one of you dies—for example, whether the deceased's interest in the house will go directly to the other owner, or go to an heir.

7. What will happen if one of you wants to move out or sell the house sooner than the other would like to. (Many buyers include what's called a "right of first refusal" in their co-ownership agreement, giving the nondeparting owner first crack at buying the other owner's share of the property, at a specified value, usually either the original purchase price or the currently appraised value.)

8. How you will handle disputes.

OTHER:

CD-ROM

Make sure your discussion covers all the bases: Use the "Cobuyer Discussion Worksheet" included in the Homebuyer's Toolkit on the CD-ROM. A sample is shown above.

CHECK IT OUT

Looking for details on buying a house with someone other than a spouse? For ideas and practical suggestions on sharing living space and other resources, see *The Sharing Solution*, by Janelle Orsi and Emily Doskow (Nolo). If you and your cobuyer are a couple, you'll also find useful information and sample forms in either *Living Together: A Legal Guide for Unmarried Couples*, by Ralph Warner, Tony Ihara, and Frederick Hertz (Nolo); or *A Legal Guide for Lesbian & Gay Couples*, by Denis Clifford, Frederick Hertz, and Emily Doskow (Nolo).

Subdivide Your Space: Renting Out a Room

If total privacy is a luxury you can sacrifice, at least in the short term, it may help you afford a home. In fact, if you've already got a roommate who you enjoy living with, that person might be content writing the rent checks to you, instead of to your current landlord.

You can often charge almost as much as what renters would pay for an apartment and set down rules regarding which rooms they can use, kitchen cleanliness, and more—it's still *your* place. The rent will help you pay the mortgage, and you can charge for a portion of the common costs, like utilities. Of course, you'll want to protect yourself with good tenant screening and a written rental agreement.

If you can't face the thought of a stranger having your front door key, look for a duplex, a place with a cottage in the back or a basement apartment, or another multiunit building.

CHECK IT OUT

Planning to be a landlord? Get help from:

- *Every Landlord's Legal Guide*, by Marcia Stewart, Ralph Warner, and Janet Portman (Nolo). Although aimed primarily at off-site landlords, this book will help you find and screen tenants and draft your rental agreement.
- *Every Landlord's Tax Deduction Guide*, by Stephen Fishman (Nolo). Find out how to save even more money by taking advantage of favorable tax laws.

Hey, Where's Their Agent? Looking for FSBOs (For Sale by Owners)

Another way to broaden your search is to visit FSBOs, that is, houses sold directly by their owners. Just how many sellers go the FSBO route is impossible to say, but most estimates put it around 15% of all U.S. houses. That's a lot of houses your real estate agent might not, under ordinary circumstances, be showing you.

In a few cases, FSBOs can also save you money. The seller may have underpriced the house or be willing to share the commission savings with you. But don't count on either—sellers going through the effort of advertising and showing their houses aren't always interested in parting with any of their earnings.

Your Agent's Role in Buying a FSBO

Most agents don't routinely search for FSBOs, so you'll need to work out whether you want this service in advance. One option is to do the searching yourself, using the resources listed in the next section. If you see an ad for a FSBO that looks interesting, the appropriate next step is to tell your agent about it before visiting the house.

That lets the agent deal with the next important issue, which is how he or she will get paid. Your agent will call and ask whether the FSBO seller will "cooperate" regarding the commission (that means paying the portion of the commission that the seller's agent would normally hand over, usually

2½%). If the answer is no, the agent will come back to you and discuss the commission, to see whether you're willing to pay it. You should agree on the rate in advance.

Finding FSBO Houses

Because FSBO sellers aren't represented by real estate brokers, they don't have access to the MLS database (unless they've made a special effort to find and pay a broker for the discrete task of listing the house). That means you'll find most FSBOs either listed on independent websites (like those below) or advertised by more-traditional means (local newspapers or yard signs).

 CHECK IT OUT

Your best bets for finding FSBOs on the Web are:

- www.ForSaleByOwner.com
- www.owners.com
- www.craigslist.org ("real estate for sale" is right there under "housing"—they're not all FSBOs, but some are), and
- www.fsboguide.com, for links to FSBO websites in your area.

Dealing With FSBO Sellers' Varying Personalities, Skill Levels

A FSBO seller doesn't have an agent to educate him or her about the real estate market and act as a buffer in negotiating with buyers. That means that the success of buying a particular FSBO house—from setting a price to closing the deal—depends largely on the seller's own personality, real estate knowledge, and skill set.

In the best-case scenario, you might find a FSBO seller who is a knowledgeable, fair-minded lawyer or retired real estate professional, who sees no reason to enlist extra help for a familiar process. In the worst case, you might find a seller who is a skinflint curmudgeon know-it-all or a total flake, who has overpriced the house, refuses to discuss commissions, and cancels the sale the minute you bring up inspections or repairs. And even the most expert sellers sometimes approach negotiations based on emotion.

Best thing we ever did **Get to know our FSBO seller.** Maria and her husband had been keeping their eyes open for a house that would not only fit them and their two girls, but include an in-law unit for an elderly parent. "We knew such a house would be hard to find," says Maria, "so when we heard that my husband's sister's best friend's mom's house was sitting empty—she'd recently moved into an assisted-living center—we contacted the family to sound them out. They'd just begun thinking about selling and were intimidated by the amount of work it would take to clear out the place (the mother was a packrat) and to fix it up (it desperately needed a new roof, not to mention cosmetic fixes like replacing the orange shag carpet). But after my family and I saw the house—which was just what we wanted—I talked to the mother directly, and we hit it off. In fact, eventually she told her daughter that selling the house to us was almost like keeping it in the family. We agreed to buy it without an agent, at a price that was reasonable given all the fix-ups and the commission savings. The whole arrangement was mutually beneficial in many ways—including when we began picking up the seller at her assisted-living center and driving her to the house so she could sort through the lifetime of possessions."

Buying a FSBO With No Agent

If you don't have or want an agent yet, you can buy a FSBO on your own—but be prepared for a steep learning curve. Unless you're already friends, a canny seller might try to take advantage of you. And any deal can get mired in disagreements. There's a reasonable chance you will be friends or acquaintances, however—common when someone hears about a house for sale before it's advertised. But you'll still need a standard, written sales agreement to protect both of you.

If saving money is a key concern, consider hiring an attorney for limited parts of the transaction. (In a few states, you'll have to use an attorney for certain tasks, anyway.) A few hours' worth of advice can save you from later heartache and expense and still cost you thousands less than an agent's commission. Michigan attorney Fred Steingold says, "One option is to hire a lawyer to serve as your coach. Ask the lawyer to give you a purchase agreement form that's widely used in your community and that fairly protects both you and the seller. The lawyer can also explain how to complete the form yourself, and then review your handiwork."

And whatever you do, don't go without the services of an escrow or title company to help guide you toward the closing, as described in Chapter 11.

> **TIP**
>
> **If no agent is involved in a FSBO, some states don't require seller disclosures.** In that case, bring in the most thorough professional home inspectors you can find to assess the property's physical condition.

On the Auction Block: Buying Short Sale, Foreclosure, or Probate Properties

Particularly following a huge drop in house values, you may find the market littered with tempting real estate bargains. The lowest-priced homes are often short sales, foreclosures, or probate properties.

Purchasing one of these types of properties is not for the faint of heart. As we'll explain, the already-stressful process of buying your first home can be exacerbated by complications in the process at every step.

Buying a Short Sale

A "short sale" is real estate lingo for a house that's being put up for sale for less than the homeowner owes on the mortgage—usually, a homeowner in financial distress who is trying to avoid foreclosure. Sometimes, but not always, the seller has already defaulted on the loan.

Don't assume that the lender has already agreed to this arrangement, however. In fact, the normal way that a short sale works is for the seller to find a willing buyer, and then present the lender with the buyer's offer, often on a preprinted application form, and accompanied by an appraisal showing the property's estimated market value. The hope is that the lender will agree to forgive what remains on the loan and let the sale go forward, as a way to get rid of a mortgage that it would probably never have been able to fully collect on anyway.

As you might guess, the need for the seller's lender to approve the sale adds a potential hurdle to the process. After you've submitted your offer and the seller has accepted it, the lender must run some numbers, trying to balance the amount that would be lost on the loan against the probable loss (and cost and hassle) if the property continued on into foreclosure.

What's not so intuitive is how long it typically takes lenders to perform this analysis. When this book went to print, they were commonly taking from four to six months to provide answers.

A short sale may have an alluringly low price—especially in comparison to what the seller owes—but that doesn't necessarily make it a good deal. The seller may have overpaid to begin with, or the market may have fallen significantly. And as we'll explain below, as the buyer you may be responsible for significant additional costs that aren't accounted for in the selling price.

And you run the very real risk that the lender will say no, particularly if the seller has advertised the property for much less than is owed on it, desperately fishing for any offer.

Making an Offer on a Short Sale

If you're interested in a short sale property, choose an agent who's dealt with them before. The agent should do some homework before you make an offer. You want to know how much the homeowner owes on the property; if it's a lot more than you're willing to pay, the lender is unlikely to approve the sale. Lenders reportedly favor offers of at least 85% of the property's appraised market value, but in very badly distressed real estate markets, have been known to accept as little as 50% of this amount.

You also want to know whether the homeowner has more than one loan. If so, you'll need the approval of all lenders to make the sale, and the more lenders there are, the harder that will be to get, because they must each agree to taking a smaller piece of the pie. Ask your agent to research this for you.

Also, make sure your agent talks with the seller's agent about what kind of legwork has already been done. Banks will approve a short sale only if the seller is in financial distress. Even though you're going to need the bank's ultimate approval, you want to be sure the seller has at least contacted the bank and gotten confirmation that the bank will consider a short sale. Unless you're not in any particularly hurry to buy a place, you don't want to waste your time waiting for a bank to respond to an offer if you're fairly certain it will just be rejected anyway.

What to Expect With a Short Sale

If you decide, after obtaining the information above, that you still want to buy a short sale, expect it to differ from a regular sale in a few different ways:

- **You'd better be first in line.** Short sale sellers will often approach the lender with the first offer received, even if it's on the extremely low side. Why? Because once they've started the long process of gaining bank approval, they don't want to derail it by bringing in an alternate offer; nor do they want to give the bank any ideas about how they could actually get more for the house than the offer on the table.

- **Lower commissions paid by the seller to your agent.** The lender, who is ultimately paying the real estate agent commissions, may negotiate them down with the seller's agent, and your agent will get paid less as a result. If you agreed to pay your agent more in a buyer's brokerage agreement, you'll have to do so out of your own pocket.

- **The property will be sold "as is."** Lenders offer the property in its present condition, with no reductions for repair needs. To make sure you know what state things are in, you should be certain you have an inspection contingency in the contract, allowing you to have the property profes-sionally inspected and back out of the deal if you're not satisfied with the results. (We discuss inspections in greater detail in Chapter 12.) Just don't expect to negotiate any of the repairs with the bank.

- **You'll pay all closing costs.** These fees are usually split with the seller, but the bank will likely refuse to pay any of them.

- **The transaction will take longer.** You may spend months waiting for your offer to be approved or rejected by the bank. Make sure your offer terminates at some realistic point in the future. A few short days probably won't do it, but if you let the offer remain open-ended, it's sure to end up parked on a desk somewhere.

- **Last-minute unhappy surprises.** When the lender finally approves your offer and sends the seller the paperwork to finalize the deal, it's not uncommon for the seller to discover that the lender has inserted language saying that even after releasing the mortgage, the lender can come after the seller for the difference in what is owed—which, for the seller, defeats the purpose of the short sale, and may make the deal fall through.

As you can see, short sales are extra work and hassle. Unless you're going to get a property at a deep discount—even after adding up the costs of your real estate agent's commission, repairs, and closing costs—and you have enough time to wait around for the bank to respond to your offer, you're probably better off buying a house that isn't conditioned on an unusual form of bank approval.

Buying in Foreclosure

Even more challenging than buying a short sale is buying a foreclosure. Foreclosure occurs when a homeowner can't pay back a mortgage loan, and the lender exercises its legal right to force a sale. But they've become especially common with recent meltdowns in the bank and mortgage industries, leading to renewed interest by bargain-hunting homebuyers. Foreclosures happen in every market, from the highest-end houses to the lowest. The bank or lender doesn't usually foreclose right away—they give borrowers a grace period first. When a lender does move toward foreclosure it creates opportunities for new buyers at three stages of the process: preforeclosure, at a public sale or auction, and by buying directly from the bank (called real-estate-owned, or REO).

Where Most Foreclosures Happen

The five cities with the largest percentages of homes foreclosed upon in mid-2010 included:

- Chicago, Illinois
- Las Vegas, Nevada
- Los Angeles, California
- Miami, Florida
- Phoenix, Arizona

Source: www.RealtyTrac.com

Regular Sellers Are Starting to Try Auctions

Some ordinary home sellers are deciding that auctions—either live or on-line—are the fastest, most profitable way to sell. This is most common on the East Coast, but catching on in the West.

Live auctions are usually handled by professionals who let potential buyers visit an open house first and hire inspectors before making a bid. The buyer pays the company a premium, usually 7%–10% of the house price.

The online auctions are usually handled on sites like eBay, and the procedures vary depending on the sellers: Horror stories are already emerging of naïve buyers who purchased houses sight unseen. The bottom line is you might get an auction bargain, but there are unusual up-front costs and risks.

The main advantage in buying a foreclosure is price—you're likely to get some sort of a discount no matter what stage you buy at. The main disadvantages to buying foreclosure properties are:

- **Going without usual buyer protections.** As we'll explain further below, at most stages in the foreclosure process you'll forgo at least some of the normal protections available in a typical transaction; for example, you may not get to see the property before you buy, have to accept it "as is," and have to go without title insurance.

- **Waiting to make sure the owner is protected.** Most states have laws to make sure banks can't rip properties out from under late-paying owners on a moment's notice. For buyers, that means deadlines, delays, court rules, and uncertainty—particularly in the many states that allow the former owner to "redeem" or buy back the property within a certain period of time after it was sold in foreclosure (usually from ten days to one year). Of course, if that happens, your money will be refunded. But as attorney Fred Steingold notes: "Do you really want to be held in limbo, unsure of whether you'll ever be able to occupy the house?"

CHECK IT OUT

To find out your state's redemption period and get other summaries of your state's law regarding foreclosures, see:

- www.realtytrac.com
- www.foreclosureforum.com.

- **Competition from experienced real estate investors.** If there are good deals to be had, you can bet real estate investors will be lined up in front of you.

- **Risks of undisclosed repair needs, tax liens, or other issues with the property.** Remember, these homeowners were probably financially stressed for a while. They may have held back on maintenance, gotten behind on their taxes, or used the house as collateral for other debts.

Still interested in pursuing foreclosed properties? Find an agent who specializes in them—most don't handle them at all, while some go so far as to arrange bus tours of local foreclosures A good source is www.reonetwork.com. If you still have a regular real estate agent, explain to both what you're doing, so that you can agree on each agent's limited role. You'd also be wise to hire a real estate attorney to help navigate this somewhat touchy area.

Buying a House in Preforeclosure

When a house is in preforeclosure, the owners have received a notice of default from their lender, saying they have a set period of time (depending on their state's law) to either sell the house, pay all late mortgage payments and fees, or work out some other agreement.

Preforeclosure listings are publicly available even if the homeowner hasn't listed the property for sale. Online services like Foreclosures.com or RealtyTrac.com compile this information from public records and members pay a modest monthly fee ($40–$50) to get the information. Some aggressive homebuyers or investors use this information to find homes in preforeclosure and then approach the defaulting homeowners to make an offer. Of course, they'll be interested only in properties that are worth more than the homeowners owe, because they'll be able to offer less than market value but still help the homeowners get out from under the mortgage. (If the seller owes more than the property is worth and can't make up the difference or negotiate an agreement with the lender, the only alternative short of foreclosure is a short sale, discussed above.)

EXAMPLE: Lucas wants to buy his first home, and is looking for a bargain. He uses an online service and finds a house in the neighborhood he wants to live in that is in preforeclosure. The owners, Jean and Greg, owed $155,000 on the house and Lucas thinks it's worth about $180,000. Lucas approaches Jean and Greg and offers them $160,000: more than they owe on it, but less than it's worth.

Whether a homeowner will appreciate this, if you attempt it, is questionable. Some may feel like you're circling like a predator, waiting for misfortune to befall them. Others might be grateful that you're helping them get out of a tough predicament. Either way, it's a gamble, and the less experienced you are at it, the more likely you are to make mistakes.

If you do find a homeowner ready to sell, you can negotiate just as you would any other transaction. But you'll probably be very pressed for time. Depending on the state you're in, the homeowner could have as little as 30 days from the time the Notice of Default is filed to catch up on the mortgage (meaning you'll have to close the deal by then), or the lender will put the house up for auction.

Buying a House at Public Sale or Auction

If the seller doesn't pay what's owed and the lender forecloses, the property will be sold at a public sale or auction. This is rarely a good time for a first time homebuyer to get a good deal, for several reasons.

First of all, the lender will probably make the first bid on the house, for the amount owed on the mortgage. Unless the amount owed is low in relation to the home's value (rarely the case), you won't want to bid any higher. And if the price is right and you want to bid, you'll be competing with savvy real estate investors who know what they're doing. Even if you're the highest bidder, you have another giant hurdle to overcome: You'll be expected to have come with cash in hand, without a traditional loan or financing, which is rarely a realistic option for first-time buyers.

Add to this the fact that you'll know very little about the house itself. You may never have even seen the place, and you'll have to take it "as is," without the benefit of an inspection. It isn't uncommon for disgruntled homeowners to trash their former homes or to strip them of all valuable assets when foreclosure happens (light fixtures, appliances, even copper wires). Or if the house has sat vacant for a long time, thieves may have done the same thing. Even worse, you may have to go without title insurance, leaving you open to the risk of an unpaid lien or a later claim to title.

Unlike a preforeclosure, when you buy a foreclosure, you aren't working directly with the homeowner anymore. But that doesn't mean the homeowner isn't involved. If a stubborn homeowner or tenant hasn't moved out, you will likely have to proceed with an eviction action or exchange "cash for keys"— that is, give them some money to vacate the place, to avoid the hassle and expense of the eviction.

Buying a Bank-Owned House

If no one else buys the property at the foreclosure sale, the bank will then own it and likely try to sell it, usually by listing it with a local real estate agent. You may come across these deals if you browse MLS listings. At this point, the bank may be willing to sell the house for less than the seller owed, because it isn't in the business of owning property, and wants to get as much of its cash out of the place as possible. Still, lenders want to get as close to market value as possible, and that may mean it's not such a great deal for you.

Even if the price is a little lower than you'd find on a house that isn't bank owned, a bank-owned property comes with additional complications. By the time the bank gets to selling it, it may have been vacant for months, which means it probably won't be in the best shape. Banks usually do little more than pick up debris and do a basic clean up, so you won't see any expert staging here, and you may find that the lower price is balanced by the hard work you'll have to put in to make the house liveable.

Best thing we ever did

Buy a bank-owned home. Anjanelle and Alan were looking to buy a house in the Sacramento, California, area. "When a wave of bank-owned properties flooded the market at rock bottom prices, we thought it might finally be affordable," says Anjanelle. "But it was an uphill battle, and it took several months." They bid on three houses before striking a deal, offering a little above the asking price to avoid being outbid. But then the house didn't appraise for the amount of their offered price. "We thought the deal was going to fall apart, but the bank was so anxious to get rid of the place, and we already had a deal on the table, so they dropped the price. It worked out great for us, and then we had enough cash to do some of the major repair work the house needed, like painting the smoke-damaged walls and having the worn-out hardwood floors refinished."

Also, banks usually sell properties "as is." At this stage, you'll at least have the benefit of an inspection contingency (discussed in more detail in Chapter 11). That means that while you can't expect the bank to do anything about repairs that are needed, you'll at least be able to have the property professionally inspected and back out of the deal if you don't like what you see.

If you do find a good deal on a bank-owned home, chances are you're not the only one. It isn't unheard of for well-priced bank-owned properties to garner as many as ten to 20 offers. (Your real estate agent should be able to find out this type of detail on properties you're interested in, with a little legwork.) To make your offer stand out, you may have to pay more than other bidders. You'll definitely want to be preapproved for a loan, and it could help if your preapproval letter comes from the selling lender—they'll trust their own assessment of your finances better than anyone else's.

Houses Sold at Tax Sales

When a homeowner fails to pay property taxes, the state may take title to the property, then sell its claim (its "lien") at auction. The buyer of the lien will have to allow the current owner a legally specified amount of time to pay off the lien and reclaim the property before stepping in to claim title. The procedural requirements are complex and definitely not recommended for first-time buyers. For related articles, go to www.lienexchange.com.

CHECK IT OUT

For information on foreclosures, see the following sites.

- www.propertyshark.com (you'll need to register for some information)
- www.realtytrac.com (includes state-by-state statistics)
- www.homesales.gov (for listings of houses foreclosed upon by the federal Department of Housing and Urban Development after owners failed to pay their FHA loans)
- www.foreclosure.com, and
- www.foreclosures.com (note the "s" after "foreclosure").

Buying in Probate

Usually if a homeowner dies, and either left a will or didn't leave any instructions at all, the property must be "probated." A court reviews the case, orders a division of assets, and more. Without getting too deep into the legal details, some properties end up being sold, usually at a court-supervised public sale or auction. This is the classic "probate sale." Another variation on this theme is that the estate's executor, administrator, or personal representative may sell the house privately, with or without a broker, so that cash can be distributed to the heirs.

It's possible to get a bargain on a house in probate whether it's sold at auction or through negotiation. If it's sold at auction, a minimum bid is set based on its appraised value, and you may be the only bidder. Even if you're not, California real estate agent Annemarie Kurpinsky points out that, "Unlike competing for nonprobate properties, you know exactly how high the other bidders are willing to go, and you therefore have no feeling of having overpaid." And with a negotiated purchase, you may benefit from the heirs' desire for a quick sale—they may regard any money that they get as a windfall.

But the disadvantages of buying a probate property include:

- **Legal and procedural hassles.** Court procedures vary by state but almost always involve paperwork and deadlines—and often a trip to court to bid on the house.

- **Risks of undisclosed repair needs.** You're waiting for a property whose physical condition may be going from bad to worse. And many states lift their disclosure rules for houses in probate. Worse yet, in many probate sales you must buy the property "as is," without making the sale conditional on the results of inspections.

If you're interested in probate houses, find an agent who specializes in them. Or, if you happen to know about a person who has died, there's nothing wrong with checking the probate court records to find out who's administering the estate and contacting that person. Attorney Fred Steingold explains, "The executor (or "administrator" or "personal representative") is probably an amateur—a relative of the deceased—and may be grateful for a way to liquidate the real estate without the expense of a commission or the hassles of an auction."

Housebuying Fantasies

For when reality hasn't yet delivered the house of your dreams, here are some fantasies to indulge in:

- **Buy an island.** Whether you'd fancy an Irish island with a castle or a coral reef atoll in Belize, they're listed, with photos, at www.vladi-private-islands.de.

- **Buy an airplane.** A California woman paid $100,000 for a 747; disassembled it; and turned it into a curvy, eco-friendly cottage. (The plane's nose was used as a meditation temple.) See http://news.bbc.co.uk/2/hi/americas/4926216.stm.

- **Build a treehouse.** You can buy plans—including for a treehouse that's 64 square feet and requires two trees to support it—at www.thetreehouseguide.com.

- **Convert a caboose.** They're available at www.cabooses4sale.com.

- **Live on a houseboat.** You provide the boat, and lease the dock or slip. But first, visit Amsterdam's House Boat Museum: www.houseboatmuseum.nl.

Okay, now get back to reality.

What's Next?

Your home search may continue for a while, but that's all right. Don't settle for anything less than a home that meets your minimum requirements (even if those had to be adjusted), one where you'll be happy living for long enough to strategize your next move. Once you find the right house, things will move quickly—and your first step will be to make an offer to the seller, as described next.

Show Them the Money: From Offer to Purchase Agreement

Meet Your Adviser

Richard Leshnower, a New York-based attorney with specialized experience in real estate.

What he does Helps buyers and sellers negotiate and close on the purchase of co-ops and houses in New York City and surrounding areas. Richard not only represents people at the front end of property sales, but helps some who come to him with postsale problems—for example, a buyer who didn't understand what she was signing and discovered that she'd bought a house without buying its side yard.

First house "I bought it in 1974, a beautiful colonial in Woodmere, New York. I asked my boss (another attorney) to represent me at the closing. Closings in 1974 involved a lot fewer documents than you'll encounter today! But what I remember most about the closing was the behavior of the husband seller, who was retiring and moving out of state. He flipped out under the pressure of the moment. He stood up, grabbed the table and threw it over. Papers went flying all over the floor. His wife jumped on him to calm him down. The good news is that he returned to his gentlemanly self, and the deal closed—and I lived in that house for 30 years."

Fantasy house "A majestic house with an ocean view, like you might find in Big Sur, California. In addition to the usual rooms, I'd like a small hideaway room where I can read, view television, and use the computer. And let's pack the house full of other good stuff like a game room, swimming pools (outdoor and indoor), bowling alley, gym, movie theatre, and a slip for a boat. Not that I really 'need' all of this—my wife Karyn and I are empty nesters and already have a house we love in Delray Beach, Florida, and a co-op apartment in Hewlett, New York."

Likes best about his work	"Helping people who are otherwise intelligent and cautious find their way out of a tough situation—for example, afford a home when they thought they couldn't qualify for a mortgage. And nothing thrills me more than when I get a call out of the blue from a client who's moved elsewhere, to tell me how he or she is doing."

• •

Top tip for first-time homebuyers	"Pick good advisers who you know are on your side and will be available to you for consultation. Don't let anyone tell you that something is too difficult for you to understand—you don't have to read every word of every document, but ask your advisers to educate you on their meaning. Also, walk the property and look at every nook and cranny yourself. That avoids situations like one where some buyers (whom I didn't represent) bought a big house on a large area of land one summer but didn't walk beyond the thick shrubbery in the backyard. After moving in, they heard trains rumbling—and sure enough, there was a train track right behind the rear property line, which came into full view that autumn, when the leaves fell off the trees."

Y ou've found it, the place you love, the home you want. Now all you have to do is tell the seller you'll take it, sign a few papers, and move in, right?

Not quite. First, you'll need to decide on the terms of your offer; most important, whether you'll pay the asking price. And maybe you'll want to ask the seller for a short closing period so you can move in soon or request that the custom-built kitchen table be left with the house. You'll figure out whether you and the seller can agree on such terms once you start negotiating. In this chapter, we'll explain how to:

- submit an offer, negotiate with the seller, and reach an agreement
- decipher the typical language in a standard home purchase contract
- decide on the contract's basic terms like price, contingencies to protect your interests, and deposit
- make your offer the best it can be, given the market you're in, and
- work with a developer to buy a new home.

Start to Finish: Negotiating and Forming a Contract

Buying a house is nothing like most of the financial transactions we make— unlike groceries, clothing, or most consumer goods, the price and other terms are largely negotiable. As adviser Richard Leshnower says, "This isn't like putting a dollar into a vending machine and getting a can of soda." To understand the options and get the best deal, it's good to know how the process works before you begin.

Submitting an Offer

Once you say, "This is the house!" your real estate agent will probably suggest you sit down together to draft an offer. (In a few states, however, your attorney will do the drafting, or the opening offer may be verbal.) You'd normally go back to your agent or attorney's office, but if there's time pressure, perhaps from competing buyers, drafting an offer in the agent's car is not unheard of.

Are You Ready?

Use this checklist to decide whether you're ready to make an offer on a specific house, or whether you should do more legwork first:

☐ This house is in my price range, and I have my down payment cash available.

☐ I'm preapproved for a mortgage, and I know what kind of mortgage I want—or the seller is willing to take back a mortgage.

☐ I've hired or am already working with a real estate agent, mortgage broker or lender, and/or attorney.

☐ I'm ready to devote much of my time over the next several weeks to closing the deal and preparing to move (unless it's a yet-to-be constructed house, in which case the time period may be longer).

In many states, a buyer's initial offer eventually serves as the complete contract, after both the buyer and seller have approved and signed it. Such offers are written in great detail, including not only a proposed price, but what conditions (contingencies) must be met for the deal to finalize, how disputes would be resolved, and who will pay what fees. It may be accompanied by a sum of money called an earnest money or good faith deposit.

In other states, the offer is a very short document or is not written down at all—the point is just to communicate to the seller that you'd like to buy the house. The full contract is written later, sometimes with the seller's attorney creating the first draft. (In which case you should read it extra carefully!)

 TIP

Ask your agent to explain the standard contract ahead of time. Says Illinois Realtor® Mark Nash, "When working with first-time buyers, I show them the standard form, and all required disclosures, before we even start looking at properties. I answer questions they have about what each clause and phrase means, and I encourage them to read it over and make sure they really understand it. That way, when it comes time to actually write up the contract, they're less overwhelmed—they're dealing with the specific terms they want in the agreement, not the basic meaning of the contract language itself."

Presenting Your Offer

Once you have an offer together, someone (usually your agent) must present it to the seller. A great agent can present your offer in the best possible light. Perhaps your offer isn't as high as the seller would like, but you're preapproved for a mortgage and are including few contingencies that could slow the process. Whatever your strengths, it's your agent's job to highlight them.

Normally, your agent will contact the seller's agent and arrange for a time to meet and present the offer. The seller may come to this meeting, too. The seller may hear just one offer (yours) or may hear multiple offers from several potential buyers, sometimes on the same day.

Occasionally, a seller will request that offers be sent by email or fax, maybe because the seller is out of town or expects multiple offers. In that case, include a personal cover letter outlining your qualifications and the strengths of your offer.

The Seller Responds

After you've submitted your offer, you'll probably be on pins and needles, wondering how the seller will react. The seller is eventually going to do one of three things: (1) accept, (2) reject, or (3) make a counteroffer.

> **CAUTION**
>
> **The seller might not respond right away.** Particularly if you're offering to buy a house sold in a "short sale" (requiring bank approval) or making an offer on a bank-owned property, it could be weeks or even months before you hear back from the seller. If you're patient, you can wait for the response and maybe get a good deal. If you're in a hurry to move, however, you may have to withdraw your offer and look elsewhere.

The Seller Accepts Your Offer

If the seller accepts your offer in writing, you have a contract. You and the seller can begin to perform all the tasks that take you up to the closing, as described in Chapter 11.

The Seller Rejects Your Offer

Sometimes, the seller will flatly reject your offer, usually because someone else made a better offer, and yours simply didn't rise to the top of the stack. The seller's agent should contact your agent with the bad news.

You Might Make the B-Team

Instead of rejecting your offer outright, a seller may suggest that you make a backup offer to purchase the house if the chosen deal falls through. Your backup gives the seller a little extra security and saves the hassle of readvertising.

If you submit a backup offer, ask the seller to give you a final yes or no within a few days or to specify that the exact terms of the agreement are to follow. This protects you in case you find another property, lose interest, or want to renegotiate terms with the seller.

The Seller Counteroffers

The seller may decide that your offer is okay but needs improvement (usually a higher price). The seller may then give you a counteroffer, with an expiration date for your reply. A counteroffer is a good sign—it means the seller is interested in negotiating with you. But Massachusetts broker Nancy Atwood warns, "Sometimes the buyer and seller forget that they have the same goal in mind, which is the purchase of the home. I was once involved in a transaction where the buyer and seller were fighting over a couple thousand dollars, on an $800,000 property! Eventually they did relent and split the difference, but it caused some unnecessary stress on both sides of the table."

The counteroffer may be structured like a whole stand-alone contract, or it may incorporate your original offer, essentially saying, "I agree to the terms of the offer, except with these changes." If the new terms are satisfactory—for example, you're willing to pay a higher price or give the seller extra time to move out—you can accept the seller's counteroffer.

When a seller receives multiple offers, the seller may return multiple counteroffers, asking people to submit new, better offers. It's kind of like being outbid on eBay: You can then decide whether you want to put in a new offer, but your competitors will be doing the same thing.

> **Mel:** *Which reminds me, where's your report card?*
>
> **Cher:** *It's not ready yet.*
>
> **Mel:** *What do you mean, "It's not ready yet?"*
>
> **Cher:** *Well, some teachers are trying to low-ball me, Daddy. And I know how you say, "Never accept a first offer," so I figure these grades are just a jumping-off point to start negotiations.*
>
> From the movie *Clueless*, 1995

If the seller gives you a counteroffer that you don't like, you can reject it and simply walk away, or you can counter the counteroffer. Leshnower counsels, "Don't feel that walking away is failure. It's just another step in the hunting process."

You and the Seller Negotiate

You and the seller can continue to exchange counteroffers until you reach agreement or give up. Each time, you'll include expiration dates for your counteroffers. If an expiration date passes, negotiations are over—no deal. If, however, one of you accepts the other's counteroffer, you'll put that agreement down on paper, as described next.

More Than Words:
What's in the Standard Purchase Contract

When you and the seller agree and write a contract, it will probably look like pages and pages of a legal document—which it is! Luckily, you'll probably be spared creating it from scratch. Your state's Realtor® association may provide a standard preprinted form for your use, called something like "Contract to Purchase" or "Offer to Purchase." These fill-in-the-blanks forms contain state-specific legal language so you won't forget to deal with important issues. But they usually leave space for you to customize, too. If you're using an attorney, he or she may start with some boilerplate and customize it to your purchase. Leshnower adds, "Never believe anyone who tells you that this is a standard contract and you cannot amend, change, or add to it."

To form a legal contract, your final agreement must be in writing and signed by both you and the seller. So if the seller or the seller's agent calls you and says, "We accept your offer," wait for that signed agreement before taking further action.

Whether you use a standard form or a fully customized document, certain key terms and phrases are likely to be in it (though these, too, vary by state). Read it carefully, using the summary of common terms below for both decoding and making sure it contains the protections you want. We'll discuss many of these terms further in this and later chapters.

> **TIP**
>
> **Ask questions.** If you don't understand the meaning of a term or document, don't hesitate to ask your real estate agent or attorney for a plain-English explanation.

- **Parties.** The names of the buyer and seller.
- **Property description.** The property address and a simple physical description ("a single-family house").
- **Offer or purchase amount.** The price you'll pay, as long as the seller agrees and all the other terms are met.
- **Earnest money amount.** How much you'll deposit when the transaction begins but forfeit to the seller if you back out of the transaction for a reason not allowed in the contract.
- **Down payment amount.** How much you'll pay in cash toward the purchase price (unless your agreement simply includes a contingency that you qualify to finance a certain percentage of the purchase price).

- **Contingencies.** Conditions that must be met for the sale to be finalized.

- **Loan amount and conditions.** How much you'll borrow, and on what terms and with what restrictions, to finance the purchase.

- **Title.** The seller promises to be in a legal position to sell you the property, without any outstanding debts.

- **Seller representations.** You may require the seller to make certain promises about the property, for example, that to the seller's knowledge, the roof is free of defects or, in a condo or co-op, that the seller knows of no mold or pest problems in the building.

- **Fixtures and personal property.** Fixtures (items permanently attached to the property, like built-in appliances or fences) stay with the house unless you or the seller specify otherwise, while personal property leaves, unless you and the seller agree otherwise.

- **Rights of use.** If you're buying a condo, co-op, or townhouse, you may have the right to use portions of the property that you either don't own yourself or that you own jointly with others, such as a specific parking space.

- **Possession.** The date you can possess (move into) the property.

 TIP
Your lender may require you to occupy the home within 30 days after closing. That's to make sure you're using the property as a home, not an investment. (Mortgage interest rates on investment properties are normally higher and have special qualification requirements.)

- **Prorations and assessments.** How you and the seller will split recent and upcoming fees like mortgage interest, property taxes, and community association fees.

- **Closing agent (or "escrow holder").** Who will act as intermediary, assisting with preclosing tasks and holding onto any money that you or the seller deposit in advance. This may be a title company, escrow company, or attorney(s).

- **Fees.** A list of the various fees to be paid before and during the closing—including escrow fees, title search fees, deed preparation fees, notary fees, and transfer taxes—and who will pay them.

- **Expiration date.** The time limit for the seller to accept your offer.

- **Closing date.** The date the transaction finalizes and the house is legally yours. In some states, instead of an actual date, the contract will give a certain time window or say "on or before" or "on or after" a certain date.

- **Agent payment or commissions.** What payment will be made to the real estate agents representing you and the seller.

- **Damage to property.** How damage to the property during escrow (such as a fire) will affect the agreement.

- **Resolving disputes.** How you and the seller will resolve any legal disputes, and whether you'll use alternative methods before going to court (such as mediation or arbitration).

- **Entire agreement.** A statement that you and the seller don't have any other agreement and that if you want to alter the one you have, you'll do it in writing and both sign it.

- **Time is of the essence.** This confirms that if a date was important enough for you to write into the agreement—for example, the closing date—it's a fundamental part of it, and if either you or the seller don't make the date (or modify the agreement), then you'll have breached the contract.

- **Signatures.** No matter who goes first, you don't have a contract until both of you have signed.

> **CAUTION**
>
> **Put co-op agreements in writing.** When buying stock in a co-op, your state's laws may not require a written agreement. But to prevent any "he said, she said" disputes, get it in writing, anyway.

Your agent or attorney can tell you of any special contract requirements in your state. Your contract may also include other terms—for example, it may address an existing lease if the property is being rented to a tenant or may specify whether all documents must be transmitted in person, by fax, or by email.

Too Much? Not Enough? How Much to Offer

The most important, and visible, term of an offer is the price. If you offer far less than a seller thinks the house is worth, your offer might be rejected outright. But if your offer is very high, the seller might snatch it up quickly—and you might overpay. To find a balance, look at:

- whether the market is hot or cold
- the amount that comparable properties have sold for
- your agent's opinion
- the seller's position (confident or desperate?), and
- your own state of mind.

Whether the Market Is Hot or Cold

Part of what determines a house's relative worth is how hot or cold the market is. In very hot markets, some sellers set prices deliberately low, and you'll have to decide on a price that will outdo the competition without going overboard. In a cold market, many sellers accept offers below the asking price.

> **CAUTION**
>
> **Stick to your budget.** If a house costs more than you can afford, it's not the house for you—even if it's a great deal. You don't want to land in dire financial straits.

Unless you're in a really hot market or facing multiple bidders on a hot property, it's best to offer less than you're ultimately willing to pay, because the seller will probably counteroffer. If you leave room for that, you may get a better deal than you'd hoped for. If you can't reach a compromise, you can walk away.

EXAMPLE: Soledad tours a home and decides to make an offer. The asking price is $385,000, but she thinks it's worth between $365,000 and $375,000. Soledad offers $360,000. The seller counteroffers for $367,000, which Soledad accepts.

That being said, don't offer an amount so far below market value that you insult the seller: You might not even get a response. Or the seller may push right back, resisting compromise on the asking price or other terms. Of course, "insultingly low" depends on market conditions, too. In many markets throughout the country of late, where prices have dropped dramatically and there's lots of competition, motivated sellers may be more willing than ever to accept, or at least negotiate, a very low offer.

How Much Comps Have Sold For

To gauge a property's worth, you'll want to know how much houses with similar features have sold for in the area in the last six months. Your real estate agent should provide you with a list of comparables. Make sure the comps really are comparable—for example, an older home with an original kitchen isn't worth the same amount as a similar home with a remodeled, state-of-the-art kitchen in the same neighborhood.

If you spend several months searching and your agent gave you a list of comps at the beginning, ask for an updated list.

> **CAUTION**
>
> **Offering too much may get you nowhere.** If you offer more for a house than it's worth, either because you don't know any better or because you desperately love the place, it could cost you the deal. Your lender will eventually require you to have the house appraised and won't lend you more than its appraised value.

Your Agent's Opinion

Ask your agent about the value of the home you're interested in and what a reasonable offer price is. Your agent should be experienced enough, and familiar enough with the market, to express a helpful opinion. The agent will also know how to take other variables into account—for instance, the seller's eagerness to get rid of the place.

Of course, this assumes you're working with your own agent. A dual or seller's agent is obligated to get the most money possible for the seller and might encourage you to bid more aggressively than is necessary.

Clues That a Seller Might Accept a Lower Price

Here are some signs that a seller may be motivated to unload a house:

- The house has been on the market a long time, with no real interest.
- The seller has put in an offer on a new home that's contingent on the sale of the current home.
- The MLS or other listing describes the seller as "motivated" or says "seller will consider all offers."
- The seller has already moved out.
- The seller has dropped the price at least once.
- The seller has changed real estate agents at least once.
- A previous offer on the house recently fell through.
- The house is being sold in winter, when buyer interest is generally low.
- The seller plans to move out of the area by a specific date.
- The seller has a major life change on the horizon (getting married, having a child, divorcing, or retiring).
- The seller inherited the house but doesn't live in it.
- The house is an investment property and rents are falling.

The Seller's Position

When you make an offer, think about what the seller wants from the deal. For example, if you know that the seller has rejected several offers, the seller may be holding out for top dollar—but if the house is overpriced, you can possibly get around this by asking for other concessions, like payment of closing costs. Or if you know the seller has already put in an offer on another home but needs money from the current sale in order to proceed, you might get away with offering less.

> **TIP**
>
> **Find out all you can about the seller.** Your real estate agent may know some information—like why the seller put the house on the market, how long it's been for sale, and whether the seller is particularly motivated to sell.

Your State of Mind

Fatigue ("I'm so tired of looking at houses"), anxiety ("If we don't get this house, real estate prices will go up"), and excitement ("I love this house!") may all affect the terms you're willing to offer. Don't let your emotions control the process. Instead, focus on the externals: the objective value of the house based on market conditions and comparable properties, your agent's opinion, and the seller's position. Remember, if this house doesn't work out, another one will come along.

Best thing we ever did **Sleep on it.** Ross and Yasmin found an okay house for sale on the fringes of a great neighborhood. Ross says, "We liked the place, but we weren't sure we wanted to make an offer. Then we discovered that another buyer was writing up an offer that night. 'We're going to lose it!' we thought, and drafted our own offer, submitting it that very day. The counteroffer from the seller came back to us with less-than-thrilling terms, including the full asking price. We decided to sleep on it this time. The next morning, both of us realized that we'd worked ourselves into a frenzy over a house we didn't love, just because we were so anxious that someone else was going to get it. We walked away and have since bought a home we like much better."

Keeping Your Exit Routes Open: Contingencies

Let's say you agree to purchase a house with a beautifully remodeled bathroom. But then you learn that underneath the shiny exterior, old pipes are leaking and rusting—an expensive repair job. Suddenly, you feel like you're overpaying.

You can avoid this trap, and others like it, by including a list of *contingencies* in your offer: conditions that must be met before the deal will be finalized. For example, to protect against the above situation, you'd make your offer contingent on a professional inspection of the property and your satisfaction with the results.

Most offers include a set of standard contingencies that protect either you or the seller. You and the seller will agree on a date by which each contingency must be met. They're a big part of the reason that most house purchase agreements allow several weeks before the closing.

Financing

Unless you're paying cash, your contract should include a financing contingency, stating that the agreement will be finalized only if you obtain adequate financing. Of course, if you're already preapproved for the loan you want, removing this contingency will hopefully not be a problem. But remember that your preapproval probably came with conditions, such as an appraisal. This contingency lets you make sure you actually get the loan. You can also use the financing contingency period to shop around for a better deal.

Usually, the financing contingency requires you to submit a loan application within a reasonable time period, such as five days. You can protect yourself from having to accept any old loan by specifying not only how much money you must succeed in borrowing (on one or more loans), but at what interest rate and with how many points, or other terms.

Your financing contingency should be realistic. If the going interest rate is around 5%, and you condition your offer on getting a 4% loan, you're not likely to be able to meet that contingency, and you'll look less attractive to the seller.

TIP

If you pay all cash, add an appraisal contingency. Your lender usually requires a property appraisal, which you can avoid by buying with cash. But as real estate attorney Richard Leshnower notes, "You still want to make sure the house is worth the price. Include a contingency allowing you to have the house appraised and back out if the appraised value is less than the negotiated price."

Inspections

Most homebuyers have their potential home examined by at least one, and more likely two or more, inspectors. You'll want a general inspector to find any defects that can affect the property's value; a pest inspector to check for termites, dry rot, and more; and possibly other inspectors to check for things like soil stability or environmental hazards like lead-based paint or radon gas.

Your contract should include a contingency allowing you to conduct inspections and to back out of the agreement if you don't like the results or you and the seller can't agree on how to deal with needed repairs. Some contracts will also allow you to ask for approval of a survey of the property boundaries. If you're buying a newly built home, ask that several inspections be done over the course of construction.

TIP

In some states, buyers routinely do a precontract inspection. For example, in New York, after submitting an offer, the buyer has some time before the seller drafts the contract—and may use this time to schedule an inspection, so that by the time the contract is signed, there's no need for this contingency. Attorney Richard Leshnower notes, "The advantage is that you know what you're getting into, and the seller knows you won't be pulling out of the deal based on a defect found during an inspection."

Co-op buyers are in a different situation. You're not buying the property itself, you're buying shares in a corporation, and the corporation bears responsibility for the physical property. However, Richard Leshnower advises, "Getting an inspection is the prudent thing to do. If something is found to be wrong that's the responsibility of the cooperative corporation, you want to know that they will make the repair. For example, if the floor sags or creaks, support beams may have to be installed. You want to know before you purchase that this will be done and not have to fight about it later." You will also want to make sure the building is well-maintained and in good condition, by checking the co-op records and talking to the property manager, board of directors, and residents.

Attorney Review

If anyone other than your attorney drafts the final contract, you can include a contingency giving your attorney time to review it and requiring that you be satisfied with the results. You'll ordinarily set a time limit of several days after the seller accepts the offer. Being able to call in your legal eagle is especially useful when the deal is complicated or you need help understanding legal terms.

Review of the Preliminary Title Report

When you purchase a property, you normally assume that the seller has good title—meaning full ownership and the right to sell it to you, without any debts (technically called liens or encumbrances) against it. To be certain, your contract should give you the right to hire a title officer or attorney to review the title history (if a problem turns up, you can back out) and to obtain actual title insurance in case of later surprises.

Review of CC&Rs or Other Documents

If you're buying in a common interest development, you need the time and opportunity to review documents like the CC&Rs (if you haven't already), master deed, bylaws, rules and regulations, meeting minutes, and budget. If you're buying a co-op, you'll want to examine the proprietary lease as well.

These documents will tell you how well funded and well run the association or co-op is, affecting how much you can expect to pay in fees and special assessments. You'll also see what the rules are, whether you can live with them, and how they've been applied. For example, a co-op's proprietary lease may specify who can live in the unit or whether rooms can be subleased, while the minutes from a board meeting may tell you that a former owner tried unsuccessfully to challenge the sublease provision. If you don't like what you see, this contingency allows you to back out.

Board Approval

If you purchase a co-op, the transaction will have to be approved by the co-op's board of directors, which will want to make sure you can afford to make maintenance payments. If you're unable or unwilling to pay your fair share, the others in the co-op will be financially responsible. This contingency says that the board must accept you, or the deal is off.

Appraisal

Sometimes part of the financing contingency, an appraisal contingency says that you'll buy the home only if its professionally appraised value is at least as much as the amount you've contracted to pay for it. This both protects your lender and ensures you don't overpay.

Obtaining Homeowners' Insurance

You'll be required by your lender to get hazard insurance—possibly including flood insurance, depending on where you live. Making the sale contingent on actually getting it protects you if the property is uninsurable. You can also require the seller to provide a CLUE ("comprehensive loss underwriting") report. Drawn from an insurance industry database, it details the house's history of claims and damage awards. The more claims, especially serious or water-related ones, the harder it will be for you to get insurance. Even if an insurance company initially agrees to insure you, it can rescind that promise *after the closing* if it investigates a prior claim and discovers a significant risk.

Reviewing the Seller's Disclosure Report

In most states, you don't need this contingency—state law itself will condition the sale on the seller filling out a form disclosing property conditions, defects, environmental hazards, and more, and on your being satisfied with what you read before closing the sale. But in a few states, no such laws exist, or they make an exception for certain properties such as condos. One way to protect yourself is by asking the seller to provide written disclosures about the property's condition. (The other way is to get a thorough inspection.)

Final Walk-Through

Also called the buyer inspection, this allows you to take a last look at the house, usually a day or two before the closing. If it's an existing house, the purpose is for you to make sure the seller has made any agreed-upon repairs and left the place in good condition. If it's a new house, it's your opportunity to make sure the place is finished and meets your specifications. We discuss this in Chapter 14.

What About Home Warranties?

Some offers are contingent on the seller purchasing a home warranty for the buyer (a service contract mostly covering repairs to major appliances). Don't let this become a sticking point; home warranties are of questionable value, anyway (see Chapter 12).

Other Contingencies

Although we've discussed the typical contingencies, others may be included in preprinted offer forms, or you can draft your own (with the help of your agent or attorney). You may, for example, want to make your offer contingent on verifying that zoning laws allow you to convert the detached garage into a small apartment. We've even heard of cases where buyers made offers after having viewed the house only through an online, virtual tour—then added a contingency giving them a chance to see, and like, the house in person!

Keep in mind that the more contingencies you have and the less reasonable they are, the less attractive your offer becomes. If the seller has multiple offers, particularly at similar prices, the ones with the most contingencies usually lose.

Putting Your Money Where Your Mouth Is: The Earnest Money Deposit

Once you've gone to the trouble of making an offer, you want to show the seller that you're really committed to buying the property. Traditionally, you do this by putting up a cash deposit called an "earnest money" or "good faith" deposit or a "binder." If all goes well, that money is either returned to you or is applied toward your down payment or closing costs (you'll specify which in advance).

But if you inexplicably back out after you have a contract, you forfeit your earnest money (or you may have to negotiate with the seller, or even go to court, to get it back). The rationale is that the seller may have lost other opportunities to sell to other buyers by relying on your deal.

The amount of the deposit will vary depending on where you're buying; your real estate agent can advise you. For example, if local practice is to draft only a brief offer, you might submit only a small earnest money deposit offer, but then submit a larger amount when the contract is signed.

From your perspective, it's best to keep this amount as small as possible while still showing good faith and remaining competitive for your market— just in case you do end up not going through with the deal. (Even if it's for a valid reason laid out in the contract, if the seller contests it the money could be inaccessible to you until the dispute is resolved.) You'll normally place the earnest money with your escrow agent or attorney, who will hold it in a special account, inaccessible to the seller.

TIP

Know your state's laws regarding earnest money. For example, in California, a maximum of 3% of the purchase price can be kept as a non-refundable deposit.

Divvy It Up: Who Pays What Fees

An inspection fee here, an insurance premium there. Your purchase contract should deal with who pays every dollar of every charge involved in buying the house. Common ones include:

- closing agent's or escrow agent's fees for services
- title fees (title search, title insurance, and attorney's fees if needed to clarify title)
- transfer taxes (city, county, and state)
- inspections
- administrative fees (deed preparation, notary, or recording fees), and
- home warranty policy premium (if any).

Who normally pays which fees depends on local custom, which your agent can advise you on. Many preprinted forms have these fees already listed, and you'll check the box to indicate who pays what. You could just ask the seller to pay for everything, but unless you're in a cold market, the seller probably won't agree to this and it could start negotiations off on the wrong foot. Additionally, your offer will likely address real estate agent or broker fees separately from the costs discussed above.

Deal or No Deal: Picking an Expiration Date

Your offer to the seller should include an expiration date—language that says, "After this, the offer is no longer on the table." Without this, the seller could take his or her sweet time before accepting your offer. (You can also leave the expiration date open, then revoke your offer in writing later, but using an expiration date is easier.) Another good reason to put a little pressure on the seller is if you're preapproved for financing for 30 or 60 days or face other time constraints.

Some agents advise giving the seller a very short time—like 24 hours—to respond to your offer. That's to prevent the seller from using your offer to "shop" for others—telling other potential buyers, "You better get in now, and for more than this." In a hot market where a seller might be able to move a property quickly, a short expiration period can be a good idea. But if you're in a relatively balanced market, this may be interpreted as a pressure tactic.

If you're making an offer on a bank-owned property or a property advertised as a "short sale" (requiring bank approval), you may not hear from the seller for several weeks or even months. In that case, you may choose not to have an expiration date or choose one in the more distant future, then revoke your offer in writing if you find another house in the meantime.

Think Ahead: Closing Date

Your offer may also include a closing date: the date the transaction will be completed and the house become yours. (This may not be an actual date; it could also be "within 30 days of signing," "no later than" a certain date, or "on or before" a certain date, for example.) Richard Leshnower notes that, "Each of these wordings has a special meaning and should be considered carefully so that you know what to expect or how to comply." Assuming you set an exact or near-exact closing date, consider:

- **How much time you'll need.** You'll need time not only to complete all the contingencies, but also to prepare yourself to move. Between four weeks and two months is normal.

> **TIP**
>
> **Don't agree to close within a "reasonable time."** Some contracts use vague phrases like this. But what's reasonable to you may be different from what's reasonable to the seller. Far better to set a date, then later agree with the seller (in writing) to change it.

- **Impact on your first interest payment.** Loan interest is paid in arrears—meaning the beginning of one month, you pay for the interest that accrued the previous month (on October first, you pay the interest that accrued in September). You'll prepay that cost when you close (so if you close September 15, you'll prepay the interest that accrues between September 15 and 30). If you close at the end of the month, you pay only the few days left before month's end. If you close at the beginning of the month, you pay interest for the entire month. Closing at the end of the month keeps some cash in your pocket—at least for a short while.

- **Moving date.** If you plan to move the day you close (which is ambitious), schedule the closing as early in the day as you can.

- **Year-end tax concerns.** If you're buying toward the end of the year, keep taxes in mind. Any points and interest paid before the new year can become deductions for this year's taxes. On the other hand, if you don't expect to itemize your deductions this year but will the next, it's probably worth waiting. Check with a tax adviser for the timing of any other deductions.

- **Property taxes.** Depending on what state you live in, you may be able to lower your property taxes through a "homestead" or "principal residence" exemption. (Some states limit this to certain groups, like the elderly or disabled, and other states don't have it at all.) If such an exemption is available, you may need to be living in your home by the 1st of January. Check with a tax adviser.

- **Your lender's patience.** Make sure the closing date is set before your lender's commitment—or any interest rate lock—expires. You may be able to extend the commitment, but at a price.

Strategies in a Cold Market: What to Ask For

If you're buying in a cold market, your offer may be the only one the seller sees, which you can use to your advantage. Virtually every aspect of the purchase agreement—price, closing date, who pays various fees, and what the seller leaves behind (such as custom decorations)—becomes negotiable. Your agents can suggest other things to ask for, such as a $5,000 to $10,000 credit at closing, a year of paid property taxes, or a year of paid assessments (for a condo).

Of course, notes adviser Mark Nash, "Your number-one priority is a reduction in the sales price. Many sellers resist that, but it raises fewer questions with both the IRS and your lender." In Massachusetts, adviser Nancy Atwood reports, "I've also noticed sellers coming up with their own incentives—for example, offering to leave their car or widescreen TV behind!"

If your offer is well below the asking price, one way to soften the blow is to write a letter of explanation. You could, for example, highlight recent home price trends assure the seller that you love the home and have no wish to insult them, but explain that for the price that they're asking, you can get more house elsewhere.

Strategies in a Hot Market: Making Your Offer Stand Out

If you're in a particularly hot market, or just know that other buyers will be aching to get their hands on a particular house, you've got to work harder to make your offer the top pick. Here are some steps you can take:

- **Act quickly.** Chances are you're not the only one who likes this house, so you may have to submit an offer immediately.

- **Have your agent personally present your offer.** Unless the seller refuses, this can show the seller why you're better than the rest.

- **Offer more money.** Your offer will stand out if it's the highest, even by a few thousand dollars.

- **Tell your personal story.** When you submit your offer, include a letter explaining why you want to purchase the property and what you like about it. Include information that you think will be important to the seller, based on both the home itself and what you know about the seller personally. For example, if the garden is lovingly cared for, your letter might mention your own green thumb. Although some real estate professionals scoff at this idea, it's not ridiculous if it works—and a seller who is attached to a home will appreciate knowing that it will be cared for by the next owner.

★ **Best thing we ever did** **Tell the sellers our story.** Aaron and Sasha were buying their first house in a particularly hot housing market. Aaron says, "We were trying to be realistic—a friend of ours had made nine offers before one was accepted. But we pretty much fell in love with the first house we saw. In our offer, we included a letter about how much we loved it and were looking forward to raising a family there. But we didn't submit the highest offer: A developer who was going to gut and flip the property offered more. I think the sellers couldn't stand the thought of having the place ripped apart, though, because they accepted our offer instead."

- **Limit contingencies.** While contingencies like financing and inspections are normal, try not to go overboard. In some very hot markets, buyers are even willing to forgo inspections—but this is a risk we wouldn't advise taking, since the house could have serious, but not immediately obvious, structural or other problems.

- **Get preapproved.** This shows that a lender has proclaimed you loan-worthy—and the seller can be confident that you'll likely meet the financing contingency.

Best thing we ever did **Start with an all-cash offer.** Octavio and Gina were trying to buy a house in a hot market and had already been outbid twice. Octavio recalls, "On our third offer, we not only bid more than we ever thought possible, but we made a high down payment (emptying our savings) then got both our parents to lend us the rest on a short-term basis. That let us make an offer with no financing contingency. It worked—we got the house, and then were easily able to get a mortgage and repay our parents."

- **Offer better nonmonetary terms.** You might find a seller motivated by things other than money, such as the need to close quickly (perhaps to pay the mortgage on a new house) or to rent the property back from you for a while (to look for a new house).

Contracting to Buy a Brand-New Home

If you're buying a newly constructed home from a developer, the process will probably differ from what we've described above. Whether or not you've got an agent representing you, the developer is likely to pressure you to use its standard purchase offer and maybe a separate form for the contract as well. While these might look like what you'd get from a local real estate agent, they can be very different, and the variations won't be written to benefit you.

The developer's form contract may, for example, allow the developer to substitute comparable products for the products you select (so if the flooring you chose is no longer available, the developer will select "comparable" flooring). It will also likely allow a big cushion for late delivery. If you see these terms, you'll have to argue to change them—and ignore the developer's insistence that the standard form can't be altered (it can).

To add to the challenge, you might not have a real estate agent to help you negotiate, understand, and interpret the contract language. In that case, you should either have the document reviewed by an attorney before signing or include a contingency allowing your attorney to review it before the deal is done.

If you feel the agreement is too one-sided, you can alter or write in additional terms—the developer, like any seller, can decide whether it wants to deal with you on those terms. For example, you might:

- **Limit your earnest money deposit.** If you put down less cash, you'll have less at stake if the developer's performance is lacking.

- **Add a drop-dead date.** Choose a date by which the house must be completed, or you have the option of walking away.

- **Negotiate a holdback.** Add a clause requiring that a portion of the purchase price be set aside if the house isn't complete at closing, which you can then use to have the work completed.

- **Request several inspections and walk-throughs.** If your house will be constructed according to your specifications, negotiate to have professional inspectors *and* you (by yourself) go through it several times—not just right before closing. That's to make sure the installations are happening on time, and that everything is being done right.

- **Get the same quality.** If you're buying a home that looks like the model, add a clause saying that you'll get the same or better quality, not simply that the quality will meet local building codes.

TIP

Don't back down. Realtor® Mark Nash advises, "Buyers need to go head to head with pushy developers. If they don't, they're asking to be taken advantage of."

Always Late ... But Worth the Wait?

One of the most frequent complaints from buyers in new communities is that their homes aren't built on time. Even reputable builders can get pushed back due to rain or other problems. Here are some terms you can include in your offer to compensate you for delays:

- pro rata rent, based on your current home

- pro rata hotel rental, based on the market price of an acceptable hotel

- pro rata mortgage payment

- credit toward upgrades based on pro rata mortgage costs, or

- reduced price or free upgrades in exchange for allowing late delivery.

What's Next?

Once you and the seller have signed a contract, it binds you both. Now it's time to arrange your inspections, pull your financing together, get homeowners' and title insurance, remove contingencies, and close the deal. We discuss these topics in Chapters 11 through 14.

Toward the Finish Line: Tasks Before Closing

Meet Your Adviser

Sandy Gadow, a nationally recognized expert on real estate closing and escrow, and author of *The Complete Guide to Your Real Estate Closing*, widely considered the "bible of escrow and closing." Sandy maintains a website, www.escrowhelp.com, where she shares real estate articles, tips, and advice.

What she does Sandy travels all over the United States and abroad in order to continue researching and tracking the latest developments in escrow and closing. With over 25 years experience as an escrow officer, Sandy has become a frequent contributor to newspapers and other publications nationwide, including *The Wall Street Journal* online (www.realestate-journal.com), and the *Washington Post*. She's also been a guest on CNN's *Open House* and a speaker on national radio. Sandy continues to have direct contact with homebuyers as a licensed sales associate with Sotheby's International Realty in Palm Beach, Florida, and a mortgage broker with Palm Beach Mortgage. She is a featured columnist at realestatejournal.com.

First house "It was a shack, really, on two acres of land that I discovered during a hike in California's Point Reyes National Seashore. I was intrigued by the established trees, including redwood, apple, quince, and cypress; the small vineyard; and the investment potential. With a little research, I found that it was an abandoned estate, left to heirs in the Azores. I tracked down some U.S. relatives and negotiated to buy the property—it all wrapped up within 14 days, with no inspections or disclosures. This was my introduction to the property market, but it went smoothly, and I was so excited that I had no time to be nervous. When we moved in, we found cobwebs everywhere, white lace curtains hanging in shreds, beds still made, dusty dishes and glasses on the table, and jars of preserved fruits from the apple and quince trees—a scene frozen in time. It was a huge fix-up effort but is now worth many times more than what I paid for it.

Fantasy house "It would have to be two houses: one in the countryside, in the South of France preferably, where I would work on the land, relax, and eat very well. The other would be in a city, such as London, where I could work and enjoy all the cultural activities, such as museums, theatres, ballets, and concerts, with the bonus of being able to take short-break trips to neighboring countries."

Likes best about her work "First I should say that, after my first house purchase, I got the 'real estate bug' and decided the best way to learn about investing in real estate was to become an escrow officer. I started working at a local title company shortly thereafter and have been doing that ever since. I wrote my first book, *All About Escrow,* in 1981 because I saw a need to have a training manual for buyers, sellers, realtors, and escrow trainees and officers. And I still enjoy the fact that the real estate field is always changing, is always interesting, and involves meeting and dealing with new people every day."

Top tip for first-time homebuyers "Just go for it—the best way to learn how to buy your first home is to buy your first home. But I also do mean for people to do their homework, ask a lot of questions, and never take 'no' for an answer."

CD-ROM
For more tips from Sandy Gadow, check out her audio interview on the CD-ROM at the back of this book.

H aving signed a written agreement with the seller, you're in the home stretch—literally. But before you send out invitations to your housewarming party, let's focus on the few (but important) steps that remain before the sale closes:

- **Removing contingencies.** You'll need to make sure all the conditions you placed on the transaction (like getting financing and approving your inspections) are met.

- **Getting title insurance.** This is to verify that the seller has good title to the property and to protect you from claims to the contrary.

- **Deciding how to take title.** Especially if you're buying with someone else, you'll need to choose what legal form your shared ownership will take.

- **Getting ready to move.** Prepare yourself, and anyone going with you, for the big change ahead.

Some of your other responsibilities—like arranging inspections and choosing insurance—will require more discussion, provided in future chapters. Then in Chapter 14, we'll describe what actually happens on closing day.

What Have I Done?!

There are a few moments in the homebuying process where buyer's remorse —that sinking feeling that you've made a *huge* mistake—is common. If you're feeling panicked, try:

- **Calling a homeowner.** Talking to a happy homeowner reminds you that it's worth it and that your fears are completely unoriginal!

- **Driving by the house.** Take another look and imagine living there. Bring a loved one who will be excited for you.

- **Watching a home improvement reality show.** Even if you're buying a brand-new house, or not changing a thing, it's fun to see others get creative. Try the DIY Network (www.diynetwork.com) or HGTV (www.hgtv.com).

- **Doing something different.** You've probably spent too much time talking with businesspeople and reading official papers. Take a break: a long hike, a movie, or a massage.

Your purchase contract probably gave you at least a few weeks before the closing, unless you're waiting for a new house to be built. To help out, you and the seller will either hire a closing agent or one or more attorneys. They'll assist and monitor the process from start to finish.

CHECK IT OUT

For a detailed chart of who typically handles the closing in your state: Refer to *The Complete Guide to Your Real Estate Closing,* by Sandy Gadow (McGraw-Hill).

Wrappin' It Up: Removing Contingencies

One of your main objectives for the period before the closing is removing (checking off as "done") contingencies in your purchase agreement. While you might be securing a loan and getting inspections, the seller may be working on performing repairs and finding a new place to live. Each of you will need to advise the other of your progress and, with the help of your real estate agents or attorneys, provide written releases when a contingency is removed. If either of you fails to meet or remove a contingency, you can either call off the purchase or renegotiate.

TIP

If you need more time, ask. If, for example, a general inspection reveals that another specialized inspection is needed, you can ask the seller for additional time (in writing). The seller may say no, perhaps as an excuse to back out of the deal. Most sellers, however, are motivated to close the deal and will agree to a reasonable request.

Removing Your Inspection Contingency

Your purchase contract should include an inspection contingency. In Chapter 12 we'll explain what the various types of property inspections include and what problems they may reveal. Here, we're just going to talk about what to do when you get the inspector's report that explains the problems. Don't worry: Every house has hidden flaws or defects that you won't know about until the inspection.

After reviewing the report, you'll have to decide whether the problems can be fixed and whether you can live with them if they can't; who should pay for repairs; and what you'll do if you and the seller can't agree on who pays.

Whether the Problems Can Be Fixed

Discuss with the inspector or outside contractors whether the problems can be fixed and how much repairs are likely to cost. A pervasive mold problem, for example, sometimes can't be fixed, but a pet door that violates a fire code shouldn't require a team of specialists.

If a problem can't be fixed, you must decide whether you still want the property. Sometimes—like if repairs will take several weeks—the answer may be "no." In some states, your standard inspection contingency will say that you must give the seller a chance to fix a problem before backing out of the deal. But if the problem truly can't be fixed, you should be able to walk away.

Who Pays for Repairs

Your first inclination may be to ask the seller to pay for everything ("Hey, it's *her* cat that needed the pet door—I don't even have a pet!"). You can certainly try, but don't be so unreasonable that the seller says, "Forget it!"

> **TIP**
>
> **"Don't expect the house to be brought up to 'new' condition,"** **advises Nancy Atwood, of ZipRealty.** "All homes (except new construction) have issues that we refer to as 'the price of homeownership': loose faucets, old paint, and so forth. Asking for every little thing to be fixed is simply unreasonable."

If you've got some leverage—for example, you know the seller needs to move fast or that the house sat on the market for months before your offer came along—you can push harder for the seller to take responsibility. But if you know that the seller got a later offer that was higher than yours, you might want to keep requests to a minimum.

If the seller agrees to be financially responsible for all or some repairs, the two of you can handle it in one of a few ways, including:

- **Have the seller credit you a portion of the purchase price.** Normally, when a deal closes, the seller gets paid the full contract price. Instead, you can have the seller agree to have the amount needed for repairs transferred directly to you at closing or put into a special account, which you'd draw on after closing. (Lenders prefer this, because it gives you an incentive to make the repairs rather than pocket the money.) Of course, this assumes you and the seller agree on the estimated repair costs and that those estimates will be accurate enough that you don't get stuck with a big bill.

- **Reduce the sale price by the estimated cost of repairs.** The advantage to this is that, with a lower purchase price on record, your annual property taxes will be lowered, as will your transfer tax if you live in a state where they're required (and from the buyer, not the seller). And you can do the repairs whenever you like—though you'll have to come up with the cash on your own.

- **Trust the seller to hire someone to make the repairs before the closing.** This tends to be a bad idea. The seller may do the repairs on the cheap or, worse, attempt a do-it-yourself job.

- **Hire someone to make the repairs before the closing, with the seller paying.** This may raise more problems than it solves—if the repair takes longer than expected, you can bump into your closing date.

Your lender may require certain repairs to be done before the deal is finalized. If you're paying for those repairs, discuss this with your mortgage broker—creative solutions are possible, such as taking out a larger mortgage to cover the repairs or reducing your down payment to free up the cash.

New Construction: Removing the Final Inspection Contingency

If you're buying a new home, you hopefully negotiated a "final inspection" contingency, which allows you to bring in a professional to approve the completion of the house before closing. Be prepared for unpleasant surprises—legions of homebuyers have discovered unfinished construction or major defects just days before they were supposed to move in.

If this happens, your most obvious choice is to delay the closing. However, that may be impossible if you've arranged to move. Your next-best bet is to go ahead with the closing but insist on a written agreement that says the money needed to complete your house will be taken from the purchase price and put into a trust account that the developer can't touch until the work is done. To keep the developer's feet to the fire, also add new deadlines to this agreement and state that if the work isn't done by these deadlines, the money must be returned to you. You can then hire outside contractors to finish the job.

Get an attorney's help drafting an addendum to your agreement. If the developer's contract prohibits this kind of agreement or if the developer won't agree, your final option is to make a list of the remaining tasks, assign each a completion date, and insist that the developer sign it before you agree to close. This is normally called a "punch list," and developers commonly agree to it. Unfortunately, you'll have to chase down the developer to get the work done.

TIP

The developer will bring in a city inspector to do a separate final inspection—and you'll need a certificate of occupancy by the closing. Realtor® Mark Nash says, "The developer normally schedules such an inspection a couple of days before closing—you may not even know it's taking place. If the house fails, your lender won't fund your loan. Failures are usually due to basic safety or habitability issues, such as potable water, sewage, or heating." (In some communities, a closing can go forward with a "temporary certificate" that says the house is habitable, even if lacking some features.) Because the lender requires this certificate to close the deal, check with your closing agent to make sure the developer has forwarded it.

Removing a Financing Contingency

To remove a financing contingency, you must obtain financing (a loan) on the terms stated in your contract. That means either following up with whichever lender preapproved you or finding another lender that offers a better deal. (If you aren't preapproved, collect the documents described in Chapter 3 and listed on the "Financial Information for Lender" form in the Homebuyer's Toolkit.) In any case, your mortgage broker or loan officer should help you.

If you were preapproved, your lender will probably add a few requirements for your "final" approval, including verification of your credit, income, and employment; a property appraisal; and, in some cases, a property survey.

The appraisal assures the lender that you're not borrowing more than the house is worth. While the lender or broker will probably coordinate the appraisal, you'll receive a copy of the report.

Once the various requirements are met, the lender will give you an "approval" or "commitment" letter mentioning the exact dollar amount, which you can show to the seller as you remove the financing contingency. If you're borrowing from a family member or friend, you'll need a letter from that person explaining how much you're borrowing and on what terms (as described in Chapter 7). Attorney Fred Steingold counsels, "Never remove a financing contingency until you have the lender's written approval or commitment in hand."

TIP

It's not final until closing day. All commitment letters have some conditions attached, allowing the lender to back out if your financial status changes before closing. And, adviser Russell Straub warns, "I know of homebuyers who stopped paying their credit card bills, thinking they already had their loan commitment—thereby destroying their eligibility." Similarly, quitting your job or emptying your savings account could disqualify you for the loan.

What If the Appraisal Comes in Low?

When the market was hot, appraisers by and large felt safe in confirming that most houses were worth the amount they were being sold for. But ever since the mortgage meltdown, and the FHA's drafting of the Home Valuation Code of Conduct (HVCC), appraisers have had to adopt greater caution—with sometimes disastrous results. It's no longer surprising if the appraisal report comes in at tens of thousand dollars below the price that the buyer agreed to pay.

If your appraisal comes in a minor amount below the purchase price, but is still higher than the amount you wish to borrow, your lender should be willing to go through with the loan—after all, it could still foreclose and sell your house for enough to cover the outstanding balance.

But if the appraiser says the home is worth less than you plan to borrow, you may have a problem getting a loan. But don't give up yet.

Remember, appraising homes is an inexact science at best, since no two—even if they're "comparable"—are exactly alike. What's more, attempts to comply with the HVCC's new requirement that lenders hire "independent" appraisers led to situations where the chosen appraiser wasn't actually familiar with the geographic area where the house is located. (This issue should start to go away, however, thanks to recently issued Fannie Mae guidelines.)

If a low appraisal threatens to kill your deal, here's what to do:

- **Request a copy of the final report.** Lenders are required to give this to you.

- **Check for mistakes or oversights.** In particular, look for errors concerning the property's square footage and other key facts that contribute to its value. Also check whether the appraiser failed to notice upgrades, improvements, or special features about the property, such as new granite countertops or fabulous landscaping. And look at what comparables the appraiser chose to list—are they in fact inappropriate, because, for example, the sales happened before recent pending sales, or some houses are in a worse school district, or were foreclosures of uncertain condition?

What If the Appraisal Comes in Low?, cont'd

- **Check out the appraiser.** Google the name on the report. Try to find out where the appraiser's office is located and where the appraiser does most of his or her work.

- **Recheck the comparables.** Ask your agent to prepare an updated comparative market analysis, to make sure that the house isn't actually worth much less than you thought. If the appraiser's analysis turns out to be correct, you might want to either back out of the deal (which you can do without losing your earnest money deposit, based on your loan contingency) or use the appraisal to negotiate a lower purchase price.

- **Contact the appraiser directly about any issues.** For example, you might inquire further about the appraiser's knowledge of the house's geographical area, and point out (politely) any mistakes and overlooked comparable properties. Ask that, after rechecking the facts concerning the mistakes that you're alleging, the appraiser prepare an amended report.

- **Get a second appraisal.** You may be able to convince the lender to pay for this, if you can show the lender that the appraiser was wrong for the job, perhaps because he or she lacks local experience—or much experience at all. If that doesn't work, you and the seller might agree to split the cost of a second appraisal. Get a list of approved appraisers from your lender before choosing one. Have your agents prepare a list of comparable properties and key property features to give the new appraiser. Then, assuming the new report is favorable, submit it to your lender.

Both your agent and the seller's agent should get involved in this process, since you've all got the same goal—to convince the lender that lending you money with which to buy this house does not present an unreasonable risk. If all else fails, and you're still convinced the house is worth what you offered, you may want to come up with a higher down payment in order to reduce the amount you're borrowing.

Community Interest Developments: Special Contingencies

If you're buying into a community interest development (CID), you may have some additional contingencies to take care of:

- **Approval of documents.** Your contract should require that you be given, and have a chance to approve, documents such as the CC&Rs or master deed, budget, rules and regulations, and meeting minutes. This is your last opportunity to critically examine (with the help of your real estate agent or attorney) whether you're ready to be subject to the rules of the community association and whether it's financially stable.

- **Membership in the community association.** You'll likely need to submit an application to join the community association and to pay a move-in fee. Try to do this as many weeks as possible before the closing. Your application will need to be accepted before the sale can be completed.

- **Co-op board approval.** This is required for you to join a co-op and usually involves an application and interview. You'll have to provide detailed financial information about yourself, plus letters of personal and professional reference, possibly including a recommendation from your landlord. You'll also need to provide details regarding your transaction, like a copy of your contract and a commitment letter from your lender. You may also be rejected if you're caught lying on the application; if you can't comply with requirements of the proprietary lease (for example, you have a pet, which the lease prohibits); or if you seem difficult, inflexible, or hard to live near—which they'll discover by interviewing you.

> **TIP**
>
> **Interview a co-op's board, too.** "The interview is your chance to see whether you like the board," says New York attorney Richard Leshnower. "Although they ultimately decide whether you're allowed in, you should use the opportunity to find out as much as you can about the co-op, like whether any special assessments are coming up, or what condition the building is in."

Removing Other Contingencies

Other contingencies can be removed in much the same way as described above. For example, your agreement should contain a final walk-through contingency, allowing you to give your property (whether newly built or old) one last look to make sure it's in good shape and the seller has moved out. Because this often happens right before closing, we address it in Chapter 14. And getting title insurance was probably another contingency in your contract—you'll find a whole section on it below. You may have made the sale contingent on your successfully obtaining homeowners' insurance, which is fully discussed in Chapter 13.

Review your purchase agreement, particularly any deadlines for completing and removing any other contingencies. If you fail to follow the agreed-upon timeline, for example, because you didn't get around to hiring an inspector, that contingency may not be enforceable anymore. Your real estate agent or attorney should help you understand, keep track of, and meet these deadlines, but you should be well informed, too.

If You Can't Remove a Contingency

If you can't remove a contingency—for example, your loan falls through or you can't find adequate homeowners' insurance—your range of options include waiving the contingency so that the deal will go through, settling for less than you hoped for (for example, getting a higher-interest loan), or pulling out of the deal. (Of course, you can't waive contingencies that the seller negotiated for in order to protect the seller's own interests.) To waive a contingency, you'd execute a written release form. This form notifies the seller that even though you agreed to terms that can't be met, you'll still go through with the deal.

If the seller is eager for the deal to go through, you may be able to renegotiate the terms and offer less money for the house.

If, however, you decide based on the unmet contingency to pull out of the deal, you and the seller should sign a release cancelling the contract (your state may require this). You'll get your earnest money deposit back, provided the seller agrees that the contingency can't be met and the deal is over.

Aack! If the Seller Won't—Or Can't—Transfer the Property

Some deals go sour even when you've done everything you're supposed to. Here's what will happen next, if:

- **The seller calls it off.** The seller may have a change of heart about moving or think a better offer is around the corner. If so, try to resolve the dispute according to the terms of your agreement—which may mean an arbitration, mediation, or a lawsuit. You'll probably be able to recover the amount you spent getting into the arrangement, but a court is unlikely to order that you get the property.

- **The seller dies.** In theory, the dead seller's estate must honor the purchase contract. Still, the transfer may slow down, especially if the executor or administrator of the estate doesn't understand the law and doesn't want to sell. Get an attorney's help.

- **The seller won't move out.** Despite the change of ownership, some sellers just decide to stay put! You might have to go to court to evict the seller, just as you would a tenant, and to recover some of your costs. Adviser Nancy Atwood recalls, "We had a case where the seller's mother, who lived in the in-law apartment, simply refused to move. The buyers ended up renting to her for a year, by which time they'd all gotten very friendly, and the buyer was sad to see her go!"

- **The house is destroyed.** If fire, flood, or another calamity severely damages or destroys the house, look to your purchase agreement for guidance. If the seller still has legal title or physical possession, you probably won't be responsible, but if you've already received title or physical possession, you will be.

Will It Really Be Yours? Getting Title Insurance

Soon after your purchase agreement is signed, your closing agent will launch the process of getting you title insurance. (Except for a co-op, where it's not needed.) Usually your closing agent or attorney will choose your title insurer for you, from whichever of the five major U.S. title insurance underwriters it always works with or is affiliated with.

Title insurance protects you from the possibility that your seller, or previous sellers, didn't really have 100%, free and clear ownership of the house and property and can't rightfully transfer full ownership to you.

How Much Title Insurance Will Cost

On average, premiums are a one-time fee of around 0.5% of a house's purchase price, with a national average of about $605. A few states' laws set baselines—but not limits—on premiums (thanks to industry lobbying). The policy limit, or maximum payout, is usually set as the purchase price of the property.

In most Western states, the seller pays for title insurance; elsewhere, it's the buyer's responsibility. You probably settled this when you negotiated the purchase contract. To learn more, see adviser Sandy Gadow's article "How Your Title Insurance Dollar Is Divided Up," available at www.escrowhelp.com.

TIP

Buying in Iowa? By law, you can buy only state-sponsored title insurance (called a title guarantee), which costs about half as much as a private policy.

How a House's Title Can Get Clouded

Before we talk about what title insurance covers, let's focus on how a house's title can have problems ("clouds" or "defects") in the first place. At the most extreme, the seller doesn't really own the place—there have been instances of renters posing as sellers. Typical title issues are less worthy of a crime show, but more complicated. For example, the seller might have copurchased ten years ago with a brother he hasn't talked to since and doesn't realize that he needs his brother's signature to sell. Or a problem might be lurking in the more distant past.

Not all title problems involve the whole house, either. For example, liens may have been filed against the house—that is, people or agencies may have, within the public records, legally claimed the right to be paid from the proceeds of the property's sale, in order to settle the owner's debt to them. Typical debts include taxes, child support, and contractor's fees. These liens stick to the house like glue, until the house is sold or foreclosed on.

Or your new neighbors, the public, or the government may have the right to walk across or use parts of your property. This right is called an "easement." Most properties have some easements attached to them, usually by utility companies. They can be a good thing for you as the owner— perhaps your property comes with an easement to access your house using a private road belonging to someone else.

Uncovering and Removing Clouds on Your House's Title

You probably want the security of knowing the title is clear before the house is yours, right? That's what the title insurance company wants, too, to avoid paying later claims to you. Accordingly, a "title search" will be your title insurance company's first task (or your attorney's, depending on which state you live in—we'll just use the term "title insurer" from now on).

The search involves combing through as many as 50 years' worth of public records concerning the house, including past deeds, wills, trusts, divorce decrees, bankruptcy filings, court judgments, and tax records. According to the American Land Title Association (ALTA, at www.alta.org), its members find defects or "clouds" on the title in 35% of title searches.

The resulting preliminary title report (sometimes called a "title insurance commitment," "commitment of title," or "encumbrance report") gives everyone a chance to eliminate trouble spots before proceeding with the sale—or to call the sale off, if anything too serious is uncovered. It also lets everyone know the conditions under which you'll be offered insurance. For example, some things that can't be known or cleared up will be excluded from coverage.

Your closing agent should send you (and your agent and attorney) the preliminary report. Review it and ask your attorney or closing agent questions until you understand it. If the report refers to recorded documents such as easement agreements or building-and-use restrictions, ask for copies of the actual documents to see what they contain.

Also look at the included plat map (showing the boundaries from when the area was first subdivided). It's easy to read, showing the property's location and size. Look for any inconsistencies—for example, between the map and what you've observed in person ("Wait, there's a fence there!"). Don't take this map as the last word, however, because only a surveyor can tell you exactly where the boundary lines are drawn (see "Is That Tree on Your Side or Ours?" below). If any easements are mentioned in the report, ask the title insurer to point out where they are on the plat map (they won't be shown).

> **TIP**
>
> **Big reason to read the preliminary title report:** Only you know your plans for the property. Says expert Sandy Gadow, "What if you're fantasizing about building a swimming pool, but never bothered to tell anyone? Finding out there's an easement in the way later on could prevent you from building the pool. Make your future plans for the property known to your closing agent, attorney, or real estate agent."

Fortunately, you shouldn't be the one who has to act on any title defects. You won't, for example, have to call the seller and say, "Hey, pay off your taxes and child support already." Since you're being promised clear title, it's the seller's problem, not yours. The closing agent will normally call the seller's real estate agent if the report shows a defect. Most sellers agree to pay off any liens through a deduction from the purchase money at closing.

After All That Prelim Work, Why You Still Need Title Insurance

After the title search process, you can feel pretty comfortable that the house will be yours alone (subject to a few easements and exclusions). So why do you need a title insurance policy? It's protection for you and your lender in case the report missed any clouds on the title.

If you're taking out a mortgage loan, your lender will require, at a minimum, that you buy a "lender's policy" (also called a "mortgagee's policy"). This reimburses the lender for any mortgage payments you can't make because you've lost the house to someone else's claim on it. The lender may also require you to buy an "owner's policy," covering your own legal fees and other losses, as yet another step toward protecting its collateral.

Even if you're not taking out a loan from an institutional lender, you should still buy an owner's policy. No title search, no matter how complete, can predict when a long-lost relative will turn up or whether paperwork buried for years under a misspelled name will reveal a claim concerning the property.

Why Buyers of Newly Built Houses Need Title Insurance

If you're the first owner of a newly built house, you still need title insurance. The land your new house will sit on may have had a string of past owners, and what's more, if your own developer fails to pay its subcontractors or suppliers, they can file liens against your property.

You may, however, qualify for a discount if your developer previously bought title insurance on the land. The title insurer may also ask that your developer sign an affidavit stating no knowledge of judgments or liens attached to your property and that all people who supplied labor or materials for the house have been paid in full.

What's Excluded From Your Title Insurance Policy

Any issues revealed by the title search that can't be wiped out will be listed as exclusions in the preliminary report—and ultimately within the title insurance policy itself. If you aren't happy about what's going to be excluded, you can cancel the sale. Some issues won't be worth the fuss, however, such as easements allowing your local power company to come check your meter.

One of the most important limitations on coverage concerns future events. Once the policy's effective date is established, anything you do to cloud your property's title—for example, failing to pay your mortgage or a contractor who then files a lien—is considered your own problem. Your title insurance policy covers you only for events that arose before you bought the house.

You'll also find some standard, boilerplate exclusions in your title insurance policy, such as for boundary line disputes, unrecorded easements, taxes, special assessments and mechanic's liens, and mineral and water rights. You'll need to decide (probably with input from your lender) whether to buy extra coverage (endorsements) for these items if it's available. Lenders often require you to buy endorsements against unrecorded easements and liens, defects that might be found only by an inspection or survey of the property (which your title insurance company won't do), mining claims and water rights, and rights of people currently living on the property (for example, if you're buying a duplex with rental tenants).

Is That Tree on Your Side or Ours?

One of the biggest sources of homeowner angst is figuring out where your property ends and the neighbors' property begins. Bad news here: Your title insurance policy won't help forestall such boundary line disputes. Most policies include a basic plat map, but it's nothing you can draw a precise line by (although if it's clearly wrong, your title insurance will cover you). If you want certainty, call in a professional surveyor, who can put in markers denoting the exact boundaries. Many lenders insist on having such surveys done.

Unfortunately, surveyors' fees can run into the thousands of dollars, so it's best to figure out before closing whether any boundary issues might exist. Start by asking the seller whether past disagreements have arisen with the neighbors over property lines, trees, driveways, and the like. Also, review the report, especially the plat map, and take a look around the property. Note any lines that don't seem to match the map, as well as oddly placed fences, large trees that seem to straddle both properties, and neighbors' cars or possessions on your side of the supposed line. If you find any of these, ask the seller to pitch in for the survey. You can save money by asking the seller whether a previous survey was done and getting it updated. For more information, see *Neighbor Law: Fences, Trees, Boundaries & Noise*, by Cora Jordan and Emily Doskow (Nolo).

TIP

Get some additional coverage for free. According to attorney Fred Steingold, some title companies are willing to issue an owner's policy "without the standard exceptions," giving you coverage against boundary encroachments and construction liens. In return, the seller must sign an affidavit stating that there's been no construction recently that wasn't paid for, and you must provide a report from a surveyor—which your lender may order, anyway.

Yours, Mine, or Ours? What to Say on the Deed

The final step in the transaction will occur when your escrow agent or attorney prepares a new deed and files it in the public land records office. We're not there yet—but you'll need to decide in advance what the deed should say about how you've decided to legally own the place. Depending on where you live, your and any cobuyers' choices as to how to take ownership may include:

- sole property
- joint tenants with right of survivorship
- community property
- community property with right of survivorship
- tenants by the entirety, or
- tenants in common.

Your closing agent or attorney should be able to tell you which options are available in your state.

TIP

Your choice isn't permanent. Be careful about how you take title—it can affect important things like tax liability and division of the property if you die. But you can change your deed later (though you may need all the other owners' consent first).

Sole Property

If you're buying a place on your own, you'll hold it as your sole property, and your deed will reflect that. The property belongs to you alone. If you're married but nevertheless purchasing the house on your own, you can still own it as sole property. In that case, talk to an attorney, to discuss not only what to put on the deed, but how to make sure it remains your sole property. For instance, this may require you to make all the payments on any mortgage or other house-related expenses like property taxes, repairs, and upgrades. Your spouse may also need to sign a quitclaim deed giving up any interest in the house. However, that won't necessarily preclude your spouse from claiming an interest based on later contributions—for instance, if you use community property (like your salaries) to make mortgage payments.

Joint Tenants With Right of Survivorship

If you buy the property with at least one other person, you can take title in joint tenancy with right of survivorship. In most states, joint tenants must always own an equal interest in the property (50/50 if there are two of you). The most important feature of such ownership is that if one of you dies, the co-owner automatically gets the other share of the property, without the need for probate.

It's common for married couples, domestic partners, and those in committed relationships to take title this way. It's not so popular among other cobuyers, who may not want to leave their half-interest to their co-owner. Some states restrict joint tenancy—for example, in Texas it can be created only by a separate written agreement.

Community Property

This one's for married couples (and in some places, registered domestic partners) only, and then in only a handful of states (listed below). But it's usually the most beneficial option where available. Couples that own their homes as community property each own half of the property, which they can pass on to whomever they please through their wills. They can't sell or give away their share while living unless the other spouse consents.

Community property ownership often comes with significant federal tax advantages, but currently only to married couples, not same-sex couples who are married, in a civil union, or registered as domestic partners (to whom federal tax rules don't apply). Some of these same-sex couples will enjoy state tax benefits, but these are beyond the scope of this book.

When one spouse dies, the *entire* property is revalued, for capital gains tax purposes, to its current market value. This new value is sometimes referred to as a "stepped-up basis." When the house is eventually sold, the stepped-up basis is treated as if it were the original purchase price to determine the amount of profit on the sale. The higher your stepped-up basis, the lower your profit, and the lower your capital gains tax obligations. This beats the tax benefits available to buyers in joint tenancy—they also get a stepped-up basis, but for only half the property when one owner dies. For more information, see IRS Publication 555, *Community Property*, available at www.irs.gov.

Community Property States

The states that currently have community property laws include Alaska (a somewhat unusual law, in which community property is never automatic but can be chosen), Arizona, California, Idaho, Louisiana, Nevada, New Mexico, Texas, Washington, and Wisconsin.

Community Property With Right of Survivorship

In a few states, another way to hold title is "survivorship community property" (currently available in Alaska, Arizona, California, Nevada, and Wisconsin). Property held this way doesn't have to pass through probate when one spouse dies, but instead goes straight to the other spouse. It's similar to joint tenancy but limited to married couples (or registered domestic partners). It still carries the other benefits of community property, as well.

Tenants by the Entirety

Another option usually reserved for married folk—and in some states, those in registered civil unions or similar "official" relationships—is tenancy by the entirety (available in about half of the United States). Its main advantage is protecting the property from creditors. You and your spouse each own the *entire* property and can sell it only with the other's consent. In most states, if one spouse is in debt, creditors can't come against that person's share of the property—a major difference from joint tenancy. However, it's similar to joint tenancy in that if one spouse dies, the other gets the place without probate hassles.

Tenants in Common

If you're unmarried and buying with another unmarried person, you might choose to own the property as tenants in common (TIC). This allows you to hold property together in unequal shares. For example, if you're buying with a friend and have agreed on a 60/40 ownership split, your deed can reflect that. If you don't specify your shares in the deed, the split will be assumed to be equal.

With a TIC, you really have to trust your buying partner. The law will allow either of you to sell your share of the property without the other's consent, unless you make a separate arrangement. That means you could find yourself with a new housemate, perhaps one you don't like. Also, each of you owns an undivided portion of the entire property—you own 60% of the entire house, not just the large upstairs unit you and your co-owner have agreed you'll live in. You'll have to separately agree on who lives where.

If one of you dies, the other doesn't have any right to the deceased's share of the property. Instead, that person's share will pass according to the will or living trust or, if there is no such document, according to state law (which would normally give the property to a close family member). Discuss all these issues before purchasing, and write up a separate written agreement—preferably with an attorney's help—covering the use and possible sale of the property. For a refresher on the legal and practical issues of joint ownership, see Chapter 9.

Get Ready, 'Cause Here I Come: Preparing to Move

Even as you're busy with these preclosing tasks, you have another logistical issue to take care of: moving. Don't wait until the last minute to plan for how you'll transition from your old home to your new one.

Renters: Give Notice

If you're renting, you'll need to give your landlord proper notice that you're moving out. How much notice varies by state, but if you're a month-to-month tenant, one month is normal. If you can afford to pay both rent and a mortgage for a little while, plan some overlap. This will lower your stress in case the sale is delayed or repairs take longer than expected. It will also allow you to focus on the sale instead of on the move—more time reading agreements and handling contingencies, less time searching for boxes and bubble wrap.

If you have a roommate who won't be coming along, be sure to work out details such as finding a replacement for you and getting the security deposit back.

CHECK IT OUT

Every Tenant's Legal Guide, by Janet Portman and Marcia Stewart (Nolo), covers the legal rules and procedures for ending a tenancy, including situations where only one tenant is leaving.

Arrange Your Move

Even if you've always used three friends and a pickup truck, your first home might be the time to consider hiring a mover. It's much easier (especially if you're moving in or out of a space with a lot of stairs), usually faster, and not always more expensive.

Within the "move your stuff for money" arena, you have several options. The most expensive is the full-service mover, who packs everything for you and whisks it away. Another option is to pack everything up yourself, then have the mover pick it up—this tends to be cheaper. Finally, there are companies that deliver storage units to you, then pick them up and ship them to your new pad. These are typically the cheapest, but of course you do most of the heavy lifting.

> **TIP**
> **Need to access a condo unit using an elevator?** If so, Mark Nash cautions, "You'll probably need to plan ahead for moving day by reserving use of the elevator. And you can do this only after you've paid your move-in fee."

If you decide to use a mover, get in-person, written quotes from at least three different companies. If you're being quoted extremely low rates over the phone, be suspicious—reputable moving companies are usually in line with each other, and looking at the goods allows them to make reasonable estimates based on the amount of stuff you actually have.

If you're moving a long distance or interstate, choose an interstate mover licensed by the Department of Transportation (DOT). Ask for a license number, and look up basic information at www.protectyourmove.gov (by the Federal Motor Carrier Safety Administration). Your state may also have licensing requirements for in-state movers, and it's a good idea to check up on those.

Long-distance moves are charged by weight. Plan for the truck to be weighed twice—once when it's full of your stuff and again when it's empty. And know this: Movers regulated by the DOT can't charge you more than 10% over a given nonbinding estimate, so don't let the mover pull a fast one.

> **TIP**
> **Can you live without your stuff for a few days?** Some movers offer a discount if you'll allow a pickup or dropoff that coincides with another customer's. For example, if you can wait three days for someone moving to the same area, the company can move you together.

If you decide to move yourself, you may want to rent a truck big enough to accommodate your worldly goods, especially if you're going a significant distance. You might also want to call friends and family now, to ask for help.

CHECK IT OUT

For more moving help and quotes, see:

- www.moving.com, where you can compare up to six prescreened movers' rates

- www.homebulletin.net, a directory unaffiliated with any moving companies

- www.mymovingquote.com, another directory

- www.movingease.com, which gives quotes from top movers: American Red Ball, Wheaton, and Bekins.

Get the Kids Ready

A move can be traumatic for little people. According to child and family therapist Debbie Essex, "One of the reasons moving is tough on children is that they've usually had very little input into the process—they just feel like their lives are being disrupted. You can help counter that by letting them play some small role in decision making, for example, choosing a new color to paint their bedroom or where to place their bed or the posters on their wall." Here are some other ways to help make the transition easier.

- **Share it.** If you live far away but you've got pictures of the new place, show them. If you can drive by, do it. For the younger ones, remind them frequently about the new move. Reading children's books about moving can also help.

- **Keep the comforts close by.** Pack comforting items—toys, games, pictures, whatever— in easily accessible places.

> ### Children's Books on Moving
>
> Here's some comforting material for kids of various ages:
>
> - *Because of Winn-Dixie*, by Kate DiCamillo (Candlewick; Ages 9–12). A stray dog helps Opal make new friends among the unusual residents of her new hometown.
> - *The Monster in the Third Dresser Drawer & Other Stories About Adam Joshua*, by Janice Lee Smith (HarperTrophy; Ages 4–8). A spunky boy copes with moving, the strange boy next door, and a new school.
> - *Moving Molly*, by Shirley Hughes (William Morrow & Co; Baby–Preschool). Molly's new neighbors help her adjust to her new country home.

Though you may be tempted to get rid of a ratty blanket, don't do so now if it's something your child treasures.

- **Get schools squared away.** Particularly if it's the middle of the school year, do what you can to make your child's transition comfortable. Order school records. Find out whether your child is likely to be ahead of, or behind, the current curriculum and whether adjustments should be made. Take the little one to see the new school.

- **Make sure there's time to say goodbye.** You may wish to plan a going-away party, or just go out to your favorite local restaurant.

- **Get medical and dental records.** If you're going to be changing providers, make sure you have records to hand over.

- **Research activities in the new home.** Especially if you're moving during the summer, research opportunities for the kids to get involved in activities that will help them make friends.

Get the Pets Ready

For those of you with furry, scaly, and many-legged friends, here are a few important tips for making the transition:

- **Arrange transport.** Moving companies don't take pets, so plan ahead. If you're moving a long distance, some animals can be shipped as cargo on airplanes, in a pressurized (though dark) cabin. You may have to be the one to transfer your pet between planes, if you have a stopover. If driving, make sure your car is equipped to handle your pet comfortably. You may wish to get a nervous cat a pet-carrier or make sure the pets in your aquarium will get sufficient fresh water or oxygen during the transport.

- **Get vet records.** Get a copy of your pet's medical records, if you'll be seeing a new animal-care provider.

- **Get a new license or tags.** Get your pet a new identification tag—some pet stores have engraving machines. Also get a current animal license (if applicable), or update the current license to reflect your new address. If your pet is found wandering, authorities will be able to contact you in your new location. Finally, if your pet has an identifying microchip, update your contact information with the microchip company.

- **Set up space.** Keep your pet's immediate physical needs in mind as you pack, keeping food, a litter box, or other tools accessible.

- **Make sure enclosures are safe.** If your new house has an enclosed area like a fenced yard where the pet will stay, make sure there are no escape routes or hazards. You can check this out when touring the property with your home inspector.

- **Don't leave animals alone.** Unlike humans, animals don't understand why you packed up and shipped out. Leaving pets alone in a new environment can cause them anxiety. Plan to be home as much as possible in the first few days.

- **If you're moving to a new state, check its laws on bringing in pets.** Some states require you to obtain entry permits, or to undergo inspection at the border, at which time you may be asked to present a health certificate from a veterinarian. Pets traveling to Hawaii must spend time in quarantine.

- **Make sure the new house has been cleaned of old pet odors.** Otherwise, your dog's or cat's territorial instincts may be aroused—and it may start marking the space.

 CHECK IT OUT

To find out more about moving your pet, visit:

- www.petswelcome.com (under "Travel Tips" and "Moving With Pets")
- www.sspca.org (click "Pet Info"), and
- www.ipata.com (click "FAQs and News").

What's Next?

You're almost ready for the closing itself—but not quite. First, we need to explore the ins and outs of property inspections (Chapter 12) and homeowners' insurance (Chapter 13).

Send in the Big Guns: Professional Property Inspectors

Meet Your Adviser

Paul A. Rude, owner of Summer Street Inspections, based in Berkeley, California (www.summerinspect.com).

What he does Paul is a member of the American Society of Home Inspectors who has performed home inspections and consultations for Bay Area homeowners since the late 1980s. As a licensed general contractor, he has also done extensive work repairing structural damage and leaks. Besides all this, he says his most important qualifications include being both nosy and unafraid of spiders.

First house "It was a big old place, built around 1912, in South Berkeley. I bought it before I'd become an inspector—in fact, before the modern inspection industry really got started. I called a contractor I knew, who walked around the house and said, 'It's probably all right.' Then I spent the next ten years dealing with the house's incomplete brick foundation, illegal additions, and ancient roof, plumbing, and electrical systems."

Fantasy house "I'm a big desert fan, so I'd like a place in Baja California, overlooking the ocean. Let's make it complete with a swimming pool, solar power, and a self-contained sewage system. And no matter what or where the house is, I need a good-sized utility area—a basement or a big garage—to keep my tools and do my stuff."

Likes best about his work

"I left the contracting business because once you get into a project, you can't leave, no matter how difficult the clients or other aspects of the job are. With inspections, I can do one in a day, then it's over. Also, what keeps me going is the satisfaction of helping people understand things that were formerly mysterious to them—such as the difference between a standard and on-demand water heater. It's like a teaching profession. People respond, and appreciate the help."

● ●

Top tip for first-time homebuyers

"Get a professional inspection! And no matter where you're buying, watch out for water—whether it's in the basement, the roof, the siding, or whatever. Water is the most destructive element affecting homes, and water damage is difficult or expensive to fix."

CD-ROM

For more tips from Paul Rude, check out his audio interview on the CD-ROM at the back of this book.

Your purchase contract should have included a contingency saying you could back out if you weren't satisfied with the results of one or more professional inspections. While many sets of eyes—the seller's, your real estate agents', and yours—have all examined the property, it's entirely possible that no one had the expertise to identify certain problems. And even if your state requires seller disclosures, these might not be enough to cover all the bases.

This close to the finish line, you might be tempted to close your ears to your prospective home's dirty little secrets—but you'd regret it later. Horror stories abound: people who moved in only to discover that the attic becomes an all-night dance club for squirrels or the basement floods. Avoid this by picking up the phone, scheduling an inspection or two, and paying attention to the results.

This chapter will explain:

- what inspections your home needs, and how to arrange and budget for them

- what's involved in a general house inspection

- how to interpret and follow up on your general inspection report

- what's involved in a termite or pest inspection

- when you should hire additional, specialized inspectors, and

- why inspections of newly built homes—before and after they're done— are a must.

TIP

You'll be happy you did: Over three-quarters of all homebuyers obtained a home inspection before buying their homes, and nearly 100% of these people believed the home inspection was a good value. (*Source:* American Society of Home Inspectors, www.ashi.org.)

Inspection Overview: What, When, and at What Cost?

Most buyers arrange one general inspection of their house's physical and structural components, and one pest inspection (which institutional lenders usually require). In addition, buyers may also commission specialized inspections, perhaps to take a second look at a problem area like the foundation or roof, to bring in a structural engineer, or to check out something that general inspectors don't, like the condition of the hot tub. In areas where certain house features or problems are common, such as septic tanks, swimming pools, or radon, local home inspectors may add these to their inspection (at a price).

No state's laws require you to have a home inspection, so how many inspectors you bring in and how much you ask them to inspect is mostly up to you. But even if you feel confident that the seller has provided complete disclosures, or even if the seller has given you a copy of an inspection report that he or she commissioned, you should get your general inspection done. The same is true if you're buying a property "as is." Just one overlooked problem can end up costing you thousands.

 SEE AN EXPERT

The tighter your budget, the more important the inspection. According to our adviser, California home inspector Paul A. Rude, "If you have gobs of money and something wrong turns up after you move in, you can simply fix it. But if a $1,000 repair is going to break the bank, then you need to not only have the inspection, but to choose your inspector carefully."

General inspections are a relative bargain—usually between $200 and $600, depending on the house's square footage, sale price, age, and number of rooms, as well as local market conditions. Specialized inspections vary more in price, from around $100 for a radon test to $2,000 for an engineering inspection. You won't necessarily need to pay on the spot; inspections can usually be paid through escrow, and sometimes the cost can be folded into your loan. (Or you may have already gotten the seller to agree to pay for them, as discussed in Chapter 10.)

TIP

Don't rely on a home warranty to cover undisclosed defects. Most cover only appliances and other mechanical systems (such as heating) and leave out expensive structures or problem areas (such as the foundation, walls, or roof). Chapter 13 provides details on home warranties, both for preowned and newly built houses.

House Calls: Your General Inspection

The general inspection will usually be the most important inspection your house has. Its findings could make a difference to both your current negotiations with the seller and your future home maintenance budget.

What a General Inspection Includes

Assuming you use a professional inspector (licensed in states where that's offered), the investigation and resulting report will probably cover all the items listed on the Standard Inspection List, below. The report will describe the items' condition and any defects or damage.

But not all home inspections are created equal. In fact, many states don't offer an inspector's license, so people with varying specialties—or lack thereof—can decide what services to charge you for in the name of a "home inspection." Most good general inspectors started out as either contractors, builders, or engineers. (We're assuming you've already evaluated the inspector's basic qualifications, as covered in Chapter 5.)

Before hiring the inspector, confirm exactly what will be inspected, what won't be (perhaps because the inspector isn't licensed to do so), and what inspections (such as radon, or simply the inspector crawling into the subspace or attic) are optional for an extra fee.

CD-ROM

Check out an actual inspection report: You'll find one (with personal information removed) in the Homebuyer's Toolkit on the CD-ROM. A sample of this inspection report is shown below.

Sample From Home Inspection Report, by Paul A. Rude

ROOF, GUTTERS, AND ATTIC

My roof inspection is limited to a visual evaluation of the overall condition. I do not guarantee that the roof will not leak. Roof leaks are commonly due to defects that are concealed by the roofing surface. Identification of leaks typically requires testing or removal of roofing materials, which are beyond the scope of my inspection.

Roofing

The roofing is of modified bitumen. This is a petroleum-based material applied in sheets sealed at the edges with heat. I used a ladder to reach the roof and walked on the surface.

I was told that the roofing was installed about seven years ago, which is consistent with the appearance. It shows moderate wear. This type of roofing may last from 10 to 20 years, depending on environmental conditions and the quality of installation. I offer no warranty as to the remaining service life.

The roofing is wrinkled and loose from the sheathing at the left front corner. This usually indicates an installation defect. These areas should be checked regularly in routine maintenance, and may need repair sooner than the rest of the roof.

The roofing has a reflective coating to reduce deterioration due to sunlight. This coating is worn. I recommend that a qualified roofer apply a new coat. Depending on the material used, it will probably need to be renewed every few years to achieve the maximum useful life from the roofing. There are several trees near the roof. Plants touching the roofing can damage it, and leaves on the roof hold water, increasing the chance of leaks. I recommend that you keep trees and other plants trimmed away from the roof.

All roofs require routine maintenance and occasional repairs. You should have a roofer examine the roof periodically and perform any repairs required to keep it waterproof and extend the service life. After initial repairs and maintenance, a maintenance check every two or three years should be adequate. As the roof ages, maintenance will be needed more often.

Flashings

Edges, openings, and intersections in a roof should be protected by transition pieces called "flashings," usually made of metal. Visible portions of the flashings appear to meet generally accepted standards. Much of the flashing material is concealed by the roofing, siding, and other surfaces.

Part of the tile liner for a "patent" flue that once served a kitchen range has been removed at the rear. The metal shroud for the flue is still in place but it is not weatherproof; rain could blow into it, resulting in leaks. I recommend that a roofer modify it as needed to prevent leaks.

Roof Drainage

The main roof has a single drain opening through the parapet wall to a downspout at the right rear. There is a second opening for the small roof area above the front porch.

The drain opening is small and could easily be clogged with leaves. I recommend that it be cleared regularly as needed and the downspout flushed with a hose to ensure it is not clogged.

Standard Inspection List

Most inspections that meet industry standards will evaluate the house and garage, from top to bottom, including the foundation; electrical and plumbing systems; roof; heating, ventilation, and air-conditioning systems; water heater; waste disposal; doors, windows, floors, and ceilings; walls; exterior, including grading, drainage, retaining walls, porches, driveways, walkways, and any plants or vegetation affecting the house's condition; insulation; smoke detectors; floor surfaces and paint; and fireplaces and chimneys. If you're buying a townhouse or condo, some of the exterior items, such as drainage, may not be included, because they're not part of your property.

What a General Inspection Doesn't Include

Although the list above looks pretty comprehensive, it doesn't cover every possible problem area of a home. When you get the inspection report, you'll see that it lists items or areas the inspector couldn't or wouldn't investigate.

Don't worry—it's not because the inspector is slacking. Instead, many of these disclaimers arise because the inspector can't see through walls, pull up carpeting, or dig underground. And no one expects the inspector to take a dip in the pool or hot tub. Also, because the average home is estimated to contain 60,000 bits and pieces, inspectors may look at only representative samplings of things like electrical outlets and windows.

Safety is another important limitation. The inspector isn't required to risk injury. Exactly where the line gets drawn might vary: One house's crawl space, for example, might be accessible, but another's too narrow or wet. And further limitations can arise if unscrupulous or lazy sellers create barricades, for example by piling up boxes in front of the door to a room or leaning bicycles near the back of a garage. If this happens, contact the seller and ask that the blockage be removed immediately. If that doesn't work, follow up with a request that the seller clear the area and allow it to be inspected again, at the seller's expense.

If your property has unusual features such as a swimming pool, hot tub or sauna, playground equipment, security system, seawall, breakwall, or dock, the inspector will probably not evaluate these. The exception would be if the inspector happens to have specialized expertise and is willing to put it to use. If you know these will be issues for you, seek out inspectors with those specialties.

Finally, every property has a unique array of appliances, furnaces, water heaters, and other manufactured items—some of which may have been recalled due to safety concerns. Most experienced inspectors know about major recalls and will mention them in their reports. But to be thorough, do your own search by noting the brand name, manufacturer, model, and serial number, then searching the site of the U.S. Consumer Product Safety Commission, www.cpsc.gov.

Tagging Along at Your General Inspection

You and your real estate agent normally can—and should—follow along while your house is being inspected. There's nothing like seeing problems for yourself and being able to ask questions.

> **TIP**
>
> **"If an inspector asks you not to show up until he or she is finished, hang up the phone,"** advises retired Austin, Texas, inspector Paul MacLean. You should wonder why someone you hired doesn't want you—the paycheck—to watch how he or she works.

As a bonus, the best inspectors will tell you practical tips above and beyond the report, such as advice on future maintenance and potential remodeling. Plan on spending two or more hours at the general inspection, and definitely not less than one hour. Many unhappy consumers tell stories of inspectors who took only an hour to complete a general inspection and missed something important.

Here's how to make the most of the inspection:

- **What to bring.** Bring pen and paper, and make a list of any potential trouble spots you saw on prior visits—such as cracks in the walls or signs of basement leakage. Also bring copies of any past inspection reports provided by the seller, as well as any disclosure form that the seller filled out. That way the inspector can follow up on the issues mentioned.

- **What to wear.** Wear comfortable clothing that you don't mind getting scuffed, and bring a dust mask in case you venture into the crawl space or attic or onto the roof. You aren't obligated to follow along everywhere, and the inspector might not encourage it (you'll be doing so at your own risk—no fair suing the inspector if you're injured).

- **Bring a camera or video recorder.** Pictures and videos of the inspection will remind you of problems that the inspector said didn't need immediate attention but should be watched. Ask the inspector for permission first— some aren't comfortable with being photographed or recorded.

- **What not to do.** Don't crowd the inspector or interrupt with questions about your remodeling plans. Be attentive, but give the inspector space to do his or her job. Try not to be one of the buyers who blurts out nervous questions like, "Is everything okay?" before the inspector has even had a chance to look. Save unanswered questions for the end of the inspection, or ask the inspector to orally summarize the findings.

> **TIP**
>
> **Don't make it a family affair.** We asked California inspector Paul A. Rude what he wishes people would do differently during the inspection. His reply: "Bring fewer people along. Often the whole family wants a chance to see the house, and they're feeling festive, planning for new curtains, and maybe taking care of a crying baby. All of this is distracting if I'm trying to explain why the house may need $100,000 in repairs."

Say What?
Understanding Your General Inspection Report

Within two to three days of the general inspection, you should receive a written report, several pages long. It may go straight to your agent, so be sure to get a copy. (We know of at least one horror story where an agent went on vacation and forgot to forward an inspection report containing information about sewage issues—the buyers had to spend thousands of dollars on repairs after moving in.)

The best inspectors give you a descriptive narrative report. (The Home-buyer's Toolkit on the CD-ROM includes a sample, from inspector Paul A. Rude.) Some include digital photos (nice, except that some inspectors use them to replace actual explanations of the problem). At the other end of the spectrum, cookie-cutter franchise operations give you a computer-generated, check-the-box report, where each item may be simply marked "serviceable," "not serviceable," "repair or replace," or something equally vague.

No matter what your report looks like, read the entire thing, even if your agent summarizes it for you. Realize, however, that some of the report is just boilerplate—for example, disclaimers regarding areas that the inspector takes no responsibility for. The purpose is usually to head off lawsuits.

Lesson learned the hard way **Shoulda read the report.** After the inspection, Julian's real estate agent told him that the report showed "no major defects." Julian's exact words were, "Awesome." He closed the sale and moved in. That winter, Julian watched water leak into the house through its aged roof. He says, "I finally read the report, ready to yell at the inspector for incompetence. But no, the leaky roof was right there! There went hundreds of dollars that I could have asked the seller to pay if I'd been paying attention."

How Bad Is It, Really?

Every house has problems, and most can be fixed or lived with. The seller has no obligation to provide you with a flawless house, and the inspection isn't a repair list—it just gives you an opportunity to negotiate. Plus, the inspector wouldn't be doing the job right without describing everything from a missing cover plate on an electrical outlet to a crack in the foundation. And the inspector has to worry that if the report leaves something out, you might one day respond with a lawsuit.

The inspector should be able to prioritize the necessary repairs and explain whether they need immediate work. But don't expect the inspector to tell you that your house has "passed" or "failed." While buyers and agents frequently ask whether a problem is serious or is a "defect," some inspectors rightfully shy away from making such judgments. One buyer's defect is another buyer's "no big deal." The inspectors don't want to scare you unduly—nor do they want you to later complain that they didn't ring sufficiently loud alarm bells.

Don't ask the inspector to give you an exact estimate of repair costs, either. That's partly because you shouldn't be hiring the inspector to do the repairs (that would create a conflict of interest), so any cost estimate is hypothetical. It's also because some repairs may need a closer look and can be approached in more than one way—for example, crumbling mortar between chimney bricks might be fixed with either a quick patch or a complete teardown and rebuild. You and a separately hired contractor would decide on the solution.

It's okay to contact the inspector after reading the report and ask for clarification or more information. Like every professional, inspectors have their own jargon, and you may need a translation of some of the report's more arcane language. Other common questions include, "How important is this really?" or "How soon do I need to fix this?" And if you notice something missing from the report, ask for a written addition.

Getting Estimates for Repair Needs

If not to the inspector, to whom do you talk about the cost and other details concerning repair needs that turned up in the report? You'll need to make some educated but quick decisions about whether the problems justify backing out of the sale or at least asking the seller to pay for the repairs (as discussed in Chapter 11). Your inspector may be able to recommend follow-up professionals. Your real estate agent can also help here.

Termite or Pest Inspections

Years ago, most everyone got a pest inspection, to check for fungus, dry rot, and "wood-boring organisms"—creepy crawlies that dine on homes, such as termites, carpenter ants, powder-post beetles, and carpenter bees. And almost no one got a general home inspection. Today, the pattern has reversed. The standard home inspection is the broader, structural type, while pest inspections remain a separate specialty.

In regions with pest problems, it's common and wise to get both types of inspections. Most parts of the United States do have some sort of pest trouble, whether it's termites in the West, old-house borer beetles in the East, or carpenter ants in the Midwest and South. In fact, your bank or lender will probably insist on a pest report, and that any problems be corrected before you move in.

Your seller may have had a pest inspection done before putting the house on the market—and if you're lucky, has already had the repairs done. But, as with every inspection, you may still want to have your own, independent one done. Ask your real estate agent about the reputation of the seller's pest inspector. Your bank or lender, in fact, may demand a second inspection after the first one is more than 30 days old (these house pests are quick eaters).

How Gross Are They? Termite Facts

- Termites actually eat wood (well, technically, protozoa in their gut do the digesting). All that wood gives the termites gas—enough, some believe, to boost global warming.

- Termites move slowly but will keep on trekking for up to one-half an acre in search of a tasty wood source.

- A termite colony may contain between 100 and 1 million-plus termites.

- Subterranean termites can, in a major infestation, destroy a house in two years.

- At least you're not househunting in Africa—one species there builds cement-like mounds that are the largest non-man-made structures in the world. If the termites were as big as people, their towers would be 180 stories high.

In a few states, a mixed pest/home inspection is common or even standard. But it's worth trying to find separate specialists if you can, since finding one who is truly expert in both house structure and the various pests is difficult. Adding to the confusion, a regular home inspector may alert you to obvious signs of pests. (Though they may have to be careful how they word this: In Washington State, for example, it's illegal for anyone but a licensed pest inspector to make any determinations about pests in your home.) The general inspector will then likely suggest a follow-up pest inspection.

Budget around $150 to $300 for the pest inspection. Plan to tag along—it won't take as long as the general inspection, usually no more than one hour.

When to Get Other, Specialized Inspections

Your general inspection and pest inspection may be enough. But, as Texas inspector Paul MacLean notes, "Your general inspector is like a family physician, who gives you the big picture—but may need to refer you to a heart specialist or brain surgeon for potentially serious conditions or complications." Consider hiring more inspectors if:

- your inspector recommends them, such as for electrical or plumbing issues; structural engineering issues like a damaged foundation; a house on a steep hillside; unusual construction types like a house built on a pier; a defect in a retaining wall; drainage or soil problems; and toxic substances like asbestos, lead, or radon

- you know you're allergic or sensitive to, or are worried about, particular toxic substances such as mold

- you notice a potential problem in an area your inspector's report doesn't cover, such as unpleasant aromas around the septic tank

- the property has special features such as a swimming pool, septic tank, or boathouse, or

- the seller's disclosure report revealed potential problems, such as lead or asbestos, that your general inspector didn't test for.

> **TIP**
>
> **"What's the 800-pound gorilla in your area?"** According to adviser Paul A. Rude, every geographic area has some potential natural disaster. How your home stands up to this gorilla's pounding should be among your first priorities in a home inspection. On the West Coast, it's earthquakes, floods, or mudslides; in the southeastern United States, it's hurricanes; in the northern states, it's extreme cold weather and snow.

Trouble in Paradise: Inspecting Newly Built Homes

If you're buying a house that hasn't yet been built, you have every right to expect something in mint condition—like a shiny new raincoat. But if you're like many homebuyers, you may soon discover missing buttons and leaking seams. It's been called an epidemic of bad workmanship: In a 2005 sample, *SmartMoney* magazine found that one in ten new houses had problems the owners were sufficiently mad about to contact their state licensing board. (See "Heartbreak Houses" in *SmartMoney*, September 2006.) And the down economy hasn't improved the situation.

It's not hard to understand the source of the problem: Developers respond to buyer demand, and everyone wants their house built *today*, or at least tomorrow. Buyers also want hard-to-build luxury features like vaulted ceilings and giant windows. Meanwhile, experienced contractors or subcontractors are in short supply. So, some developers cut corners; hire unqualified, inexperienced workers; or just plain make mistakes.

Worse still, once developers finish a project, they usually move on—and try to avoid phone calls. Some even set up shell corporations and intentionally go bankrupt. And some states' laws (lobbied for by developers' associations) allow the developer a chance to fix the property before you sue, without necessarily specifying a timeline. That gives the developer every incentive to delay fix-ups.

The upshot is that you need to monitor the process well before the house is built. Get not only a general inspection of the completed house, but interim inspections during its construction. Yes, this will cost hundreds more than an average general inspection, but it's worth it—the average newly built U.S. home needs over $5,000 in repairs. And don't count on a city inspector or the developer's so-called "third-party" inspector to do the job—they're not necessarily on your side. Plus, the city inspector is looking only for code compliance, and won't comment on many other issues.

Problems With Newly Built Homes

Here are some all-too-common defects:

- **improper weather detailing** around windows, doors, chimneys, and decks, and improperly installed siding (causing leaks)

- **poorly graded land or faulty sewer and water main connections** (causing flooding, sewer and drain backups)

- **roof problems,** such as improperly installed shingles and poor design

- **ventilation problems,** most often in the attic, roof, kitchen, and bathrooms, such as blocked or improperly installed vents (leading to mold and moisture problems)

- **building code violations,** such as improper rail heights on stairs, ungrounded electrical outlets, loose wiring, flues too close to wood, and pipes that don't extend to the drain.

TIP

"I inspect a couple of new homes every week, and I always find problems," says Texas inspector Paul MacLean. "The worst was in a two-story house, where the master bedroom upstairs had a whirlpool. I filled up the tub and turned on the jets. Next thing I know, a subcontractor who happens to be downstairs is yelling, 'Hey, do you know you've got water coming through the ceiling?' The plumber hadn't hooked things up correctly."

Hopefully, your purchase contract included the right to make all these inspections. Now you just need to follow through and schedule them. Remember, no one has lived in this house before, and you don't want to be the first to find out that the chimney top was cemented over, the drains flow under the house without connection to further piping, or the hot water or power turns off without warning (all real stories).

Unfortunately, even if your purchase contract allows inspections—and even if state law backs up your right to an independent inspection—you may encounter extreme resistance from your developer. When demand for their properties is high, developers have been known to refuse outright, figuring someone will be in line behind you, ready to buy with no inspection. In a slow market, however, you have more leverage. Do what you can to claim your rights.

 CHECK IT OUT

Still not convinced of the need for new home inspections? Find out about real complaints or class-action lawsuits against specific builders, at:

- www.hadd.com, by Homeowners Against Deficient Dwellings, and
- www.hobb.org, by HomeOwners for Better Building.

What's Next?

Completing the inspection, and negotiating over repairs and removing the inspection contingency, is a major step toward buying your first house. Now take steps to protect its future physical condition by learning how to select the best homeowners' insurance policy.

Who's Got Your Back?
Homeowners' Insurance and Home Warranties

Meet Your Adviser

Mary I. Husk, Vice President of Faculty Development for The National Alliance for Insurance Education & Research in Austin, Texas (www.scic.com). The mission of The National Alliance is to provide insurance and risk management professionals of every experience level with integrated, practical continuing education, timely research, and designation opportunities—advancing the profession through education. This organization offers over 2,500 insurance and risk management programs and courses a year in all 50 states, Puerto Rico, and Mexico. Mary's professional designations include being a Certified Insurance Counselor (CIC), a Certified Risk Manager (CRM), and a Chartered Property Casualty Underwriter (CPCU).

What she does   In addition to developing course curricula for The National Alliance, Mary teaches courses to insurance agents, agency representatives, and insurance company personnel. In addition, she manages the CRM Mexico Program. Mary also writes articles for magazines and trade journals on personal insurance coverage, trends, and issues. When she's not helping people understand insurance requirements, Mary enjoys ice skating, tennis, coaching a Miracle League baseball team, and growing African violets for show.

First house   "It's the house my family and I still live in, 23 years later! At the time, it was in the outskirts of Austin, Texas, but the city has grown to where it's now the area many homebuyers look at first, because of its convenience to schools, downtown, and more. The house was brand-new when we bought it, a two-story place with high ceilings and a very open design. One of its best features turned out to be the large game room. We bought a pool table, which made our house a favorite gathering spot for my son and his friends. We could get to know who he was spending time with, and always had a house full of kids."

Fantasy house "Just a one-story place, somewhere near the beach, where it's calm and peaceful. It doesn't matter what style. I'd choose practical furnishings, nothing fancy. The idea would be to find a place that's easy to maintain, so I could spend my time walking on the beach and relaxing."

Likes best about her work "All the people I get to work with, not only within the office but around the United States and other countries. Recently I've been traveling to Mexico on work-related projects, where I can practice using the Spanish I spoke with my parents and grandparents growing up."

Top tip for first-time homebuyers "Do your research—check the location, and make sure the style of the house is something you'll be comfortable with over the long term. We didn't expect to be in our house for this long, but it worked out that way, and mostly for the best. Realize also that your needs may change over the years. For example, the open design of our house was great when my son was a baby and I needed to hear what he was up to, but not so great when he became a teenager and wanted privacy!"

Once you own a home, you'll want to guard against all kinds of bad stuff, be it fires or thieves or lawsuits. While you can't prevent everything, you can protect yourself by buying insurance to cover potential losses. In this chapter, we'll explain:

- hazard insurance, or the portion of your homeowners' insurance covering physical damage or loss involving your property and possessions (required by lenders)

- liability insurance, or the portion of your homeowners' insurance covering injuries to people on your property or caused by members of your household (including pets), and

- home warranties, or service contracts for your house's appliances and systems.

CD-ROM

For further help on insurance terminology: See the "Homeowners' Insurance Terminology" list in the Homebuyer's Toolkit on the CD-ROM.

Damage Protection: Hazard Insurance

Hazard insurance compensates both you and your lender for physical damage to your property and its contents caused by fire and smoke, wind, hail, lightning, explosions, volcanoes, riots and vandalism, theft, water damage, and similar events. For example, it will cover roof repairs after a tree falls during a windstorm, replacing your stereo after a break-in, and fixing ceiling damage from your leaking tub.

Personal property that you've temporarily taken outside your home may also be covered under the standard policy—for example, items stolen from your car or even your child's dorm room.

Beyond the House: Property That's Separately Itemized

The core of your homeowners' insurance covers hazards to your house and everything attached to it. That's not enough! The insurance company will tell you exactly how much more you'll need to pay for coverage of:

- Structures on your property other than your house, such as a garage, shed, pool, or cottage, as well as fixtures attached to the land such as fences, driveways, sidewalks, and retaining walls.

- Personal items such as jewelry, clothing, artwork, and computers, up to a certain dollar limit.

- Property and inventory used for a home business.

- Loss of use. Your daily necessities such as motels or rent and meals, minus the amount you'd normally spend on necessities each day, while your house is undergoing major repairs after a loss.

- Your trees, plants, shrubs, and landscaping.

You can decline coverage of a few of the above items, but in most cases you'll need to include them in the package of what you pay to insure.

Damage Your Hazard Insurance Won't Cover

Between the hail storms and volcanoes, you'd think every type of physical damage to your house and property would be covered—but it isn't. Take a close look at the mostly boilerplate section of the draft policies called "exclusions." Flooding, earthquakes, mudslides, police activity, power outages, sewer backups, dry rot, vermin, war, nuclear perils, losses if your house is vacant for 60 days or more, or losses caused by your own poor maintenance or your failure to preserve or protect the property after it's been damaged are all likely excluded.

Insurance companies usually don't want to sell you coverage for these high-risk, high-expense types of damage at any price. But there are exceptions, where you can buy extra coverage from the insurance company or another source (like flood and earthquake insurance, which we'll talk about shortly).

Most Dangerous U.S. Town

Hogan's Alley, Virginia, averages two bank robberies a week and is a hotbed of criminal, terrorist, and mob activity. Don't worry, you can't buy a house there—it's owned by the FBI, for use as a training ground. Built by Hollywood set designers, it has all the classic small town features: a bank, a post office, a laundromat, houses, and more. See www.fbi.gov.

The key is to buy added coverage for hazards that can cause huge damage (like sewer backups) or are big risks in the area where you live—like earthquakes in parts of California, hurricanes along the Gulf Coast and Eastern Seaboard, or local concerns such as sinkholes in parts of Florida.

Who Should Buy Flood Insurance

Standard homeowners' policies don't cover damage from flooding, though your lender will require you to get it if you're in a designated flood zone. But more than half the people whose homes were damaged by Hurricanes Katrina and Rita weren't in a flood zone and had no flood insurance. Unfortunately, flooding is the United States' most common natural disaster, affecting people who live nowhere near water. Melting snow, overflowing creeks or ponds, a weak levee, or water running down a steep hill can all cause flooding. The good news is, flood insurance is cheaper if you're not in a flood zone.

Flood insurance is available from the National Flood Insurance Program (www.floodsmart.gov), but many consider the coverage limits too low—currently a maximum of $250,000 for a one-to-four-family structure, and $100,000 for personal property. You can buy additional coverage, called "excess" flood insurance, from specialized companies (some available through your insurer).

CHECK IT OUT

Could your house be flooded? After checking the seller's disclosures, get more information from www.floodsmart.gov (enter your address under "How can I get covered?"). Also check with your local flood control board or city building department.

Who Should Buy Earthquake Insurance

Standard policies also don't cover earthquake damage—and you don't have to live in San Francisco to experience one. The U.S. Geological Survey estimates that earthquakes pose a hazard to 75 million Americans in 39 states. The top five earthquake-prone states include Alaska, California, Hawaii, Nevada, and Washington. And scientists think the Midwest may be overdue for some major quaking, in Arkansas, Illinois, Kentucky, Missouri, and Tennessee.

To cover earthquake damage, either add an endorsement to your homeowners' coverage or buy a separate policy. Expect high costs—but given the level of potential damage, it's worth it.

CHECK IT OUT

Is your house in earthquake territory? After checking any disclosures from your seller, go to the U.S. Geological Survey website at http://earthquake.usgs. gov (Click "Earthquakes," then "Earthquake Info by State").

How Much You'll Receive

Most insurance doesn't give you a blank check but sets a dollar maximum on your coverage. And the limit isn't your only concern: How your house or property is valued before you reach the limit can be just as important. For example, a $100,000 personal property limit might sound okay—but you'll never reach it if the policy treats all your old property as nearly worthless. Keep reading to pick up crucial tips for making sure you get enough back.

Is Your Hazard Coverage Enough to Rebuild Your House With?

Let's take the most unlikely (but scary) scenario: A fire or other hazard decimates your house. You might then expect your insurance company to pay for it to be rebuilt, just as it was. But that's not usually how it works.

The Norm: Replacement Cost Coverage

The amount you receive to rebuild under a standard policy will be a set dollar figure—calculated in advance. It's called "replacement cost" coverage, but it's only indirectly connected to your actual rebuilding costs. Replacement cost coverage literally means the insurance company's representative will, when you're arranging to buy the policy, ask you about the house's size, location, number and type of rooms, building materials, amenities, and more. Then the rep will estimate your house's replacement value, often using industry software called a "costimator." You'll either be covered for the exact "costimated" amount or, if you buy extended replacement cost coverage, 125% of that amount.

Many homeowners just accept the replacement cost figure without question. But it can be off the mark, particularly if building costs go up, a widespread natural disaster increases demand for contractors, or your house has historical features that will be hard to recreate. Ask a local contractor or builder's association how much a house of a similar size, with similar features, would cost to build. If the insurance will be low, either talk up your house's value (for example, making sure the rep factors in any special features) or buy an "inflation guard," which raises the stated value of your house by a set percentage annually.

TIP

Buying a house built more than 20 years ago? Consider adding an endorsement called "ordinance or law—increased amount of coverage." This covers your extra repairs to meet modern building codes.

The Ideal: Guaranteed Replacement Coverage

If you look hard, you may find a policy that guarantees payment of 100% of your repair or rebuilding costs, without any limits. This rare creature is called a "guaranteed replacement cost" policy. But if your house has historical features that are hard to reproduce, finding such a policy will be especially difficult.

Best thing I ever did — **Get 100% guaranteed replacement coverage.** Ellie knew she'd used a good insurance agent—but until her home was destroyed in a fire, she didn't realize how lucky she'd been. Ellie says, "You can't tell by looking that the house is a total loss—its construction was partially brick, and it's still standing. But everything inside was either burnt or destroyed by smoke damage. With the 100% replacement cost coverage, we can tear down what's left and rebuild the whole thing just like it was."

To Be Avoided: Actual Cash Value Coverage

Don't buy an insurance policy that pays the "actual cash value" of your house. These are sometimes pushed on people with older houses or ones with an inadequate water supply (a fire danger). You'll get the house's replacement cost *minus* any depreciation or wear and tear that it's suffered since being built.

Will Your Living Costs Be Covered While the House Is Rebuilt?

If your house needs major repairs or rebuilding, you probably don't want to pitch a tent outside. Standard policies include a "loss of use" provision to cover the extra costs of living elsewhere, like hotel bills and restaurant meals.

Most policies limit your living-costs coverage to one year. But two years is better, giving you time to find an architect or contractor (which can be tough after a major flood or wildfire), develop plans, and actually build.

Some policies instead place a dollar limit on your living expenses, often 20% of the total insurance on your house. If so, calculate average rental and utility costs in your area and figure out whether that will be enough.

Will Your Coverage Be Enough to Replace Personal Possessions?

You'll want to be able to replace the stuff inside your house if it's lost, stolen, or damaged. Look for a policy offering "replacement value," meaning the actual cost of buying a new piece of jewelry, television set, refrigerator, or whatever.

The alternative, "actual cash value," is far less satisfactory. You'd get the amount your stuff would sell for used, taking depreciation into account. It's not far different from estimating how much your things would sell for on eBay.

Regardless of how much you can claim for each individual item, a cap will be placed on the total amount you can receive, based on a percentage of the insurance on your house itself, usually 50%–70% of your maximum payout. So if you've got $375,000 in insurance on your house, you'd get $187,500 worth of coverage for its contents. If this sounds like more than enough, great.

If it doesn't, draw up a list of all your worldly goods—furniture, clothes, jewelry, toys, sports equipment, art, light fixtures, appliances, electronics, CDs and DVDs, garden equipment, and more—present it to the insurance company, and ask how much added coverage would cost. Even if you don't create this list now, do so after you move in, in case you ever need to make a claim.

CHECK IT OUT

Free inventory software: It's available from the Insurance Information Institute, www.iii.org (under "Software," click "Home Inventory Software").

Got Expensive Items Needing Separate Coverage?

Talk to the insurance rep if you own any big-ticket items such as jewelry, furs, firearms, coins, or silver. In a standard policy, separate limits may apply to these if they're stolen, usually between $1,000 and $2,000 in total. You'll need to pay more for endorsements insuring each such item for its appraised value—but thefts are among your most likely losses. This coverage will also take care of "accidental disappearance," including dropping your emerald ring in the garden.

Protection for Other's Injuries: Liability Insurance

Liability insurance compensates you and people who visit your property for two things:

- **"Medical payments to others."** This pays the medical bills of people from outside your household who are accidentally injured while on your property or by you or a household member, including your pets, whether on your property or elsewhere.

- **"Personal liability."** This covers your legal fees and any damages the court orders you to pay, such as medical expenses and lost wages, if you get sued by someone who was injured or whose property was damaged by someone in your household (human or animal). It covers events not only within your house, but anywhere—if you land on a sheep while parachuting in Scotland, your debt to its owner is covered.

Your liability coverage has its limits, though. You'll need either additional coverage or a separate policy for injuries related to your car, home business, nanny or other domestic worker (in some states), tenants (if any), and some pets (depending on their breed, behavior, or other circumstances).

> ⓘ **TIP**
>
> **Agreed to rent your house back to its former owners?** You'll need separate liability insurance to cover your tenants for this time period; talk to your insurance company.

Pet Liability Issues

Although dog bites and other pet-related injuries are ordinarily covered, the costs have been going up, and the insurance industry is getting stricter about this. If you've got a Rottweiler, Doberman, German Shepherd, Chow Chow, Pitbull, Husky, or other breed with a bad reputation, your insurance company may refuse liability coverage or raise your premium. A few states, such as Michigan and Pennsylvania, prohibit insurers from singling out entire dog breeds. But the insurer can still exclude a "bad" dog, that is, one with a bite complaint filed against it. Also be prepared to pay more or be refused liability coverage based on your snake, alligator, spider, or exotic bird.

If you can't find a homeowners' policy that gives you liability coverage, you could buy one that's limited to hazard insurance (unless you're in a state that requires it for certain breeds). But do so only as a last resort—the average cost of a dog bite claim is nearly $25,000. Look for a company that doesn't ask about your pet or one friendly to your dog breed.

CHECK IT OUT

Don't bark up the wrong tree. When looking for homeowners' insurance that covers your dog, check out these websites:

- The Insurance Information Institute, at www.iii.org (search for "Dog Bite")
- The American Kennel Club, at www.akc.org (click "Owners," then "Homeowners' Insurance")
- The American Rottweiler Club, at www.amrottclub.org, which keeps track of all manner of dog-breed related legislation.

Get Enough Liability Coverage to Cover Someone's Injuries

A standard homeowners' policy will give you a minimum of $100,000 in liability coverage. But you can imagine how someone's medical bills could top that. And if you're sued, you could end up paying additional damages. Rather than putting your house at risk of being sold to pay a court judgment, simply increase your liability coverage to a more realistic level, between $500,000 and $1 million. That should raise the premium by only about $40.

Whether to go even higher depends on how much you have to lose. If your net worth (including future earnings) is over $1 million, consider buying an umbrella policy or excess liability coverage. This starts to pay after you've used up your homeowners' liability coverage.

> *Taking one's chances is like taking a bath, because sometimes you end up feeling comfortable and warm, and sometimes there is something terrible lurking around that you cannot see until it is too late and you can do nothing else but scream and cling to a plastic duck.*
>
> —Lemony Snicket

Your Out-of-Pocket: Homeowners' Insurance Costs

U.S. homeowners spend between about $450 and $1,300 per year for homeowners' insurance (the whole package; hazard and liability). How much you'll pay will depend on such variables as:

- where you live (Texas, Louisiana, and Florida tend to be the most expensive, and Wisconsin, Idaho, and Utah the least)
- risk factors—both the house's and yours
- how much coverage you get (what's covered and the dollar limits)
- how high a deductible you agree to
- discounts offered by your insurance company, and
- your ability to seek out the best price by shopping around.

Risk Factors That Affect Your Insurance Rates

Topping the list of factors that an insurance company will look at before quoting you a price are:

- the house's age (newer homes are considered less risky, having been built according to modern codes)
- the house's size, condition, and number of rooms
- other physical aspects of the house and property (for example, in some parts of the country, brick construction is considered lower risk than wood, because it reduces the possibility of fire damage)
- the geographical location of the property (such as near the coast, on a hill prone to mudslides, or in hurricane territory)
- proximity of a fire hydrant or other water supply and a fire station
- claims filed on the property by the current or past owners (usually up to five years ago)
- your personal credit score, and
- your history of filing insurance claims on other properties.

TIP

Trampolines and old roofs now on the "high-risk" list. According to our adviser Mary Husk, "Some insurance companies are no longer interested in insuring a house with a roof that's older than ten or 20 years, or they might quote you a higher rate for coverage. The reason seems to be that many homeowners fail to maintain their roofs, and then a storm may come through and wipe out a whole neighborhood's worth of roofing—a big expense. Also, whether you own a trampoline is now a standard question—the insurer will either list trampoline-related losses as an exclusion or refuse coverage altogether."

Reasons to Choose a High Deductible

A deductible is the amount you must pay after a loss before your insurance company steps in and starts paying. Most homeowners agree to a $500 deductible (for the hazard portion; liability insurance doesn't normally carry a deductible). However, many insurance companies now set the deductible at a higher, often percentage-based amount, such as 1% of the hazard insurance amount. Your policy may also have additional, separate deductibles for particular damages such as windstorms.

Agreeing to a higher-than-average deductible can actually be a great financial move. For one thing, it allows you to reduce your premium costs— or buy more coverage for the same premium. By raising your deductible from $250 to $1,000, you can save as much as 25% on your premiums. Some insurance companies will let you take your deductible up to $5,000 or more.

Another plus is that you may be better off not calling your insurance company for relatively small losses, anyway. Many homeowners just fix minor damage without a peep to their insurer, because of the very real risk that the company will punish them with raised premiums the following year. The raise in rates can be higher than the amount of your claim.

If only your mortgage lender weren't weighing in on the size of your deductible: Ever vigilant about protecting its collateral, your lender may place a limit on how high a deductible you agree to—often $1,000. They're afraid that if you don't keep that amount of money in the bank, you won't be able to claim any insurance after a loss, and the house—their collateral—will remain damaged.

No matter what deductible you choose, make sure you keep at least that amount of money in the bank. Otherwise, you risk being unable to use your insurance and facing major losses on your own.

Discounts for Lowered Risk

Most insurance companies will knock a little off your premium if your house:

- has smoke alarms and fire extinguishers
- has deadbolt locks
- has burglar and fire alarms that report to a central service
- has weather-resistant features such as hurricane shutters
- was built within the last ten years, or
- was built using fire-resistant construction, such as block or masonry.

Your own personal characteristics can sometimes also get you discounts or reduced rates, for example, if you're a nonsmoker or have a good credit rating (the theory being that you're less likely to start fires or to be generally irresponsible).

TIP

Don't hide a home-based business. Its inventory, equipment, and location (if it's a separate structure like a garage) will be excluded from coverage under most policies. And your business-related visitors won't be covered under the liability portion. Either buy the added coverage, or get a separate policy.

Shopping Around for Homeowners' Insurance

A lot of buyers just go with the insurance company their real estate agent recommends. But doing some price comparison—preferably between three or four companies—could save you hundreds of dollars.

Money isn't your only concern. You want a customer-friendly, cooperative insurance company that will make you feel supported after damage happens, not put you through bureaucratic hoops and delay your payment. Get some price quotes and policy descriptions for the amount and type of insurance your house will need; you have three choices:

- companies who sell insurance directly to you (sometimes at a distance, for example, on the phone or via the Internet)
- companies that sell insurance through so-called "captive agents" who represent only that company, and
- agents or brokers who represent more than one company.

The third option is often best, since the agent will give you a range of choices. But if your friends and real estate agent are pointing to one company as affordable and consumer-friendly, ask it for a quote. If you're coming up short, get online quotes from multiple companies at www. insweb.com (but it doesn't include some of the big companies like State Farm). Also, if you're happy with your car insurance, contact that company's representative to ask whether it offers a dual-policy discount (often 5% to 15%). And for information about particular companies, check with your state insurance department, which may track local insurance rates and complaints.

Jointly Owned, Jointly Insured: What Your Community Association Pays For

If you're buying a condo, co-op, or other property in a community interest development, the community association should already have bought a "master policy," including hazard and liability coverage. It will cover common areas such as the roof, walkways, furnace, pool, and building your unit is in, but not usually your actual unit. If the roof leaks, the furnace dies, or a passerby falls into the pool, you won't have to get involved—or pay.

Still, it's worth examining the master policy for completeness. Many condo owners have learned only after a flood or earthquake that their association hadn't bought insurance for these hazards. Worse yet, a clause in your association's CC&Rs may allow it to collect from you personally if its master policy doesn't cover the full extent of a loss.

Coverage for the inside of your own unit is more complicated. The master policy's coverage may stop at your unit's bare walls, ceilings, and floors, or it may also include your cabinets, plumbing, appliances, carpeting, wallpaper, wiring, light fixtures, and more. You may have to worry, for example, about a fire that burns up your cabinets and appliances, a burglary, or someone slipping in your bathroom. Check with your association for details. Then buy insurance to fill any gaps. Special condo and co-op policies are available.

CHECK IT OUT

To learn more about homeowners' insurance: See the Insurance Information Institute's website (www.iii.org). Also see *The Insurance Maze*, by Kimberly Lankford (Kaplan Business).

Home Warranties for Preowned Houses

Getting a home warranty—which provides service and replacement for certain home repairs—should be both the last and the least of your worries. (Though if you might want one, decide now, because they become unavailable after the closing.) If you're buying a newly built home, skip to the next section.

A home warranty provides repair and replacement of mechanical systems and attached appliances in your house, such as the furnace, plumbing, and electricity, and for an added fee, the air conditioner, spa, pool, and roof. If one of these breaks due to normal wear, you call your warranty company. If it believes you're covered (a big "if," which we'll discuss), it sends a repairperson. You pay a set fee for parts and labor, usually $50 to $100.

Unfortunately, you could spend all night reading consumer complaints against home warranty companies. The "preexisting condition" clause in most warranties incites the most outrage. People complain, "I bought the policy in case the house contained hidden defects—now they say it covers only new problems!"

Other common policy exclusions include inaccessible areas, your failure to have the item serviced as often as recommended (will you remember to change your A/C filter once a year?), and improper installation. The policy may also require you to pay to upgrade a system to current building code standards before it pays for repairs. And if your toddler flushes a teddy bear down the toilet, that's not "normal wear and tear," so you're on your own.

Home warranties cost around $300 to $900 per year, depending on your house. Many sellers will offer to pay for the first year, as a way of inspiring confidence. In this case, your decision is easy—say yes, unless you'd rather negotiate for something else. Or, your own real estate agent may offer to pay, in the name of customer satisfaction.

If the seller or your agent isn't paying, however, you might save your money—and put it toward your annual repair fund. Setting aside $5,000 per year for home repairs is recommended (unrealistic for most, but worth a try).

All that being said, some people love their home warranties. If a major home system breaks down, and you get a good, cooperative repairperson, and your warranty company does cover it, you'll be smiling. Just make sure to look into several different companies' warranties, and read the exclusions.

Also check whether a government agency in your state—probably either your department of insurance (as in California) or real estate (as in Texas)—regulates home warranty companies. If so, contact that agency to check complaint records. But not all states have passed regulatory laws. If regulation is loose or nonexistent, pick a company with a long history in your state.

Home Warranties for Newly Built Houses

If you're buying a newly built house, don't consider one that isn't backed with a builder's warranty. Reputable builders won't balk at this. What this often means is that the builder promises to assess any problem and arrange for repairs. (Get this in writing.) In other cases, it means the builder buys you a warranty.

No matter where the warranty comes from, read it carefully to find out what it covers. For the first year, it should cover workmanship and materials on everything from the roof to the structure to the mechanical systems. The builder is off the hook for appliances or fixtures whose manufacturers provided separate warranties. The best builders will also plan to schedule one or two inspections during the first year, in order to find and repair any nonemergency problems. After that year, most builder warranties cover mechanical systems (plumbing, electric, heating, and A/C) for two years and the basic structure for ten years.

As with any warranty, damage due to normal wear and tear isn't covered. It will also be your responsibility to take care of normal upkeep, such as annual servicing on the heating and air conditioning system, and simple maintenance like caulking the seams around windows and tubs.

CHECK IT OUT

Most states regulate builder warranties. Check your state government website for consumer information, for example, via www.usa.gov.

What's Next?

You're almost there—proceed to the next chapter, on closing the sale!

Seal the Deal:
Finalizing Your Homebuying Dreams

Meet Your Adviser

Stephen Fishman, a Bay Area attorney, tax expert, and author.

What he does Stephen has been writing about the law for over 20 years. Among his many books are *Home Business Tax Deductions; Deduct It! Lower Your Small Business Taxes; Every Landlord's Tax Deduction Guide;* and *Working for Yourself: Law & Taxes for Independent Contractors, Freelancers & Consultants.*

· ·

First house "It was a one-bedroom condo in a 30-story building in Emeryville, California. I bought it because I was tired of being a renter and particularly tired of my landlord, who, among other things, failed to provide me with a stove for about a year! The condo complex was pleasant enough, with a pool, gym, and sauna. Unfortunately, it turned out to be quite noisy, and during the five years I lived there, I never actually used the amenities. But I earned a lot on the sale!"

· ·

Fantasy house "A brownstone in Manhattan—maybe next to Central Park (on the West or East side, I'm not that picky). Those brownstones are bigger than they look. They give you all the advantages of a house, but with easy access to all that the city has to offer. Inside, I'd have an old-fashioned leather couch, wood paneling on walls, and Persian rugs on wood floors."

Likes best about his work	"The intellectual challenge is great, but what I really like best is being able to work at home any time of the day or night!"
Top tip for first-time homebuyers	"Take your time looking—don't buy the first thing that looks halfway decent, but wait to find something you really like. Enjoy the fact that, if you're buying your first place, you're probably under less pressure than someone who has to worry about selling an existing house at the same time."

At last, you're approaching closing day, when the house officially becomes yours. You should have the easiest job of anyone involved—mostly familiarizing yourself with documents that other people prepare and signing your name. That doesn't mean sitting back and putting your feet up, though. You'll need to stay in close contact with your team as they take care of the myriad tasks in the last hours before the closing. And be aware that some little surprise or bump in the road may come along on closing day. Fortunately, most house closings work out fine in the end, usually because the professionals involved have the experience to save the day.

This chapter will tell you what to expect during the last hours leading up to the closing, and on the closing day itself, including:

- what a closing is—the who, what, and where of it
- how to conduct a thorough final walk-through
- tasks that you're personally responsible for in the last days and hours before the closing
- what to expect when attending your closing, including what documents you'll have to sign, and
- when you can move in.

TIP

The world won't end if your closing gets delayed. According to Carol Neil: "In my 30-plus years as a Realtor®, I've never had an escrow where something new didn't come up at the last minute, leading to scrambles or even a delayed closing date. I worked on one sale where the lender, at the 11th hour, asked for the buyer's divorce papers—even though he'd already been divorced for about 15 years! Homebuying is like childbirth: You think you might not survive the process while it's happening but later forget the pain and love the results."

Preview of Coming Attractions: What Your Closing Will Involve

A closing (also sometimes called a "settlement") is a meeting or a nearly simultaneous series of events during which you pay the seller and the seller transfers ownership rights to you. All of this will be orchestrated by your closing agent or, in some states, your respective attorneys.

The closing can't happen until both you and the seller have either met or renegotiated all the terms of your purchase agreement. The two of you have, no doubt, been working hard to bring this about for weeks, by having inspections and repairs done, arranging for financing, and removing other contingencies. But during that time, you were still hanging onto your purchase money, and the seller still owned the house. The closing was created so that each of you could feel safe handing over what you own to the other.

Of course, if you're not paying in cash, your lender actually holds much of the money for this transaction. The lender will be doing some last-minute investigating behind the scenes—don't be surprised if your employer gets a call on closing day to make sure you still work there! And you yourself may have to fulfill some last-minute lender requests for additional documents or statements. When the lender decides that all is clear, you'll be able (as part of the closing "ceremony") to sign off on your loan and transfer your down payment to the seller. Your lender will then pay the seller the bulk of the purchase price (like you, using the closing agent as intermediary).

But enough generalities: What about *your* closing? The biggest logistical questions in the days leading up to it are:

- When will it be?
- Where will it be?
- Who will attend?

When. The exact date of your closing, or an approximate date, should have been specified in your purchase agreement. If the date wasn't made absolutely clear, your closing agent will help you and the seller decide when you'll all be ready.

*L*esson learned the hard way **Don't schedule your closing on a weekend.** Marge and her husband Theo lived a long way from their escrow agent's office, so, as Marge explains, "We thought we were lucky when the escrow officer volunteered to come in on a Saturday. But then she got really annoyed when we wanted to read everything (our agent hadn't given us drafts) and when a complication arose with our loan. Our mortgage broker wasn't available by phone, and it took three hours to sort everything out. By the end, we were all exhausted. Theo and I had to force ourselves to go out and celebrate afterwards, but I'm glad we did."

Where. The meeting will most likely take place at the office of either your escrow officer or attorney, the registry of deeds, your builder's sales office, or (in rare cases) your lender. The choice of location depends on local custom.

Who. Of course you'll be there, preferably well-rested and fresh, along with any cobuyers. Don't bring children! A closing is a serious, sometimes intense experience demanding your full attention. Hire a babysitter (for double the time you think it will take), and give yourself plenty of time for the meeting (and maybe an adult-only celebratory meal afterwards).

TIP

What if an emergency comes up and you or a cobuyer can't be at the closing? One possibility is to arrange to sign everything a few days beforehand, for example, if you'll be traveling. Another is to prepare a document called a "power of attorney" giving signing power to a trusted friend, relative, or lawyer. The power of attorney should include an expiration date—perhaps a few days after the closing. Check with your attorney or closing agent for details of how the power of attorney needs to be formatted and possibly recorded with a government office.

Your real estate agent should definitely be at the closing, offering support and carrying a packet of documents in case anyone forgot anything. You might also be accompanied by your mortgage broker and your attorney, if you have one. If you haven't used an attorney up to now, but are worried about any last-minute issues or complications—for example, if a recently completed survey reveals that the house's garage is over the neighbor's property line—you can hire one before the closing.

TIP

Save on attorney fees. Attorney Fred Steingold notes, "Bringing an attorney to the actual closing can get expensive if the attorney's time is mostly spent watching people sign papers. Often, a good middle course is for the attorney to receive the key documents for review the day before the closing—which is probably the earliest they'll be ready—and to report any findings to the buyer by phone. The attorney may also agree to be reachable by phone if a problem comes up at the closing table."

Best thing we ever did **Have our lawyer there on closing day.** Mackenzie and her husband Don had agreed to buy a fixer-upper within walking distance of their jobs on the University of Michigan campus. "But," says Mackenzie, "We had a feeling our seller wasn't the most scrupulous character. He'd been renting out even the damp, gross basement spaces to students, and the place was a total wreck. Our suspicions were confirmed on closing day, when our lawyer discovered an outstanding water bill of some $800. The seller tried first to pretend that he'd paid it (he hadn't), then to argue that it wasn't up to him to pay it! It was quite a scene. But our lawyer eventually helped make him understand that he had to pay it in order to transfer the deed."

Unless you're meeting at the lender's office, the lender won't normally send a representative, but will send the documents straight to the closing agent. If questions come up, your mortgage broker will normally contact the lender. The lender feels safe doing this because it knows the closing agent won't actually finalize the transfer (by recording the deed) until the lender gives its final okay, even if that's after you've all gone home.

TIP

Who will answer last questions about your loan? Many buyers develop new questions on closing day when all the documents are in front of them, such as why the lender is charging certain fees. Closing agents can't answer these. Make sure that your mortgage broker or, if you have none, your lender, will either be represented at the closing or give you a direct-line phone number and a promise to be available on closing day.

Another person who may be in the room is a notary public, charged with the brief but all-important task of making sure that you and anyone else signing documents are, in fact, who you say you are (the notary will check your photo ID) and stamping the documents to confirm this.

Whether the seller and the seller's agent or attorney will come to the same meeting as you also depends on local custom. They may handle their end of things separately—the seller has far fewer documents to sign. And signing documents—anywhere between ten and 75 of them—will, in fact, be your main task at the closing.

> **TIP**
>
> **Differences with co-op closings.** Co-op buyers normally meet at the co-op attorney's office, and a representative of the seller's bank or lender will be there (to bring the stock certificate proving the seller's ownership of the co-op, which they've been holding as security for their loan—and must destroy before you get a new certificate). Other folks in attendance will include an attorney or other representative of the co-op, the attorneys and real estate agents for both sides, a representative of your bank or lender, probably a paralegal who brings the checks, and the seller. Instead of recording a deed, your lender's attorney might record a UCC-1 financing statement to publicly show its lien on your co-op shares.

Is It Really Empty?
Final Walk-Through of an Existing House

Taking a last look at the house before the closing is both fun and vitally important. Never skip this step! The walk-through is your chance to make sure that the seller has (in accordance with your agreement) moved out of the house, made any agreed-upon repairs, left behind all fixtures or other agreed-upon property, and left the place clean and trash-free. Once the house has closed, it's a lot harder to run after the seller saying, "Wait, I thought you were leaving the stove?!" (You could sue, but you'll have more interesting things on your mind by then.) Be careful on your walk-through—but also don't let last-minute jitters make you see major problems when you're really looking at minor cracks or dust balls.

You'll normally want to schedule the final walk-through within the five days before the closing, most often the day before, if not on the closing day itself. The closer to the closing day, the more time the seller has to move out completely—but the less time remains to fix any problems. There's no perfect balance!

Arrive at your final walk-through with your agent. The seller's agent may also be there as well as, in rare cases, the seller.

> **CD-ROM**
>
> **Bring the "Final Walk-Through Checklist (Existing Home)" provided in the Homebuyer's Toolkit on the CD-ROM.** A sample is shown below. It lists all the things you should check out, like the windows, faucets, and appliances.

Also bring along a copy of your purchase agreement and any follow-up writings explaining what the seller has agreed to repair or leave behind.

Then take a good, hard look around. Make a list of what remains to be done, and negotiate accordingly. If it's just a matter of removing the old magazines from the garage, the seller should be able to handle that pre-closing. If you find a more serious problem—one that appears to be new or previously hidden, such as a mysterious puddle in the crawl space or a foundation crack revealed after the boxes were moved—quickly get a contractor's estimate. Then try to negotiate to withhold enough money from the seller's proceeds to cover repairs after the closing.

Depending on the timing of your walk-through, the sellers may not have actually moved out yet. In that case, focus on whether repairs have been completed, and check that nothing has already been removed that should have stayed behind. If, for example, there are holes in the wall where a mirror fixture used to hang, or the light fixtures have been downgraded, bring this up with the seller's agent. If most of the seller's possessions are in boxes, ask about trashy-looking items that no one seems to have taken an interest in

Final Walk-Through Checklist (Existing Home)

Use this checklist to walk through the house and make sure everything is in good order or repair. You'll want to make sure that the seller has made any agreed-upon repairs, left behind all fixtures or other agreed-upon property, and left the place clean and trash-free. Add any other relevant items (inside and outside) or questions you may have (such as the name of the architect who did a recent kitchen remodel) to the list. Note any problems and try to work them out with the seller before the closing. If the seller agrees to do additional work or repairs, be sure to get the details in writing, including how the costs will be paid.

❒ The keys fit in the locks, keys have been provided for every door, and you know how to use them.

❒ The lights and fans work when you turn switches on and off.

❒ The doorbell rings.

❒ The alarm or security system works, and the seller has left the company's contact information and any entry codes and remotes.

❒ The faucets turn on, no leaks are evident under or around the sinks, and all toilets flush.

❒ The stove, oven, refrigerator, garbage disposal, dishwasher, microwave, and other appliances work.

❒ The garage door opener works, and the seller has left the remote.

❒ The ceilings, wall, and floors are in the condition you expected.

❒ The heating and air conditioning work.

❒ The windows all open and close.

❒ The sump pump, if there is one, works (to turn it on, you'll normally need to fill the pit with water).

❒ None of the seller's trash or personal items remain in the house, garage, attic, basement, yard, or refrigerator.

❒ The seller has left you any brochures or warranties regarding the furnace, appliances, and other fixtures.

❒ Other.

NOTES:

packing. And if the seller has only a few hours in which to move, your real estate agent might need to get assurances about what will happen (preferably in writing) or, at worst, delay the closing or negotiate to have the seller rent the place back from you for awhile.

What if you've just noticed a problem that was probably there before and your inspector could have seen, such as cracks in the ceiling? You may just have to live with it. This isn't a new inspection, it's your chance to confirm that the house is in the same condition in which you agreed to buy it. These can be tough calls, so confer with your real estate agent before rushing to judgment.

Even if the seller moved out ages ago, you shouldn't be held responsible for any damage that occurred while the place sat empty, so long as the seller still owned the home. The seller is normally responsible, under the contract, for fixing any damage due to vandalism, dumping, spontaneous leaks, or even the seller's moving company (after all, the seller's homeowners' insurance is still operative).

 TIP

If the seller is at the walk-through, get friendly. Establishing a relationship you can draw on later, after your agents and the others are gone, can be invaluable. If negotiations were tough, try to put the business side of the transaction behind you, and ask practical questions like, "How do the burners on this vintage gas stove light?" and "Is that a fruit tree?" Also ask the seller for contact information, including a forwarding address. (You'll no doubt get some of the seller's mail, and can your conscience handle throwing away a letter from a long-lost relative?) Years from now, you may also need to call with questions like, "Where can we buy replacement tiles for the ones you installed?" or "What's this urn full of ashes in the attic?" If the seller isn't at the walk-through, you might want to get in touch or meet soon after the closing, for the same purpose.

Is It Really Finished?
Final Walk-Through of a New House

By now, you've hopefully seen your new house at various stages of construction—perhaps as recently as a week ago, if you negotiated for a series of walk-throughs in your purchase contract. But now you're at the very last walk-through, your first opportunity to see the house in its final form. Bring your original contract or addendum specifying products, extras, and upgrades.

The developer may accompany you, which is helpful for learning where things like the circuit breaker and the water shutoff valve are; how the heat, appliances, and other systems actually work; how you'll need to maintain them; and whether they're covered by any warranties. (Some builders call this the "orientation.") Expect also to be handed a pile of instruction pamphlets (or make sure to get these even if the developer isn't personally there).

> **TIP**
>
> **Gather all your new home's plans, documents, and more.** According to California inspector Paul A. Rude, developers can be difficult to contact after the home is yours. Insist on copies of architectural plans, names of all the contractors and subcontractors, and any written warranties that came with building materials and appliances. These will come in handy for later repairs, matching new materials to old, and so forth.

> **CD-ROM**
>
> **Use the "Final Walk-Through Checklist (New Home)" in the Homebuyer's Toolkit on the CD-ROM.** A sample is shown below. This will help you assess whether everything (such as flooring, landscaping, and sinks) has been finished and is in good shape.

Final Walk-Through Checklist (New Home)

Use this checklist to walk through your new house and make sure everything inside and out (from flooring to landscaping) has been finished and is in good shape. Then, create a "punch list" of what remains to be done. Work out with the developer how and when needed changes will be made and how this will affect your closing date.

❐ Construction and finishing work is complete, with no missing trim, hardware, or paint, no exposed wires, and all water gutters pointed away from the house.

❐ The landscaping is complete, with grading sloped away from the foundation (no trenches right next to the house). All agreed-upon trees have been planted (often the last thing to be done).

❐ No damage, scrapes, or gouges are visible on counters, walls, floors, appliances, or other surfaces.

❐ All fixtures, carpets, and appliances are the ones you specified.

❐ The keys fit in the locks, keys have been provided for every door, and you know how to use them.

❐ The lights and fans work when you turn switches on and off.

❐ The faucets turn on, no leaks are evident under or around the sinks, and all toilets flush.

❐ The stove, oven, refrigerator, garbage disposal, dishwasher, microwave, and all other appliances work.

❐ The garage door opener works.

❐ The ceilings, wall, and floors are in the condition you expected.

❐ The heating and air conditioning work.

❐ The sump pump, if there is one, works (to turn it on, you'll normally need to fill the pit with water.)

❐ All windows open and close, and all doors and cabinet doors are hung correctly and open and close smoothly.

❐ Other.

NOTES:

Don't let the developer rush you! Then create a so-called "punch list" of what remains to be done. Your developer may have a standard form for this.

At the end of your walk-through, the developer will review the list and should agree to make the needed changes by the closing. If that looks impossible, your best bets are to either delay the closing or get a written agreement saying that the developer will put the necessary money to complete your house into an account that the developer can collect on when the work is done. And you can add new deadlines within this agreement, saying that if the work isn't done by these deadlines, the money will be returned to you. Consult an attorney if you're not satisfied with the developer's assurances.

TIP

"Now is when you have the most leverage," says Realtor® Mark Nash. "Right before the closing, the developer is looking forward to cashing out and moving on. Be pleasant, meticulous, and assertive as you press for everything to get done— and delay the closing if you have to. As soon as the developer has your money, you're history—the developer is mentally already moving on to the next project."

ℒesson learned the hard way **Don't arrange your life around closing day.** When Flora bought a newly built condo in Portland, Oregon, the last inspection was scheduled on a Friday, with closing the following Monday. Flora says, "I arrived Friday to find workers running in all directions. I went around with my punch list of things that should have been done and kept checking off 'not done,' 'not done.' But we couldn't put off the Monday closing—I was living in someone's basement, and my husband was flying up from California. The developer never finished all the items on the punch list; we later sued."

Your Last Tasks Before the Closing

Below are the most important things for you to do in the approximately 24 hours leading up to the closing.

Check and Double-Check Final Closing Cost Amount

Your closing costs include everything that you (and the seller) will have to pay to anyone connected with the sale, including your loan fee, points, and first month's payment; title and homeowners' insurance premiums; transfer and property taxes; recording fees; and down payment. Many people are surprised by how high their closing costs go—several thousand dollars is not uncommon.

Co-op buyers may pay a little less, because title insurance isn't available to them (as owner of shares in a corporation rather than land), and the taxes are normally lower because it's not considered a real estate transfer. On the other hand, co-op owners may be required to pay a move-in deposit, a stock transfer fee, and a fee for any credit checks run by the owner's association board.

Condo owners should also be prepared for a few closing costs not owed by ordinary homeowners, such as a move-in fee or move-out deposit and fees for credit checks run by the community association.

 TIP

Remember next April: Some closing costs are tax-deductible. These include the points and any prepaid interest you pay for your mortgage, and any reimbursement you pay the seller for already-paid local property taxes. Many other closing costs, while not tax-deductible, can be figured into your house's adjusted cost basis, helping to reduce your capital gains when you eventually sell.

You should have already gotten some warning of your closing cost amount from your lender, which was legally obligated to give you a "Good Faith Estimate" (GFE) of these costs (not just the ones relating to your loan) within three days of first receiving your loan application. Remember, after January 1, 2010, your GFE should be on a standard form (a copy can be found in the Homebuyer's Tool Kit on the CD-ROM), and the lender isn't permitted to raise many of the costs on it, while others can only be raised by up to 10%.

Your current task, on the day before the closing, is to find out whether your total closing costs are adding up as you expected and get ready to pay that amount. To see the latest tally, ask your closing agent for your final draft of your HUD-1 Settlement Statement. This is a standard from developed by the Department of Housing and Urban Development (HUD) that the lender is required to give you at closing. It is set up to make it easy to compare the final costs to the estimated costs on the GFE.

CD-ROM

The Homebuyer's Toolkit on the CD-ROM contains a blank HUD-1 form. Open it to see the full list of possible closing costs. A partial sample is shown below.

At the closing itself, you'll receive a final version of the closing statement or HUD-1 form. But it's good to get an advance look, so that you can check for oddities, errors, or failures to credit you for fees you've already paid. For example, your earnest money deposit should show up as a credit, reducing what you'll owe at closing. If you're buying a newly constructed house, your advance payments to cover customizations or upgrades should be credited against your closing costs. Bring up any errors or questions with whoever is responsible (usually, the lender or the closing agent) *before* you get to the closing.

Hopefully you won't be one of the consumers who find that the fees have been added to or padded since the original estimate (sometimes called "junk fees") to pull in extra profits, usually for the lender or title company. If you see unexpected or questionable fees, realize that you may be able to negotiate them away. The most likely candidates for negotiation are those called "Items Payable in Connection with the Loan," listed on the lines numbering in the 800s on the HUD-1 form, and "Title Charges," listed on the lines with "1100" numbers. The sooner you bring these up, the more negotiating clout you have.

Sample Settlement Statement

A. **Settlement Statement (HUD-1)**

OMB Approval No. 2502-0265

B. Type of Loan		
1. ☐ FHA 2. ☐ RHS 3. ☐ Conv. Unins.	6. File Number:	7. Loan Number:
4. ☐ VA 5. ☐ Conv. Ins.	8. Mortgage Insurance Case Number:	

C. Note: This form is furnished to give you a statement of actual settlement costs. Amounts paid to and by the settlement agent are shown. Items marked "(p.o.c.)" were paid outside the closing; they are shown here for informational purposes and are not included in the totals.

D. Name & Address of Borrower:	E. Name & Address of Seller:	F. Name & Address of Lender:

G. Property Location:	H. Settlement Agent:	I. Settlement Date:
	Place of Settlement:	

J. Summary of Borrower's Transaction		**K. Summary of Seller's Transaction**	
100. Gross Amount Due from Borrower		**400. Gross Amount Due to Seller**	
101. Contract sales price		401. Contract sales price	
102. Personal property		402. Personal property	
103. Settlement charges to borrower (line 1400)		403.	
104.		404.	
105.		405.	
Adjustment for items paid by seller in advance		**Adjustments for items paid by seller in advance**	
106. City/town taxes to		406. City/town taxes to	
107. County taxes to		407. County taxes to	
108. Assessments to		408. Assessments to	
109.		409.	
110.		410.	
111.		411.	
112.		412.	
120. Gross Amount Due from Borrower		**420. Gross Amount Due to Seller**	
200. Amounts Paid by or in Behalf of Borrower		**500. Reductions In Amount Due to Seller**	
201. Deposit or earnest money		501. Excess deposit (see instructions)	
202. Principal amount of new loan(s)		502. Settlement charges to seller (line 1400)	
203. Existing loan(s) taken subject to		503. Existing loan(s) taken subject to	
204.		504. Payoff of first mortgage loan	
205.		505. Payoff of second mortgage loan	
206.		506.	
207.		507.	
208.		508.	
209.		509.	
Adjustments for items unpaid by seller		**Adjustments for items unpaid by seller**	
210. City/town taxes to		510. City/town taxes to	
211. County taxes to		511. County taxes to	
212. Assessments to		512. Assessments to	
213.		513.	
214.		514.	
215.		515.	
216.		516.	
217.		517.	
218.		518.	
219.		519.	
220. Total Paid by/for Borrower		**520. Total Reduction Amount Due Seller**	
300. Cash at Settlement from/to Borrower		**600. Cash at Settlement to/from Seller**	
301. Gross amount due from borrower (line 120)		601. Gross amount due to seller (line 420)	
302. Less amounts paid by/for borrower (line 220)	( )	602. Less reductions in amount due seller (line 520)	( )
303. Cash ☐ From ☐ To Borrower		**603. Cash** ☐ To ☐ From Seller	

The Public Reporting Burden for this collection of information is estimated at 35 minutes per response for collecting, reviewing, and reporting the data. This agency may not collect this information, and you are not required to complete this form, unless it displays a currently valid OMB control number. No confidentiality is assured; this disclosure is mandatory. This is designed to provide the parties to a RESPA covered transaction with information during the settlement process.

Sample Settlement Statement, con't.

L. Settlement Charges

		Paid From Borrower's Funds at Settlement	Paid From Seller's Funds at Settlement
700. Total Real Estate Broker Fees			
Division of commission (line 700) as follows:			
701. $ to			
702. $ to			
703. Commission paid at settlement			
704.			
800. Items Payable in Connection with Loan			
801. Our origination charge $	(from GFE #1)		
802. Your credit or charge (points) for the specific interest rate chosen $	(from GFE #2)		
803. Your adjusted origination charges	(from GFE A)		
804. Appraisal fee to	(from GFE #3)		
805. Credit report to	(from GFE #3)		
806. Tax service to	(from GFE #3)		
807. Flood certification	(from GFE #3)		
808.			
900. Items Required by Lender to Be Paid in Advance			
901. Daily interest charges from to @ $ /day	(from GFE #10)		
902. Mortgage insurance premium for months to	(from GFE #3)		
903. Homeowner's insurance for years to	(from GFE #11)		
904.			
1000. Reserves Deposited with Lender			
1001. Initial deposit for your escrow account	(from GFE #9)		
1002. Homeowner's insurance months @ $ per month $			
1003. Mortgage insurance months @ $ per month $			
1004. Property taxes months @ $ per month $			
1005. months @ $ per month $			
1006. months @ $ per month $			
1007. Aggregate Adjustment -$			
1100. Title Charges			
1101. Title services and lender's title insurance	(from GFE #4)		
1102. Settlement or closing fee $			
1103. Owner's title insurance	(from GFE #5)		
1104. Lender's title insurance $			
1105. Lender's title policy limit $			
1106. Owner's title policy limit $			
1107. Agent's portion of the total title insurance premium $			
1108. Underwriter's portion of the total title insurance premium $			
1200. Government Recording and Transfer Charges			
1201. Government recording charges	(from GFE #7)		
1202. Deed $ Mortgage $ Releases $			
1203. Transfer taxes	(from GFE #8)		
1204. City/County tax/stamps Deed $ Mortgage $			
1205. State tax/stamps Deed $ Mortgage $			
1206.			
1300. Additional Settlement Charges			
1301. Required services that you can shop for	(from GFE #6)		
1302. $			
1303. $			
1304.			
1305.			
1400. Total Settlement Charges (enter on lines 103, Section J and 502, Section K)			

Sample Settlement Statement, con't.

Comparison of Good Faith Estimate (GFE) and HUD-1 Charges		Good Faith Estimate	HUD-1
Charges That Cannot Increase	**HUD-1 Line Number**		
Our origination charge	# 801		
Your credit or charge (points) for the specific interest rate chosen	# 802		
Your adjusted origination charges	# 803		
Transfer taxes	#1203		

Charges That in Total Cannot Increase More Than 10%		Good Faith Estimate	HUD-1
Government recording charges	# 1201		
	#		
	#		
	#		
	#		
	#		
	#		
	#		
Total			
Increase between GFE and HUD-1 Charges		$ or %	

Charges That Can Change		Good Faith Estimate	HUD-1
Initial deposit for your escrow account	#1001		
Daily interest charges	# 901 $ /day		
Homeowner's insurance	# 903		
	#		
	#		
	#		

Loan Terms

Your initial loan amount is	$
Your loan term is	▓▓ years
Your initial interest rate is	▓▓ %
Your initial monthly amount owed for principal, interest, and and any mortgage insurance is	$ ▓▓▓ includes ☐ Principal ☐ Interest ☐ Mortgage Insurance
Can your interest rate rise?	☐ No. ☐ Yes, it can rise to a maximum of ▓▓%. The first change will be on ▓▓▓ and can change again every ▓▓▓ after ▓▓▓. Every change date, your interest rate can increase or decrease by ▓▓%. Over the life of the loan, your interest rate is guaranteed to never be **lower** than ▓▓% or **higher** than ▓▓%.
Even if you make payments on time, can your loan balance rise?	☐ No. ☐ Yes, it can rise to a maximum of $ ▓▓▓.
Even if you make payments on time, can your monthly amount owed for principal, interest, and mortgage insurance rise?	☐ No. ☐ Yes, the first increase can be on ▓▓▓ and the monthly amount owed can rise to $ ▓▓▓. The maximum it can ever rise to is $ ▓▓▓.
Does your loan have a prepayment penalty?	☐ No. ☐ Yes, your maximum prepayment penalty is $ ▓▓▓.
Does your loan have a balloon payment?	☐ No. ☐ Yes, you have a balloon payment of $ ▓▓▓ due in ▓▓ years on ▓▓▓.
Total monthly amount owed including escrow account payments	☐ You do not have a monthly escrow payment for items, such as property taxes and homeowner's insurance. You must pay these items directly yourself. ☐ You have an additional monthly escrow payment of $ ▓▓▓ that results in a total initial monthly amount owed of $ ▓▓▓. This includes principal, interest, any mortgage insurance and any items checked below: ☐ Property taxes ☐ Homeowner's insurance ☐ Flood insurance ☐ ▓▓▓ ☐ ▓▓▓ ☐ ▓▓▓

Note: If you have any questions about the Settlement Charges and Loan Terms listed on this form, please contact your lender.

> ⓘ **CAUTION**
>
> **Don't pay junk fees that exceed legal limits.** Certain costs can't exceed the estimates given on the GFE, and other costs can only increase by a maximum of 10%. (Many of the costs on the lines numbering in the 800s or 1100s fall within this category.) For a full list of which costs can't be changed, review the Good Faith Estimate form that appears in The Homebuyer's Toolkit on the CD-ROM in the back of this book.

Assuming you find no problems, the total on the closing statement is the amount that you'll need to show up with at closing. Have your real estate agent, closing agent, or attorney confirm that the amount is, in fact, final.

Make Payment Arrangements

For convenience, many buyers pay their entire closing costs in one lump sum. (The closing agent saves you from having to write separate checks to everyone.) We're assuming you haven't already deposited money with the closing agent, which some buyers do several days in advance—usually more than they think they'll need, with the idea of getting a refund after closing. This allows buyers to use a personal check, which you can't do at the closing itself.

Of course, if you've got money coming from different sources (a bank account here, a family member there), compiling it into a lump sum before giving it to the escrow agent might not actually be so convenient. The important thing is to make sure you'll be transferring the money—every last cent of it—in an acceptable form. That usually means either a certified or cashier's check or having funds wired directly from your bank or investment company. A briefcase full of five-hundred-dollar bills would probably work, too, depending on how many bodyguards you normally travel with.

If wiring some or all of the funds is your plan, double-check how much advance notice your bank needs. Wiring is usually a same-day deal, but not always. One of this book's authors nearly had her California house closing delayed because the wired funds mysteriously got stalled in an office in Texas.

Personal checks aren't usually accepted at the closing, because of the uncertainty over whether they'll clear. Even so, it's a good idea to bring your personal checkbook along and make sure a few hundred dollars will be in your account. This is in case any last incidentals crop up.

Best thing we ever did **Bring our checkbook.** Everything had been going smoothly with Meggan and her sister's joint purchase of a house in Massachusetts. They arrived at closing with a cashier's check for the exact amount they'd been told to bring. But, as Meggan describes, "For some reason, the amount was too low, by $500. My sister broke down crying, saying, 'I knew this was too perfect, something had to go wrong.' Since she's my older sister, I started worrying, thinking maybe I should be in tears, too! Although there was some question about whether they'd accept our personal check for $500, we had a prominent local attorney with us, who said, 'They're good for it, I'll cover it if it doesn't clear.' So the deal went through."

Read Your Documents and Raise Any Last Issues

By the time you walk in the door to your closing, all possible negotiations and issues should have been settled. Closing day is not the time to tell the seller, "You never removed the pet door!" Nor is it a good time to ask your mortgage broker what this line about "prepayment" means.

Start by reviewing the escrow instructions, and any letters or instructions from your lender, to make sure you've done everything requested. Also ask your mortgage broker and real estate agent to give you complete sets of any draft documents that have been prepared to date and to explain to you (if they haven't already) what the documents mean. Unfortunately, some documents might not be prepared until right before closing day, but you can ask for the standard templates, for example, of the promissory note and mortgage.

Finally, call your real estate agent, closing agent, and mortgage broker to double-check that they're not waiting for anything else from you. (And, just in case, that they still have tomorrow's closing on their calendar!)

Prepare What You'll Bring to the Closing

Other than money, the buyer is expected to bring only a few documents, including proof of homeowners' insurance and an original copy of any inspection reports. As a practical matter, your real estate agent may bring these or have forwarded them to the closing agent. But if you're in doubt, or think you may be the only one holding any possibly relevant document, bring it. Also bring receipts or other proof of things you've already paid (such as inspection fees or homeowners' insurance) in case any last questions arise about whether these can be deducted from your closing costs.

Finally, bring proof of your identity. Many people forget a driver's license, passport, or other photo identification. You'll need to show it to the notary, who stamps the documents after you sign them.

The Drum Roll, Please: Attending the Closing

No matter what time your closing is scheduled for, plan to take the day off work and to get there in plenty of time. Although a normal closing lasts no more than an hour or two, surprises are common. Also, your closing agent may have more than one closing scheduled that day, and an earlier one might run over.

Whether or not you're meeting in one room, who signs the documents *first* isn't really an issue. The seller could, for example, sign the deed transferring ownership to you before you'd signed anything—but would have the protection of knowing that the closing agent won't record the deed until you've signed your documents and the loan has been funded.

We'd love to tell you to read every document one last time before signing, but that's probably not realistic—it would take hours. By now, you should have seen many of the documents in draft form and read them when you weren't under time pressure. As adviser Russell Straub says, "It's important to get your questions answered, but if you wait until the closing to read everything, you're really throwing sand in the gears." Just listen carefully as your team of professionals explains what each document is; compare the filled-in portions and numbers (not the boilerplate) with your own notes;

and raise questions about things that don't appear as you'd expected. If you have an attorney representing you (and not simultaneously representing the seller), you can rely on the attorney to tell you what a document generally means and whether it's safe to sign.

Closing Documents, Part One: Your Mortgage Loan

The first set of documents you'll deal with at the closing are those concerning your loan. Makes sense: Unless your financing goes through, there's no point in continuing.

> **TIP**
> **Expect a little sticker shock.** Annemarie Kurpinsky, a California real estate agent, says, "Buyers tend to think in terms of the house's purchase price—as in, 'I'm buying it for $800,000.' But the closing can be daunting, because you're now confronted with loan documents showing how much you'll REALLY be paying, after the interest and other costs are added up. To relax, try focusing on all the reasons you chose this house in the first place, on how it will be a good investment over time, and on the fact that you don't need to pay this all at once!"

Before you sign, look at every number to make sure it's what you were expecting and that no one mistakenly added any zeros. Below is a summary of the main documents you'll be given. However, there will probably be more. For instance, your lender may have you sign an affidavit promising that you'll live in, not rent out, the house.

- **Promissory note, or "Note."** You're stating that you're borrowing X amount of money and personally guaranteeing to repay it.

- **Mortgage or Deed of Trust.** Here's where you agree to have a lien put on your house as security for the loan. It turns your house into collateral, which the lender can claim in foreclosure if you fail to repay or to otherwise follow the terms of the Note (you "default"). The lender will record your mortgage with the appropriate local government office.

- **UCC-1 Financing Statement (co-ops only).** Since co-op financing involves no mortgage, your lender may instead fill out and record this document, to show its claim on your property interest.

- **Truth-in-Lending (TIL) Disclosure Statement, or "Regulation Z form."** You should have seen an earlier draft of this, within three days after applying for the loan. Here, the lender will break down all the payments you'll make in connection with your loan. It will confirm your interest rate, the annual percentage rate ("APR"), and the total cost of the loan over its life.

- **Closing Statement, Settlement Sheet, or HUD-1 Settlement Statement.** This is the statement described above, usually prepared by your closing agent using a HUD-1 form. It itemizes each payment to be made by you and the seller, not only for the house, but for other costs such as services performed in connection with the sale, insurance premiums, paying off liens, and more. (The seller will need to sign it, too.) Before stuffing the HUD-1 statement into your files, check whether your closing agent included a refund check with it (for any extra money that you deposited ahead of time).

- **Monthly payment letter.** This tells you how much money you'll pay in monthly loan principal and interest. It may also include amounts that your lender requires you to put into escrow each month for payment to third parties such as the tax collector or insurance companies (homeowners' or PMI). Your closing agent will take care of setting up this account on closing day.

Closing Documents, Part Two: Transferring the Property

Once your financing is taken care of, it's time to turn to the documents that transfer the property to you. At a minimum, these include the items below, though others may be added depending on where you live, for example, to account for local transfer taxes. Some documents you won't even have to sign, you'll just receive them from the seller: perhaps a certificate saying that the house has smoke detectors, or a certificate of occupancy showing that the house has passed a municipal or local inspection for basic habitability and legal compliance.

- **Deed (or "warranty deed").** The seller signs this to tell the world that title of the property has been transferred to you, the new owner. Make sure your name is spelled correctly and that it accurately shows the manner in which you and any cobuyers have opted to take title (for example, as joint tenants). Your closing agent will, as the last step in closing on the property, file a copy with the appropriate public records office.

- **Co-op buyers only: Stock certificate and proprietary lease.** Instead of a deed, co-op buyers receive a stock certificate indicating how many shares they own in the corporation and a proprietary lease outlining their rights to live in a certain unit. Your lender will probably keep these in its files.

- **Bill of sale.** This document attests to the transfer of any personal property from the seller to you. In other words, if the sale includes any non-fixtures such as a children's swing set, curtains, or a floor rug, the bill of sale creates a record of this agreement.

- **Affidavit of title and ALTA statement.** Here, the seller swears to have done nothing to cloud the house's title and to know of no unrecorded contracts, easements, or leases regarding the property. The seller signs the affidavit, but both you and the seller sign the ALTA statement to finalize your request for title insurance.

Once all the documents are signed, you'll be given a complete set for your records. Some closing agents will even put them onto a CD for you. Keep everything in a safe place, such as a safe deposit box. Don't assume that your closing company will keep a copy for you—they're allowed to toss most of your records after five to seven years.

The final task, after the meeting is over, is for your closing agent or attorney to record the property deed that shows you as the new owner, in the appropriate public records office. In some areas, this is done electronically. In others, someone (the closing agent or a messenger) must go to the appropriate office in person. The sale hasn't truly "closed" until the deal is recorded, even if you're already sharing a glass of wine at a nice restaurant.

Can I Move In? Taking Possession

After waiting so long, it's hard to believe you've actually got the right to move in or, in legal terms, take possession. That right normally kicks in at the end of closing—receiving the keys is a pretty good clue. But before you tell the movers when to arrive, check two more things:

- **Your purchase contract.** Your contract will probably contain a clause titled or mentioning "possession." That clause will most likely say that the seller must deliver possession at closing (in other words, you can move in then). However, in a few states, different arrangements are common—for example, that buyers can't take possession for two days after the closing (as in Colorado), or that the seller can stay for up to seven days after paying a deposit (as in New York). Also, you may have agreed to give the seller extra time, perhaps to move out or close on another property.

- **Your state's practices around waiting for the deed to be recorded.** Although the house is yours once the title has been transferred from the seller to you, the deal isn't technically closed until the deed has been recorded with the appropriate government office. And customs regarding whether you'll need to actually wait for the recording

---

Tunes to Celebrate By

Here are some house-inspired songs to play as you dance with joy:

- "Our House," by Madness ("Our house, in the middle of our street ... Our house, was our castle and our keep ...")
- "This Is Not the House That Pain Built," by Dar Williams ("My house is hard to find, but I'll give you directions, You can visit sometime ...")
- "Our House," by CSNY ("I'll light the fire, you put the flowers in the vase that you bought today ...")
- "More Than One Way Home," by Keb' Mo' ("Well there's more than one way home, Ain't no right way, Ain't no wrong ...")
- "Come-On-A My House," by Rosemary Clooney ("Come on-a my house my house, I'm gonna give you candy ...")
- "Home," by Bonnie Raitt ("And all through my brain, Came the refrain, Of home and its warming fire.")
- "Spiritual House," KMFDM ("This house is built, On a foundation of love ...")

to receive the keys and take possession are stricter in some states than in others. In Massachusetts, for example, recording is taken very seriously, and ZipRealty's Nancy Atwood says, "You may have to wait for 45 minutes at the closing attorney's office until the messenger has recorded the deed." By contrast, in Michigan, where most closings take place at a title insurance office, Fred Steingold says, "Once all the papers have been signed, the seller receives the payment check and simultaneously gives the buyer the keys. The seller, buyer, and lender all rely on the title company to take care of recording the deed."

TIP

Now that you've got the keys, should you change the locks? Not a bad idea, as we'll discuss in Chapter 15.

What's Next?

You've done it! Time to move in, settle down, sing at the top of your lungs, and enjoy knowing that no landlord will be knocking on your door to protest. For tips on settling in, see Chapter 15.

Settling Into Your New Home

There's nothing like waking up the first morning in your new home—ready for the fun parts of homeownership, like settling in and making the space your own. We'll give you some creative ways to make your mark (without going broke), including how to:

- tell the world where you are
- get comfortable socially
- make sure your new home is as safe as it can be
- decorate, design, and remodel on a budget
- organize your records and finances, and
- get back on your feet financially.

Just don't try to do it all in one day!

RESOURCE
For more detailed information on both the fun and the responsible parts of homeownership, see: *The Essential Guide for First-Time Homeowners; Maximize Your Investment & Enjoy Your New Home,* by Alayna Schroeder and Ilona Bray (Nolo). It covers everything from hiring contractors to refinancing to decorating on a budget to filing an insurance claim.

Tell the World You've Moved

Most everyone in your daily life probably knows you've moved. Not so your phone company, bank, or third cousin. Here are some ways to remedy that.

Set Up Services

The important places to notify are:

- **Electricity, water, and gas companies.** Call your local providers and arrange for your new account. The seller has probably told you whom to contact. If not, search for "utilities" in a directory like Yahoo!'s (http://dir.yahoo.com).

- **Trash collectors.** You can find your local waste management provider by checking a local phone book or contacting your city government. If you're in a condo or co-op, this may be part of your monthly fees—check with the association.

- **Telephone, Internet, and TV provider (cable/satellite).** It may be economical to subscribe through one provider for phone, Web, and cable TV, or now may be a good time to check out the latest satellite deals. If you're interested in forwarding phone calls from your previous number, contact your previous provider to find out your options.

- **Postal Service.** Fill out a Change of Address form online at www.usps.gov, or do it at a post office. This is supposed to forward your mail for 12 months, except periodicals, which are forwarded for only 60 days. (But plan for slipups, in which your mail is occasionally delivered to your old address.)

- **Subscriptions.** You can often update your address at a periodical's website. Don't forget to contact alumni magazines or newsletters you get from nonprofits, too. And what about your favorite retail catalogs?

- **Credit card companies.** Make sure creditors know where you are—you'd hate to get behind on a payment when you've just proven how responsible you are.

- **Department of Motor Vehicles.** Go to your state's DMV website or www.dmv.org to get information on updating your car registration and driver's license.

- **Parking permit provider.** If you need a residential parking permit, you'll need to let the appropriate permit-issuing entity know. Try your new city's website.

- **Registrar of voters.** Go to www.nased.org and click "Membership" for links to every state's elections offices, which have change of address forms online.

Notify Friends and Family

To make sure you keep getting Great Aunt Margaret's holiday fruitcake or your college friends' wedding invitations, send out new-address announcements. You can send emails or make your own cards, but online vendors will also custom-print announcements on a design of your choosing; check out:

- www.thestationerystudio.com
- www.movingannouncementstore.com.

Thanks a Million! (Or $200,000)

Your real estate agent probably spent a lot of time and energy helping you find the perfect abode—and maybe even gave you a nice gift. For a good agent, consider a similar gesture: a bottle of champagne, a CD for use when driving clients to showings, or a quality pen to write up offers. And remember, the best gift of all is referring others to your agent.

A fun and cheap method of announcing your move is to share photos of your house online. Try the following free image-hosting websites, some of which will even create custom slideshows for you to share on your Web page or social networking profiles (like MySpace or Facebook):

- www.photobucket.com
- www.flickr.com
- www.imageshack.com.

Home, Hearth, and Hors d'Oeuvres: Settle in Socially

Once you're sure your old friends know where you are, it's time to have them over—and maybe meet some new friends, too. Below are a few tips.

Housewarming on a Budget

Nothing says "Welcome Home" quite like a party. A housewarming is a great way to thank the people who helped you find, purchase, and move into your home; show off your new digs, and get to know the neighbors. Some homebuyers invite the professionals who helped out: the real estate agent, mortgage broker, attorney, or closing agent.

You're probably not looking to break the bank on the first fete. Sympathetic partygoers will probably be happy to contribute a dish, but if "potluck" feels like a dirty word, try sticking toothpicks into a few of your favorite finger foods and picking up some bottles of decent wine. And while some people go so far as to register for gifts, Miss Manners has opined, "Hoping to furnish one's quarters on other people's budgets is not a proper reason for giving a housewarming party."

 CHECK IT OUT

Streamers are SO preschool. Cool party supplies and favors—everything from candles to aqua palm tree bubble lamps—can be found at:

- www.coolstuffcheap.com
- www.orientaltrading.com
- www.merch-bot.com.

Get to Know the Neighbors

Whether or not you invite the neighbors to your housewarming party, you'll probably want more intimate opportunities to get to know them. Here are some possibilities:

The Fastest Way to a Neighbor's Heart

Be the neighborhood's favorite new baker with Mom's Crunchy Granola Cookies:

1. Combine and beat with rotating mixer until creamy: 1 cup shortening; ¾ cup brown sugar, firmly packed; ⅜ cup granulated sugar; 2 eggs; 1 T hot water; 1 tsp. vanilla.
2. Add and mix with a wooden spoon: 1½ cups flour, 1 tsp. soda, 2 cups crunchy granola. Optional: Stir in ½ cup walnuts and ½ cup raisins OR a 6 oz. package butterscotch chips OR all three.
3. Drop by teaspoonfuls on ungreased cookie sheets and bake at 375° for ten minutes, or until golden brown around the edges.

- **Have a neighbors-only party.** An after-work cocktail hour, weekend high tea or barbecue, or dessert evening works well. The neighbors will probably be more relaxed among each other than with your regular crowd.

- **Knock on doors.** Don't wait for the neighbors to come to you! Bring cookies or another small gift, like a bar of handmade soap or a coupon for "one emergency cup of sugar or equivalent."

- **Look for community activities.** You may have just moved in, but you'll also want to get out sometimes. Whatever your interests (knitting, tennis, reading, cooking, running, or gardening), there's probably a local group that fits. Check out the local paper, ask your neighbors, search online, or visit the community center (if any).

CHECK IT OUT

When good neighbors turn bad. Being a neighbor isn't always about cookies: To prevent or deal with neighbor-related disputes, about things like fences, noise, easements, or joint use agreements, check out *Neighbor Law: Fences, Trees, Boundaries & Noise*, by Cora Jordan and Emily Doskow (Nolo).

Find Activities for the Kids

Your children may feel as out of the social loop as you do. Here are some fun ways to help them adjust and to meet other parents:

- **Volunteer at school.** You can participate by becoming a room parent, going on field trips, and generally helping out in the classroom (unless of course your kids are teens—then your presence might not be encouraged).

- **Start a carpool, playgroup, or babysitting co-op.** If your kids' school isn't within walking distance, start or join a carpool with nearby parents. Playgroups and babysitting co-ops are also great ways to meet and get to know other families. Check out www.babycenter.com for ideas.

- **Have a kids' party.** Just because no one's having a birthday doesn't mean that you can't have a party. Decorate the house, serve up some kiddie treats, and play a few games.

The Safest Home in Town: Yours

Given that every unfamiliar noise in a new house can sound treacherous, you're already probably thinking about home security. Take these easy follow-up steps:

- **Change the locks.** If you don't, you won't know who has keys to your front door (the seller's wacky houseguest from two years ago and several neighbors, perhaps). If you haven't already, call a locksmith or visit a hardware store.

- **Reset the alarm code.** Choose a number you'll remember, share it on a "need to know" basis, and keep the owners' manual on hand in case you're in a jam. If there's no alarm system, now might be the time to consider getting one (prices are more reasonable than you might think, and your homeowners' insurance rates may go down).

- **Check smoke detectors and sprinkler systems.** Though the inspector told you whether these were up to code, make sure they're still in good working order. For your family's safety, consider installing them in every bedroom or hallways that lead to bedrooms. And if you're in a building with a sprinkler system, make sure you know how it works and where your unit's sprinkler heads are.

- **Plan an escape route.** In a panicked situation, your halls might feel like a labyrinth. Make sure every family member knows all entrances and exits, how to get out from the second floor, and where to meet up if separated.

- **Childproof everything.** If you're a parent, you've probably done this before. Put chemicals and cleaning supplies out of reach, and add child safety locks to all cabinets. Also put important phone numbers (your cell phone, police, fire department, health care providers, and more) as well as your address on a bulletin board or refrigerator for babysitters.

> *One Way to Test Your Locks ...*
>
> **Luke:** *It's the kind of lock burglars look for.*
>
> **Lorelai:** *Why do burglars look for that lock?*
>
> **Luke:** *Because it's easy to break into. I proved that.*
>
> **Lorelai:** *You proved that by ... ?*
>
> **Luke:** *Breaking in through the back door.*
>
> *—Gilmore Girls*

- **Remind the kids how to get home.** Have your kids memorize their new address and telephone number and your full name. Make sure their school has the correct contact information for you.

Cozy Up ... Without Breaking the Bank

Decorating and remodeling—or maybe just choosing your own paint color for the first time—are probably high on your priority list. We'll give you some starter ideas and resources for:

- decorating without maxing out your credit card
- planning a remodel on your own, or finding professionals to help you, and
- beautifying any outdoor space.

Decorating on Your Budget

Though it might be tempting to buy out your nearest home furnishings store or warehouse, your budget is probably telling you to hold back. But hey, creativity thrives within constraints, right? And there's no rush—you'll need time to figure out your needs as you adapt to the space. There are hundreds (actually, thousands) of low-cost resources on decorating (TV shows, magazines, books, websites) to help you plan (or at least fantasize about) all the great things you'd like to do with your new home.

CHECK IT OUT

Outlandish and old-fashioned? Get ideas from the quirky do-it-yourself publications *DigsMagazine* (which calls itself an "online home + living magazine for the post-college, pre-parenthood, quasi-adult generation"; see www.digsmagazine.com) and *ReadyMade Magazine* ("instructions for everyday life"; see www.readymademag.com). Also see *First Digs: The Quasi-Adult's Guide to Decorating With Style Without Blowing Your Budget,* by Yee-Fan Sun (St. Martin's Press).

Other ways to be kind to your pocketbook include:

- **Inventorying.** Make a list of what you already have, and find the holes. For example, a rug you haven't used in years may fit perfectly in your new hallway.

- **Prioritizing.** Distinguish what you need to buy (a bedside lamp) from what you want (sleeker cabinet knobs). Rank your priorities from highest to lowest, and space purchases out to fit your budget.

> **TIP**
>
> **Small price, big impact.** You don't need to replace all your furniture to get a fresh look. Consider sprucing up your rooms with candles, pictures, or thrift store vases or adding color with paint, pillows, or a tablecloth. Check out www.thebudgetdecorator.com.

- **Researching.** Shop around for the best deals. Consider buying used, from Internet vendors or at discount shops, consignment stores, flea markets, or end-of-the-season clearances.

> **CHECK IT OUT**
>
> **Crafty community.** Even if you've never picked up a glue gun, you'll find easy decorating tips at www.getcrafty.com, from making felt with cat fur (eww) to quilted photo greeting cards (handy). Other resources include: www.doityourself.com and www.diynot.com.

Remodeling on the Cheap

If you bought a fixer-upper, you may be spending time and money just making the place habitable. Our book can't cover all the bases—plenty of others do—but here are some cost-cutting tips to use from the get-go. And don't forget to check out the resources in Chapter 8 on doing home repairs.

Remodeling on Your Own

If you're planning to remodel on your own, you'll need tools to do it. Some are easy to afford—you can just go to the hardware store for a hammer—but others are a larger investment. Consider renting tools; www.rentalsite.com has searchable directories. You can also borrow from your neighbors (responsibly) or buy used (check for local listings at www.craigslist.org).

Finally, find out if your community has a tool-lending library—they're available in several states.

No matter what, you'll probably have questions once you get started. Reap the benefit of others' knowledge by checking out sites like:

- www.diynetwork.com
- www.houseprofessionals.com/diy
- www.homedoctor.net.

Be sure that a project is doable before you begin. The websites listed above all have sections dedicated to user comments to help you gauge how much elbow grease and expertise you'll need for your project. Many offer detailed blogs that take you through a real remodel.

Finding and Hiring Professionals

Professionals exist for a reason, and you shouldn't be embarrassed to use one, no matter how handy you are. Bringing in a general contractor (who oversees a team of subcontracting professionals) is a smart move if you're attempting a complex or extremely large project. For more limited projects, you can hire your own carpenters, plumbers, electricians, and so forth.

> ### Watching Paint Dry Just Got Quicker
>
> Decorators are abuzz over Benjamin Moore's latest product, Aura. It's an acrylic, low-odor, water- and rub-off-resistant interior paint that needs only one coat, and that coat should last for several years. See more at www.myaurapaint.com.

Aside from getting recommendations from friends, a good place to begin looking for a general contractor is at the Associated General Contractors of America's website, www.agc.org. As with any professional, conduct a thorough interview before hiring, making sure this one has experience with the type of work you need; then sign a contract laying out what work is included and the price.

To make sure you're getting fair market value for your remodel, check out reputable do-it-yourself websites like the ones above. They'll inevitably have blogs and message boards addressing your issues, especially if you're having a common project done. And you can always post your own queries or comments.

Though it might be tempting to get the whole project done in one fell swoop, this isn't always a good strategy for the cash-strapped first-time buyer. One project will be a big enough learning experience—simultaneous ones can make you crazy. And if you have a young child (whose immune system will be sensitive to the raw materials in the air), or don't have time to work around the chaos, you'll want to keep the house livable during construction.

Get Greener Now, Get More Green Later

As long as you're remodeling, consider the short- *and* long-term benefits of making your home more energy efficient. Sustainable construction and architecture will lower both your energy consumption and the amount you spend on utilities. And when you sell, you'll be able to play up the house's upgraded insulation, sealed crawlspace, energy-efficient window glazes, or tankless water heater. Ask your contractor which features might be feasibly incorporated in the remodel, or see www.bobvila.com for more information (search for "energy efficiency").

Gardening and Landscaping

If you've just moved into a home that's beautifully landscaped, you may not realize how much time, effort, and money was put into making it just so. If you don't have a green thumb, think about hiring a professional to take over.

Ask the seller or neighbors whom they use (it's not uncommon for a whole neighborhood to have the same gardener). Local nurseries provide good recommendations, too. Realize that gardeners come with all levels of expertise and prices, from the expensive landscape architect to the college kid who likes wielding a hedge clipper. You're probably looking for someone in the middle: a gardener who specializes in maintenance rather than design but has enough experience to know a weed from a seedling and can help recognize plant diseases and suggest solutions.

Large trees, however, definitely need a professional, preferably a certified arborist. Bad pruning can kill the tree or make it look bad or grow faster. And tree pruning is dangerous work—don't risk a lawsuit by an inexperienced worker. Look for membership in either the International Society of Arboriculture (ISA, at www.isa-arbor.com), the Tree Care Industry Association (TCIA, at www.treecareindustry.org), or the American Society of Consulting Arborists (ASCA, at www.asca-consultants.org).

> *If I wanted to have a happy garden, I must ally myself with my soil; study and help it to the utmost, untiringly…. Always, the soil must come first.*
>
> —Marion Cran, gardening expert and author

If you didn't inherit a landscaped garden, you're probably going to want to use your own green thumb. Check your local nurseries for the types of plants that suit your space and ask questions about whether they're native, the type of care they'll need, whether they're susceptible to munching by deer or other natives, and their cycle (annual, perennial). And don't forget that not all plants need to be purchased—trading plant cuttings with friends is satisfying and free; see the articles at www.yougrowgirl.com.

In fact, there are plants that thrive on neglect, perfect if you've got a huge pile of dirt for a backyard and don't want to take care of a needy garden. For more ideas than you can shake a hoe at, check out the community at www.gardenweb.com.

Making It Green

Want to assuage your enviro-guilt for all the gas the moving van used? Here are some ways you can save energy and protect the environment from within your own home—and many of them cost little or nothing:

- **Hang laundry.** A $5 clothesline will cut down your gas or electricity bill, since you won't be running the dryer. And it will leave your clothes smelling fresh.

- **Wash your clothes in cold water.** Modern detergents don't need hot water to work, and heating the water uses lots of energy. Biodegradable and earth-friendly detergents are available. If you can't skip fabric softener, choose one that's soy based, or throw vinegar into the rinse cycle to soften your clothes.

- **Lower the thermostat.** Two degrees lower in the winter and two degrees higher in the summer could save up to 2,000 pounds of carbon dioxide per year.

- **Clean or replace furnace and air conditioning filters.** Keeping your furnace and air conditioning filters clean will help them function efficiently. An electrostatic filter will cost more up front than a paper or fiberglass one, but can be cleaned and reused.

- **Turn down the water heater.** Most people find 120 degrees to be warm enough, and the addition of an insulating water heater blanket (around $10–$20) can reduce heat loss by 25%–40%.

- **Switch to CFL light bulbs.** Compact fluorescent bulbs (CFLs) cost a little more than regular bulbs, but last much longer and are cheaper in the long run.

- **Use the dishwasher.** Modern dishwashers tend to be more efficient than handwashing, since they use less than ten gallons of water per load. And they're effective enough that you can feel justified in not prerinsing your dishes, which wastes water. Wait to run the dishwasher until it's completely full, and let dishes air dry if you can.

- **Reduce water use.** A low-flow showerhead will still have good water pressure, but will release (and waste) a lot less water. And if you can't yet afford a low-flow toilet, put a gallon milk jug with rocks into the tank to displace the water.

> *Ready to Discover Your Inner Martha Stewart?*
>
> *Martha Stewart's Homekeeping Handbook: The Essential Guide to Caring for Everything in Your Home*, by Martha Stewart (Clarkson Potter), covers just what it says (in over 750 pages).

- **Get rid of the junk mail.** While you're switching over your address, cancel catalogs you don't need at www.catalogchoice.org. Pay your bills—and get your statements—online.

- **Make your own cleaning products.** You can use some common household supplies—like vinegar, baking soda, and lemons—to make environmentally friendly products. For formulas, go to www.care2.com and search for "cleaning products."

- **Replace lawn with native plants.** This will decrease water use, as will watering early in the morning (to prevent evaporation) and keeping the grass three to four inches long. Getting rid of the gas mower will also have a positive environmental impact.

- **Plant trees.** A $10 annual membership to the Arbor Day Foundation (www.arborday.org) gets you ten free trees. Trees shade your home, reducing the temperature in warm spring and summer months; and deciduous trees will drop their leaves in the fall, too—letting sunlight in and potentially lowering the heating bill.

There's a Place for It: Organize Your Records

Boring, boring, but money-saving! Knowing where your home-related records are is part of the responsibility of owning a home and will help you collect on your insurance, claim tax deductions, and more. In this section, we'll run through the various categories of documents, including which ones to keep and why.

But first, a basic word on where and how to keep these documents. First, buy a locking file cabinet and keep the key somewhere secure. Then create folders with relevant titles such as "Closing Documents," "Repair and Improvement Receipts," "Product Manuals," "Homeowners' Insurance," "Tax Deductions [*year*]," and more. You'll get more ideas from the topics below and may want to put copies of some documents in more than one file.

Also find a location outside your house in which to keep copies of critical records, such as your house deed, loan, and insurance papers. If a fire or other disaster makes your house temporarily uninhabitable, easy access to these will make your life much easier. A safe deposit box is good, as is a secure place at a trusted friend's house (for weekend access).

Your Purchase and Ownership Records

Below are the basics: documents that prove you own the house, and those concerning your house's ongoing financing and insurance:

- **Closing documents.** These serve to prove your ownership of your property, a top priority.
- **Loan documents.** Keep all documents associated with your mortgage accessible, as well as documentation of other financial arrangements like promissory notes to family members.
- **Inspection reports.** These set a baseline for future comparison. If problems pop up later, they allow you to look back at whether the inspectors predicted them or overlooked something they should have caught.
- **Insurance policy.** In a minor or major emergency, you'll want to know how to contact your insurance company and what you're covered for. Having the contract handy will make dealing with company representatives much easier at a potentially troubled time.
- **Association records.** If your home is governed by a community association, keep all the relevant documents, like the CC&Rs. You'll want to be able to check on things like whether you can put up a basketball hoop or are really liable for a new fee.

Your Tax Records

Even if you've always stuffed your tax-related documents in a shoebox, homeownership gives you a good time to start over—with the incentive of some big-ticket deductions and credits. (Also, you never know when you'll be audited.) Here are some of the most important ones to keep track of:

- **Interest and points.** The interest you pay on your mortgage or home equity loan is tax-deductible, as are points you paid up front. (For more on these, turn back to Chapter 1.) Your lender will normally send you a post-year-end statement totaling your interest payments, so add these to your files.

- **Property tax.** State property taxes are deductible from your federal taxes. Keep a copy of the tax statement you receive, with notes on how you paid it (for example, a personal check number).

- **PMI.** Until the end of 2010, PMI is tax-deductible. Keep a copy of your billing statements.

- **Charitable contributions.** If you've donated to any 501(c)(3) charities, it's probably tax-deductible. Charities must send you receipts for gifts over certain amounts, but for others, or for cash you plunked anonymously into a donation box, you'll need to track and document your donations.

- **Home business.** If you work at home, your taxes are going to be more complicated than the average Joe's, but that also translates into more deductions.

- **Purchase documents.** If you're taking a tax credit as a first-time home-buyers, make sure your tax records include documentation to verify the date and amount of the purchase.

- **Energy-efficient improvements.** If you make any energy-efficient improvements that qualify for the tax credits discussed in Chapter 1, be sure to keep copies of your receipts (and make sure those receipts clearly identify what you purchased).

CHECK IT OUT

Keep what you've earned. If you're running a business from your home, learn which deductions you qualify for and which ones you don't using *Home Business Tax Deductions*, by Stephen Fishman (Nolo).

- **Other deductible expenses.** To find out more about home-related deductions (for example, moving expenses if you moved because of a job), go to www.irs.gov; download IRS Publication 530, *Tax Information for First-Time Homeowners*, and Publication 521, *Moving Expenses*.

Your Maintenance Records

All homes require upkeep, and keeping track of your maintenance and improvement efforts will help you figure out how old the roof and other things are, provide information to later potential buyers, and show the IRS why your capital gains tax should be reduced when you sell. Here are some documents to save:

- **Utility bills.** When you sell your home, many buyers will want to see about two years' worth of utility bills to see what their average expenses would be. (You can discard the older bills.)

- **Professional services.** Careful records of what's been done, who did it, when, and how much you paid will be helpful in two ways. First, you'll be able to check whom you used if you want to bring them back (or avoid them). Second, you'll be able to hand these documents over when you sell your home, so prospective buyers can see what's been done and hire professionals familiar with the property, if they choose.

- **Manuals and warranty information.** Keep all the info you'll need to replace, return, or otherwise deal with your house's appliances. Hopefully the seller left you relevant manuals and warranties; most warranties carry over to subsequent homeowners.

- **Repair and improvement receipts.** Keep records of and receipts for your repairs and improvements to the house. The distinction between them can be complicated, so for now, you might just want to save everything. When you sell, you can figure out which projects qualify as improvements that lower your capital gains tax liability. IRS Publication 530 (cited above) tells you more and includes a suggested chart for tracking home improvements.

Your Personal Records

Keeping track of essential forms was helpful in securing your home and continues to be important. Keep separate files for:

- **W-2s and other IRS-related papers.** Keeping track of your income from all sources, whether it's a salary, royalties, or eBay business, is the first step in preparing to file your taxes. Also track incoming money that might look to the IRS like income, but really wasn't, like a gift or reimbursement.

- **Health insurance records.** In case of emergency, every member of your household should know your and their health insurance information. Also consider creating documents showing who's authorized to make health care decisions for you if you aren't able to; see "What You Can Cover in Your Health Care Documents" and related articles in the Wills, Trusts & Estate Planning section of Nolo's website, www.nolo.com.

- **Auto insurance.** Though you should keep a copy of your car registration and current insurance information inside the car itself, you should also keep them on file, in case of loss or theft. Make sure you can easily find the vehicle identification number.

The Art of Organizing

Bookstores and websites are full of great resources for those who love to organize. (You know who you are—one clue is if the Container Store is your home away from home.) *Real Simple* magazine and organizing guru Julie Morgenstern both have useful books to keep your place decluttered. And if you want to hire a pro, check out the National Association of Professional Organizers, www.napo.net, for leads.

Back to the Future: Get Your Finances on Track

You've already made a budget (in Chapter 3). It may be time to revisit it to realistically account for the expenses of homeownership, which can be different from and higher than renting. (Of course, some of these expenses will be deductible, and if you alter your exemption status, this can also change your monthly cash flow.) The point is to make sure your budget is realistic and to stick to it, especially since you'll probably be tempted to do a lot at once—

like buy furniture, restock your pantry, and remodel the outdated bathroom. Here are some other ways to make the most of what you've got:

- **Hire a tax professional.** A pro can help you take maximum advantage of your brand-new investment and avoid incomplete filings with the IRS.

- **Check out additional resources.** In fact, you might want to literally check these out, at the library. See favorite books like *The Complete Tightwad Gazette*, by Amy Dacyczyn (Villard), and *Pinch a Penny Till It Screams*, by Madeline Clive (Lucerna Publishing).

- **Eat in more.** You've got a new kitchen, so experiment! There are hundreds of great websites (www.epicurious.com is one of our favorites). And if you're really pennypinching, check out *Dining on a Dime: 1000 Money Saving Recipes and Tips*, by Tawra Jean Kellam and Jill Cooper (Newman Marketing), and *The Frugal Family's Kitchen Book*, by Mary Weber (Cranberry Knoll Publishers LLC). An Internet search for "frugal recipes" will turn up plenty, too.

- **Restart your savings.** With all the financial rigmarole you've just been through, saving may sound like a pleasant dream. However, careful goal-setting can help you rebuild funds—plenty of millionaires can tell you the benefits of saving just a little at a time.

Congratulations!

It may be hard to believe, but you've reached your goal. You prioritized your needs, figured out what you could afford, researched where to find it and whom to get to help you, negotiated and closed your deal, and actually moved in. You're at the end of the road, so settle in and enjoy—this is home!

How to Use the CD-ROM

The CD-ROM included with this book can be used with Windows computers. It installs files that use software programs that need to be on your computer already. It is not a stand-alone software program.

In accordance with U.S. copyright laws, the CD-ROM and its files are for your personal use only.

Please read this appendix and the Readme.htm file included on the CD-ROM for instructions on using it. For a list of files and their file names, see the end of this appendix.

Note to Macintosh users: This CD-ROM and its files should also work on Macintosh computers. Please note, however, that Nolo cannot provide technical support for non-Windows users.

Note to eBook users: You can access the CD-ROM files mentioned here from the bookmarked section of the eBook, located on the left-hand side.

How to View the README File

To view the "Readme.htm" file, insert the CD-ROM into your computer's CD-ROM drive and follow these instructions:

Windows XP, Vista, and 7

1. On your PC's desktop, double-click the **My Computer** icon.
2. Double-click the icon for the CD-ROM drive into which the CD-ROM was inserted.
3. Double-click the file "Readme.htm."

Macintosh

1. On your Mac desktop, double-click the icon for the CD-ROM that you inserted.
2. Double-click the file "Readme.htm."

Installing the Files Onto Your Computer

To work with the files on the CD-ROM, you first need to install them onto your hard disk. Here's how:

Windows XP, Vista, and 7

Follow the CD-ROM's instructions that appear on the screen.

If nothing happens when you insert the CD-ROM, then:

1. Double-click the **My Computer** icon.
2. Double-click the icon for the CD-ROM drive into which the CD-ROM was inserted.
3. Double-click the file "Setup.exe."

Macintosh

If the **Homebuyer's Toolkit CD** window is not open, double-click the **Homebuyer's Toolkit CD** icon. Then:

1. Select the **Homebuyer's Toolkit** folder icon.
2. Drag and drop the folder icon onto your computer.

Where Are the Files Installed?

Windows

By default, all the files are installed to the **Homebuyer's Toolkit** folder in the Program Files folder of your computer. A folder called **Homebuyer's Toolkit** is added to the **Programs** folder of the **Start** menu.

Macintosh

All the files are located in the **Homebuyer's Toolkit** folder.

Using the Word Processing Files to Create Documents

The CD-ROM includes word processing files that you can open, complete, print, and save with your word processing program. All word processing files come in rich text format and have the extension ".rtf." For example, the form for the Dream List, discussed in Chapter 2, is on the file "DreamList.rtf." RTF files can be read by most recent word processing programs, including *MS Word*, Windows *WordPad*, and recent versions of *WordPerfect*.

The following are general instructions. Because each word processor uses different commands to open, format, save, and print documents, refer to your word processor's help file for specific instructions.

Do not call Nolo's technical support if you have questions on how to use your word processor or your computer.

Opening a File

You can open word processing files in any of the three following ways:

1. Windows users can open a file by selecting its "shortcut."

   i. Click the Windows **Start** button.

   ii. Open the **Programs** folder.

   iii. Open the **Homebuyer's Toolkit** folder.

   iv. Open the **RTF** subfolder.

   v. Click the shortcut to the file you want to work with.

2. Both Windows and Macintosh users can open a file by double-clicking it.

   i. Use **My Computer** or **Windows Explorer** (Windows XP, Vista, or 7) or the Finder (Macintosh) to go to the **Homebuyer's Toolkit** folder.

   ii. Double-click the file you want to open.

3. Windows and Macintosh users can open a file from within their word processor.

   i. Open your word processor.

   ii. Go to the **File** menu and choose the **Open** command. This opens a dialog box.

   iii. Select the location and name of the file. (You will navigate to the version of the **Homebuyer's Toolkit** folder that you've installed on your computer.)

Editing Your Document

Here are tips for working on your document.

- Refer to the book's instructions and sample agreements for help.
- Underlines indicate where to enter information, frequently including bracketed instructions. Delete the underlines and instructions before finishing your document.
- Signature lines should appear on a page with at least some text from the document itself.

Editing Files That Have Optional or Alternative Text

Some files have checkboxes that appear before text. Checkboxes indicate:

- Optional text that you can choose to include or exclude.
- Alternative text that you select to include, excluding the other alternatives.

When you are editing these files, we recommend doing the following:

Optional text

Delete optional text you do not want to include and keep that which you do. In either case, delete the checkbox and the italicized instructions. If you choose to delete an optional numbered clause, renumber the subsequent clauses after deleting it.

Alternative text

Delete the alternatives that you do not want to include first. Then delete the remaining checkboxes, as well as the italicized instructions that you need to select one of the alternatives provided.

Printing Out the Document

Use your word processor's or text editor's **Print** command to print out your document.

Saving Your Document

Use the **Save As** command to save and rename your document. You will be unable to use the **Save** command because the files are "read-only." If you save the file without renaming it, the underlines that indicate where you need to enter your information will be lost, and you will be unable to create a new document with this file without recopying the original file from the CD-ROM.

Using PDFs and Government Forms

The CD-ROM includes government forms in PDF format. These files were created by the government, not by Nolo.

To use them, you need Adobe *Reader* installed on your computer. If you don't already have this software, you can download it for free at www.adobe.com.

Some of these forms have fill-in text fields. To use them:

1. Open a file.
2. Fill in the text fields using either your mouse or the TAB key to navigate from field to field.
3. Print the file.

Opening a Form

PDF files, like the word processing files, can be opened any of the three following ways:

1. Windows users can open a file by selecting its "shortcut."

    i. Click the Windows **Start** button.

    ii. Open the **Programs** folder.

    iii. Open the **Homebuyer's Toolkit** folder.

    iv. Open the **PDF** subfolder.

    v. Click the shortcut to the form you want to work with.

2. Both Windows and Macintosh users can open a file directly by double-clicking it.

    i. Use **My Computer** or **Windows Explorer** (Windows XP, Vista, or 7) or the Finder (Macintosh) to go to the folder you created and copied the CD-ROM's files to.

    ii. Double-click the specific file you want to open.

3. Both Windows and Macintosh users can open a PDF file from within Adobe *Reader*.

    i. Open Adobe *Reader*.

    ii. Go to the **File** menu and choose the **Open** command. This opens a dialog box.

    iii. Tell the program the location and name of the file (you will need to navigate through the directory tree to get to the folder on your hard disk where the CD's files have been installed).

For further assistance, check Adobe *Reader*'s help. Nolo's technical support department is unable to help with the use of Adobe *Reader*.

Filling In a Form

Newer government forms enable you to fill in your form on your computer using Adobe Reader 5.1 or higher. If this feature is available, when you open the form you will see a message box about document rights. If you are using an earlier version of Adobe *Reader*, you will be prompted to download a newer version.

• Use your mouse or the TAB key to navigate from field to field within these forms.

• To complete forms without fill-in fields, print them and fill them in either by hand or with a typewriter.

Saving a Filled-In Form

If document rights are enabled, after completing your form onscreen, you can save it using Adobe *Reader* 5.1 or higher.

If document rights are not enabled, although you cannot save the form, you can print it out.

Listening to the Audio Files

This section explains how to play the audio files using your computer. All audio files are in MP3 format. For example, Househunting, an interview with Mark Nash, is on the file "MarkNash.mp3." At the end of this appendix, you'll find a list of the audio files and their file names.

Most computers come with a media player that plays MP3 files. You can listen to files that you have installed on your computer or directly from the CD-ROM. See below for further information on both.

The following are general instructions. Because every media player is different, refer to your media player's help files for more specific instructions. Please do not contact Nolo's technical support if you are having difficulty using your media player.

Playing the Audio Files Without Installing

If you don't want to copy 32 MB of audio files to your computer, you can play the CD-ROM on your computer. Here's how:

Windows

1. Insert the CD-ROM to view the **Welcome to Homebuyer's Toolkit CD** window.

2. Click "Listen to Audio."

If nothing happens when you insert the CD-ROM:

1. Double-click the My Computer icon.

2. Double-click the icon for the CD-ROM drive you inserted the CD-ROM into.

3. Double-click the file "Welcome.exe."

Macintosh

1. Insert the CD-ROM. (If the **Homebuyer's Toolkit CD** window does not open, double-click the **Homebuyer's Toolkit CD** icon).

2. Double-click the **Audio** icon.

3. Double-click the audio file you want to hear.

Listening to Audio Files You've Installed on Your Computer

There are two ways to listen to the audio files that you have installed on your computer.

1. Windows users can open a file by selecting its shortcut.

   i. Click the Windows **Start** button.

   ii. Open the **Programs** folder.

   iii. Open the **Homebuyer's Toolkit** folder.

   iv. Open the **Audio** subfolder.

   v. Click the shortcut to the file you want to work with.

2. Both Windows and Macintosh users can open a file by double-clicking it.

   i. Use **My Computer** or **Windows Explorer** (Windows XP, Vista, or 7) or the **Finder** (Macintosh) to go to the **Homebuyer's Toolkit** folder.

   ii. Double-click the file you want to open.

Files on the CD-ROM

The following files are in rich text format (RTF):	
File Name	**Form Name**
Dream List Directions	DreamListDirections.rtf
Dream List	DreamList.rtf
Gift Letter	GiftLetter.rtf
Personal Loan Terms Worksheet	LoanTerms.rtf
Questions for Seller Worksheet	QuestionsForSellers.rtf
Condo/Co-op Worksheet	CondoQuestions.rtf
Questions for Talking with Locals	QuestionsForLocals.rtf

The following files are audio (MP3 format):	
File Name	**Form Name**
Author Interviews with Ilona Bray, Alayna Schroeder, and Marcia Stewart	HTBH_AuthorsInterview.mp3
Househunting, an interview with Mark Nash	MarkNash.mp3
House Inspections, an interview with Paul A. Rude	PaulRude.mp3
Getting a Mortgage, an interview with Russell Straub	RussStraub.mp3
Closing the Purchase, an interview with Sandy Gadow	SandyGadow.mp3

The following files are in portable document format (PDF):	
File Name	**Form Name**
Debt-to-Income Ratio Worksheet	DebtIncomeRatio.pdf
Financial Information for Lenders	LenderInfo.pdf
Common Real Estate Abbreviations	Abbreviations.pdf
Real Estate Agent Interview Questionnaire	AgentInterview.pdf
Real Estate Agent References Questionnaire	AgentReferences.pdf
Mortgage Broker Interview Questionnaire	BrokerInterview.pdf
Mortgage Broker References Questionnaire	BrokerReferences.pdf
Attorney Interview Questionnaire	AttorneyInterview.pdf
Attorney References Questionnaire	AttorneyReferences.pdf
Home Inspector Interview Questionnaire	InspectorInterview.pdf
Home Inspector References Questionnaire	InspectorReferences.pdf
House Visit Checklist	HouseChecklist.pdf
First-Look Home Inspection	HomeInspection.pdf
Indiana Disclosure Form	Indiana46234.pdf
CA Disclosure Form	CADisclosure.pdf
CA Natural Hazards Disclosure	CAHazards.pdf
Cobuyer Discussion Checklist	CobuyerChecklist.pdf
Sample Inspection Report (P. Rude)	InspectionReport.pdf
Homeowners' Insurance Terminology	Terminology.pdf
Settlement Statement	Settlement.pdf
Final Walkthrough (Existing Home)	ExistingWalkthru.pdf
Final Walkthrough (New Home)	NewWalkthru.pdf

Find a Real Estate Attorney

- *Qualified lawyers*
- *In-depth profiles*
- *A pledge of respectful service*

When you want help with buying or selling a home or other real estate, you don't want just any lawyer—you want an expert in the field, who can give you and your family up-to-the-minute advice. You need a lawyer who has the experience and knowledge to answer your questions about financing arrangements, easements, lease-purchase contracts, purchasing a property in foreclosure, and if necessary, agreements to borrow down payment money from friends and family.

Nolo's Lawyer Directory is unique because it provides an extensive profile of every lawyer. You'll learn about not only each lawyer's education, professional history, legal specialties, credentials and fees, but also about their philosophy of practicing law and how they like to work with clients.

All lawyers listed in Nolo's directory are in good standing with their state bar association. Many will review Nolo documents, such as a will or living trust, for a fixed fee. They all pledge to work diligently and respectfully with clients—communicating regularly, providing a written agreement about how legal matters will be handled, sending clear and detailed bills, and more.

www.nolo.com

NOLO® *Online Legal Forms*

Nolo offers a large library of legal solutions and forms, created by Nolo's in-house legal staff. These reliable documents can be prepared in minutes.

Create a Document

- **Incorporation.** Incorporate your business in any state.
- **LLC Formations.** Gain asset protection and pass-through tax status in any state.
- **Wills.** Nolo has helped people make over 2 million wills. Is it time to make or revise yours?
- **Living Trust (avoid probate).** Plan now to save your family the cost, delays, and hassle of probate.
- **Trademark.** Protect the name of your business or product.
- **Provisional Patent.** Preserve your rights under patent law and claim "patent pending" status.

Download a Legal Form

Nolo.com has hundreds of top quality legal forms available for download—bills of sale, promissory notes, nondisclosure agreements, LLC operating agreements, corporate minutes, commercial lease and sublease, motor vehicle bill of sale, consignment agreements and many more.

Review Your Documents

Many lawyers in Nolo's consumer-friendly lawyer directory will review Nolo documents for a very reasonable fee. Check their detailed profiles at **Nolo.com/lawyers.**

Index